*Black
and White in
Colour*

Black and White in Colour

Black People in British Television Since 1936

Edited by Jim Pines

BFI PUBLISHING

First published in 1992 by the
British Film Institute
21 Stephen Street, London W1P 1PL

British Library Cataloguing
in Publication Data

Pines, Jim
Black and White in Colour:
Black People in British Television
Since 1936

I. Title
791.45

ISBN 0–85170–328–3
ISBN 0–85170–329–1 Pbk

Design: John Gibbs

Set in Bodoni and Gill by Fakenham
Photosetting Limited, Fakenham,
Norfolk
Printed in Great Britain by
Page Bros, Norwich

Cover/title page still: Jesus (George
Browne) and the Disciples in the Negro
Theatre Workshop presentation of *The
Dark Disciples* (BBC TV, 1966)

Contents

This book is based on interviews and other material which went into the making of the BFI documentaries *Black and White in Colour* for the BBC, directed by Isaac Julien. The two programmes were first transmitted on BBC2 in June 1992.

The programmes resulted from a BFI research project – 'Race and Ethnicity in British Television' – which Richard Paterson and Jim Pines started in 1985, to rediscover through archival research the struggle for representation and employment of black people in British television. David A. Bailey was commissioned to undertake a pilot research project, and a series of research seminars was organised with contributions from Stuart Hall, Kobena Mercer, Thérèse Daniels, and Chris Vieler-Porter.

First Michael Grade, then Controller of BBC1, and subsequently Will Wyatt, then Deputy Managing Director, BBC Network Television, saw the possibilities that the research offered and part-funded a two-year research programme. Under the direction of Kobena Mercer (until early 1990), and then of Tana Wollen, Thérèse Daniels and Stephen Bourne undertook the research which formed the basis for the documentaries. With the help of students on placement from Birmingham Polytechnic, they listed and traced every programme with black on-screen involvement from television's beginnings in 1936 to 1969; and they also conducted some preliminary interviews.

Acknowledgments

In the latter stages of the project, Zelda Reynolds conducted research on the period after 1970 in preparation for the documentaries. Colin MacCabe and Isaac Julien then joined the project as producer and director respectively of the two programmes.

The interviews were conducted by Isaac Julien, Colin MacCabe, Stephen Bourne and Thérèse Daniels mainly in August 1991.

Acknowledgment must also be made to Esther Johnson, who played a key role in the making of the programmes; to Eliza Mellor, the Associate Producer on the programmes; and to Jacintha Cusack for her unstinting tracking down of photographs used in this book and for her help in organising transcripts for editing. Stephen Bourne made helpful suggestions during the editorial process, and we duly thank him for his contribution.

For photographic stills reproduced in this book, we thank BBC Photo Library; BFI Stills, Posters and Designs; Central Independent Television; Channel Four Television; Granada Television; London Weekend Television; Stephen Bourne; Yvonne Salmon; and Sharron Wallace.

In addition to the aforementioned people, the editor wishes to thank especially Colin MacCabe and Richard Paterson for their tremendous support. And, finally, I would like to thank the interviewees who read a draft of their interviews and kindly made helpful amendments. I only hope that I have done justice to their stories.

The history of black people in British television can be traced back to the opening day of BBC television itself – 2 November 1936 – when the black American song and dance duo Buck and Bubbles starred in a variety show. Shortly after, the American-born singer/actress Elisabeth Welch, who already had her own BBC radio series in 1934, could be seen in 'light musical items' broadcast live from Alexandra Palace. Several landmark drama and documentary programmes followed after the Second World War, when the BBC television service resumed operation. The first of these was a production of Eugene O'Neill's play *All God's Chillun Got Wings* in 1946, featuring among the cast Pauline Henriques (in her television drama debut), Robert Adams and Edric Connor.

During the late 50s and early 60s, the popular calypso singer and actor Cy Grant became one of Britain's first black television 'stars', with his nightly appearances on the BBC TV magazine programme *Tonight* 'singing the news in calypso'. Around the same time, Pearl Connor set up an agency with her late husband, actor/singer Edric Connor, to represent and promote black talent in Britain, and to press for non-stereotypical roles for black actors and actresses in the performing arts. This pioneering agency became a vital source of personal support and professional guidance for a whole generation of black British performing artistes during the 50s and 60s.

Introduction by Jim Pines

Another early landmark was John Elliot's *A Man from the Sun* (1956). This powerful BBC drama-documentary about black working-class life in Britain featured a whole host of leading black British actors and actresses including Pauline Henriques, Cy Grant, Errol John, Nadia Cattouse, Pearl Prescod and Earl Cameron. Elliot's intention was to highlight the contrast between what he describes as the mythical image of a cosy Britain which people were receiving as part of their colonial education, and the grotty Britain which the West Indian immigrants encountered when they first arrived in this country. *A Man from the Sun* is one of the earliest attempts to look at 'the West Indian immigrant experience' from the point of view of how black people themselves were experiencing it, rather than focusing simply on the white British reaction to immigrants and immigration.

The latter approach, with its imagery of black settlement as an invasion,[1] became the dominant motif in television's subsequent handling of 'race relations' topics. But during the post-war years to about the mid-60s, racial imagery was certainly less institutionalised and, perhaps, relatively less panic stricken as well; it also exhibited a strong tendency towards humanism with definite undertones of anti-racism. This orientation is particularly evident in Ted Willis' gritty race relations drama, *Hot Summer Night* (1959), in which Lloyd Reckord played the part of a black victim of racial bigotry and intolerance – a role in which he subsequently became typecast, much to his chagrin.

In the context of the 50s, these early television representations of race were radical, in so far as they represented the stridently liberal position vis-à-vis white responses to the black presence in Britain. However, it was (and still is) essentially a moral position which was only permitted by the television establishment to exist on the margins of mainstream programme-making. It actually had precious little impact on overall institutional thinking and practice. Indeed, what comes across strongly in the interviews with 'the white insiders' in particular, is the extent to which these practitioners claimed the moral high ground and the understandably self-conscious way in which their own programmes (and mode of practice) went against the grain of a largely complacent television bureaucracy.

The 60s began promisingly, in the sense that black actors started to appear in a wider variety of programmes including soaps, serials, and one-off television plays. Thomas Baptiste appeared in some episodes of *Coronation Street* in 1963 for example, though this significant fact was somehow overlooked when the long-running soap celebrated its thirtieth anniversary in 1990. Joan Hooley appeared in more than fifty episodes of the popular hospital series *Emergency-Ward 10* in 1964, though her character's demise was shrouded in puerile anxiety over an inter-racial couple kissing on prime-time television, and signalled a much deeper problem within television drama: namely, its recurrent failure to develop black characterisation in interesting and imaginative ways.

John Hopkins' harrowing episode of the popular police drama series *Z Cars: A Place of Safety* (1964), was a notable exception to this tendency. It provided particularly challenging roles for the episode's two black stars, Johnny Sekka and Alaknanda Samarth, who played a married couple on the edge of existential despair and breakdown. The following year, Hopkins wrote a highly controversial BBC television play called *Fable*, which explored inter-racial relations in the context of Britain viewed as an imaginary apartheid state, where black-white roles are reversed. It too provided tremendous dramatic scope for the black actors in the cast which included Thomas Baptiste, Rudolph Walker (in his television drama debut), and Carmen Munroe. Significantly, Hopkins' drama led to questions being asked in the House of Commons, and was temporarily banned from broadcast because of the racially-sensitive Leyton by-election which was taking place around the same time.

The 1964 General Election had seen an important political turning-point in British politics, when Peter Griffiths, an openly racist Tory candidate, defeated the sitting Labour MP, Patrick Gordon-Walker, in Smethwick. It was the first time that overt racism actually won a parliamentary election in Britain, and as such it effectively gave racism a new kind of official legitimacy. It was inevitable that 'official' anxiety around 'race' would re-surface the following year, when Gordon-Walker stood again in the Leyton by-election (and lost, incidentally). Although racial issues (that is, anti-immigration rhetoric) evidently played a less prominent role in the by-election, the closeness of the two elections and the image of Labour as 'soft on immigration' guaranteed the continuation of a racially-charged atmosphere.

Fable was produced against this background of race relations panic. It succeeded in touching a raw nerve, by teasing viewers (and the television authority which sought to distance itself from the play's political content) with the highly provocative device of inverting the master-slave relation. By doing so, Hopkins' television play helped to further heighten official and public anxieties about 'the black presence' and British race politics. Considered analytically, this is a good example of the implicit relationship between wider race relations discourses (for example, anti-immigration rhetoric, multiculturalism, and so on) and racial representation in television.

Equally interesting though obviously less controversial politically, was BBC TV's 'Play of the Month' production of the E.M. Forster Raj epic, *A Passage to India* (1965), directed by Waris Hussein and featuring Zia Mohyeddin in the role of Dr Aziz. However, it wasn't until the early 80s that 'British nostalgia for the Imperial past' became a dominant theme in British cinema and television – with the cycle of colonial drama including Richard Attenborough's *Gandhi* and David Lean's *A Passage to India* (1984), Granada Television's *The Jewel in the Crown* (1984), and BBC TV's *The Happy Valley* (1987).

In 1967, John Elliot produced and co-wrote (with leading Trinidadian actor/writer Horace James) a six-part BBC drama serial *Rainbow City*. It starred the brilliant actor and award-winning playwright, Errol John, in the role of a Jamaican lawyer in a racially-mixed marriage and living and working in Birmingham. Elliot makes the interesting observation that by this time, the subject of West Indians in England was no longer new, compared to when he made *A Man from the Sun* ten years earlier, and that a lot could now be taken for granted in terms of representing (to white viewers) black people in television drama and documentary programmes. Certainly the relatively 'sophisticated' approach employed in *Rainbow City* suggests that it was indeed now possible to devise interesting narratives involving a wider range of black British experiences.

However, the late 60s saw a sharp reversal of this trend, perhaps in response to the rise of a new racism during the period. Television became preoccupied with promulgating a liberal notion of Britain as a multicultural society – but the proliferation of documentary programmes on race relations tended to stress a re-emerging sense of anxiety about 'the black presence'. Cy Grant and others recall how the political mood of the country changed markedly in the late 60s, following Enoch Powell's infamous 'rivers of blood' speech in 1968. 'Powellism' had had a direct and adverse impact on perceptions of black experiences in Britain, but, more importantly, it allowed what Desmond Wilcox aptly refers to as a screaming level of prejudice to enter society. Such an atmosphere was not conducive to creative expression, nor to the emergence of imaginative roles for black actors and actresses in television drama. From the black point of view, it was a creatively sterile period in British television.

Ironically, Johnny Speight's sitcom *Till Death Us Do Part* was the single most popular television programme during the period in terms of a racial thematic, though it achieved this without the presence of a recurring black character. According to Andy Medhurst, Alf Garnett, the series' bigoted anti-hero, 'is one of the few sitcom characters who has achieved legendary status. He is part of television folklore and is best known for being a walking repository of reactionary prejudices'.[2] A number of critics have also described the Alf Garnett figure as Enoch Powell's alter-ego and a liberating force for certain sections of the white working class, in the way that he embodied many of their attitudes and desires.

The 70s saw a plethora of multicultural documentary programmes which set out to 'explain' various aspects of so-called immigrant life in Britain. Blacks and immigrants (invariably Asians at the time) had thus become 'a problem' which these programmes set out to elucidate for a basically xenophobic white audience. Television's preoccupation with race and multiculturalism during this period was essentially regressive, uninteresting, and completely pointless from a creative point of view. However, these programmes did demonstrate television's ability to operate in tandem with the state in 'managing' what was then perceived as the growing race relations crisis.

Carmen Munroe talks movingly about the personal struggle which she (and doubtless many other black artistes) faced during the early 70s. The deep sense of despair that overcame the milieu both at the personal level and in terms of the sector as a whole, was only partially alleviated by some productive work which continued to be available in the theatre. But it was as though the intellectual and creative dynamism of the early 60s had suddenly evaporated, and the contribution which black artistes had been making to the medium was suddenly rendered meaningless. One is almost tempted to add that this period also marked the (temporary) demise of ethical liberalism within broadcasting institutions – the apparent collapse of a liberal motivation either creatively or institutionally, which resulted inevitably in the absence of imaginative dramas or documentaries relating to black British experiences.

Cleo Sylvestre's appearance in 1970 in the long-running soap *Crossroads* represented a significant step forward, in so far as it came at a time when the situation for black artistes was not good and involved a black character in a non-racial role in a mainstream series. Barry Reckord's full-length BBC television play, *In the Beautiful Caribbean* (1972), also hinted that things might not be all that bad. But, unfortunately, the most popular television images of 'race relations' at the time came from yet another sitcom – *Love Thy Neighbour* (1972-5). Rudolph Walker became nationally famous for his role as Bill Reynolds, the self-assured black neighbour of the irritating white bigot Eddie Booth (Jack Smethurst). Walker recalls how he insisted on making his character a stridently positive counter-irritant to the constant stream of racist abuse which typified race-related sitcoms. Many viewers are said to have enjoyed the racially-charged batting relationship between the two men, as they would a cricket match.

Love Thy Neighbour was followed by another cycle of popular situation comedies including *The Fosters* and *Mixed Blessings*. Though not ideal vehicles for displaying the breadth and depth of black acting talent, these sitcoms nevertheless helped to create new openings for black actors in mainstream television during this otherwise depressing period. But some black actors refused to appear in these programmes because of the emphasis on offensive racial jokes. However, Kenny Lynch occasionally appeared in *Till Death Us Do Part* and in Johnny Speight's short-lived sitcom *Curry and Chips*. Perhaps controversially, he offers a frank and completely different view about racial jokes, arguing that they should not be regarded as necessarily offensive but as a natural feature of humour itself. It is tempting to draw a contrast here with Lenny Henry, though I suspect the relationship between the two personalities vis-à-vis their relationship to the British comedy tradition is in fact much closer, and at the same time more complex than either of their interviews can ever reveal.

But on a wider front, the dominance of situation comedy and the absence of black representation in quality drama, are seen by many critics and artistes as the main reasons why there has not been a broader and more interesting development of black imagery in British television. Norman Beaton's general observations concerning drama are aptly applicable in this context. He suggests that roles have not been written which reflect a broader sense of black people's lives – because white writers don't seem to understand where black people are coming from, and because many black writers either lack the confidence to write this kind of drama, or they are not given the opportunity to do so.

Empire Road (1978-9) was the striking exception to this dismal state of affairs during the 70s. It was the first television series to be conceived and written by a black writer (Michael Abbensetts) for a black cast. It was also quintessentially about the British-Caribbean experience (unlike *The Fosters* for example, which was a revamped US import). In that respect, it is an important landmark in the history of black representation on British television. The series took on an almost mythical dimension, moreover, when black director Horace Ové came in to direct several episodes – suddenly it was like having a genuine black soap opera being created within a mainstream (white) television institution. But while *Empire Road* represented a major breakthrough in many respects, it was short-lived and Ové's recollections of working on the production are particularly worth bearing in mind when celebrating its otherwise historic achievements.

The advent of Channel 4 in 1982 marked an enormously exciting turning-point in black media representation. It was the first time that a mainstream television channel instituted policies specifically aimed at creating new opportunities of access for, among others, black media practitioners. There was also a recognition of the history of racial imagery and the fact that much of it had been racist, which the new channel promised to redress through its commissioning and scheduling policy. There were great expectations following the appointment of the first-ever Commissioning Editor for Multicultural Programmes (Sue Woodford), who had the onerous task of putting the channel's huge promises into operation.

The channel then commissioned London Weekend Television to produce its two new flagship current affairs programmes for ethnic minorities – *Black on Black* and *Eastern Eye*. This was quickly met with indignation and cries of foul play from a number of (black) independent practitioners, who basically felt that the channel had betrayed its innovative cultural remit which had promised greater access. Sue Woodford countered the criticisms at the time, saying:

'I felt that it was important to get programmes on the air and to get people working – and I think that in terms of what we've done I have actually managed to give more work to a lot of people. All right, there are people around who didn't get work – there's always going to be people who didn't get work – but I do feel that it was important to get programmes on the screen . . . I was very conscious of the fact that I was taking on the London Weekend Television commission (i.e. *Black on Black*, *Eastern Eye* and *No Problem!*) at the expense of bringing in new people, but I am still very keen to start working on an alternative. I certainly would like to see some stage come when I could commission, say, LWT to do a limited number of programmes, and commission an all-black independent company of, for example, black journalists to do a number of programmes in the year. That plan has not been abandoned'.[3]

Trevor Phillips and Samir Shah, the producers of *Black on Black* and *Eastern Eye* respectively, are equally dismissive of the criticisms and focus instead on the way the two programmes helped to shift the basis of news and current affairs programme-making for black and Asian audiences. Since they had both previously worked on LWT's *Skin* programme, they shared similar feelings about that otherwise innovative programme's two major weaknesses — that it collapsed the Afro-Caribbean and Asian communities into a single entity, thus losing the social and cultural distinctiveness of either community; and that it tended to 'explain' blacks to whites. In other words, following very much in the multicultural television documentary tradition mentioned earlier, *Skin* was essentially *about* ethnic minorities rather than *for* ethnic minorities. Phillips and Shah set out therefore to reverse this approach firstly by creating separate programmes for the two communities — *Black on Black* and *Eastern Eye* — and secondly by stressing that the programmes were primarily *for* ethnic minorities, but open to other viewers who would find the programmes worth watching as well.

Farrukh Dhondy replaced Sue Woodford at Channel 4 in 1984. A year later he decided not to re-commission *Black on Black* and *Eastern Eye*, and instead commissioned a newly established independent production company to produce *The Bandung File*. This became the channel's new flagship black and Asian (or 'Third World') oriented news and current affairs strand. The channel's 'multicultural' drama strand also evolved slightly under Dhondy's stewardship, in so far as he was able to commission more one-off black related dramas than his predecessor. However, the mainstay of Channel 4's 'black related drama strand' has been situation comedy, though with a significant difference — the programmes have been written and produced primarily by black practitioners. *No Problem!* grew out of the Black Theatre Co-operative and was co-written by Dhondy and Mustafa Matura, while *Desmond's*, the channel's highly successful ethnic showpiece, is the brainchild of Trix Worrell.

It is also worth mentioning Channel 4's recognition of the grant-supported black workshop sector, which provided another source of innovation in terms of facilitating new black-led film and television production. Interestingly, this came within the cultural remit of the channel's Commissioning Editor for Independent Film and Video (Alan Fountain), and as such it operated within a completely different set of parameters from that of the Multicultural strand. Since the mid-80s, the black workshop sector — that is, franchised workshops like Black Audio Film Collective, Ceddo Film and Video, Retake Film and Video, and Sankofa Film and Video — has been remarkably successful in establishing itself as an alternative, non-mainstream or commercially led framework for developing new forms of black independent media practice and black related imagery.

The new imagery which workshop practitioners promulgated during the latter half of the 80s especially, had a significant impact on public perceptions of what might constitute an alternative black British film and television culture. The numerous films and videos that were produced by these practitioners during the period proved not only that there is a highly talented and potentially prolific black independent production sector, but also that it is possible to make drama and documentary programmes which don't have to conform to the sterile conventions of mainstream 'race relations' oriented film and television.

The individual recollections contained in these twenty-eight interviews will no doubt come as a great surprise to many people, especially to a younger (television) generation who simply would have no way of knowing the extent to which black British people have been involved in, or have contributed to mainstream television output. In essence, this book is an oral history of largely unsung heroes, heroines, and pioneers in the television arts. It tries to redress what Thomas Baptiste and others poignantly refer to as the absence of any historical memory, or sense of continuity regarding their contribution to British television.

I have attempted to arrange the interviews into a loosely historical and/or generic sequence, in order to highlight the sense of interconnection which in fact links all the participants in time and space. It always struck me as intriguing that this history begins with an American entertainer, Elisabeth Welch, who came to Britain in the 1930s and participated in the first live broadcasts from Alexandra Palace, and that it ends with perhaps Britain's first truly exportable black television star, Lenny Henry, who went to Hollywood in the 1990s to star in his first major feature film.

FOOTNOTES

1 Paul Gilroy, *There Ain't No Black in the Union Jack* (London: Hutchinson, 1987).

2 Andy Medhurst, Introduction to chapter on Situation Comedies in Thérèse Daniels and Jane Gerson (eds.), *The Colour Black: Black Images in British Television* (BFI, 1989).

3 'Channel 4 – A Pandora's Box for Blacks?' Interview with Sue Woodford by Jim Pines, in *Artrage*, nos. 3/4, Summer 1983, pp. 2-4.

The Interviews
with biographical notes
by Stephen Bourne

— ELISABETH WELCH —

Elisabeth Welch was born in New York and settled in Britain in 1933. She has been featured in numerous stage revues, musicals and plays in London's West End. In 1934 she had her own BBC radio series called *Soft Lights and Sweet Music*, and in 1936 she co-starred with Paul Robeson in the film *Song of Freedom*.

Elisabeth made her first appearances on British television in light musical items broadcast live from Alexandra Palace in the late 30s. Since that time she has made over one hundred and fifty appearances as a singer in a range of musical and variety programmes including *Oranges and Lemons* (1949), *Tuppence Coloured* (1949), *Penny Plain* (1952), *Music for You* (1955), *Joyce Grenfell Requests the Pleasure* (1956), *The Long Cocktail Party* (1966) with David Kernan and Millicent Martin, *Cindy Ella* (1966) with Cleo Laine and Cy Grant, *Before the Fringe* (1967), *The Royal Variety Performance* (1979 and 1985), and *Song by Song by Cole Porter* (1980).

She has also acted in television plays and series including *No Time for Comedy* (1954), Sunday-Night Theatre: *Mrs. Patterson* (1956) with Eartha Kitt, Play of the Week: *The Grass Harp* (1957), *The Brockenstein Affair* (1962), *Crane* (1964), Play of the Week: *The Rise and Fall of Nellie Brown* (1964) with Ron Moody and Millie, *Take a Sapphire* (1966), W. Somerset Maugham's *The Moon and Sixpence* (1967), and *The Man Who Came to Dinner* (1972) with Orson Welles.

Elisabeth has been the subject of two television programmes, in 1985 *This is Your Life*, and in 1987 Channel 4's documentary *Keeping Love Alive*, described as 'a self-portrait in words and songs'.

In 1988 Elisabeth received a special Variety Club award for her services to British entertainment.

I was born in New York City, on West 63rd Street near Lincoln Square, where the Opera House is now. My father, John Wesley Welch, was a gardener and general factotum on a large estate in Englewood, New Jersey. He had to be there all the time, so he only came home on Saturdays and Sundays. My mother, Elisabeth Kay, was Scots; she was born in Leith, which used to be a large port but is now part of Edinburgh. She was brought to America when she was in her mid-teens, and worked as an assistant to the nanny of the same family that my father worked for in Englewood. That's how they met! She used to tell me about the difficulty they had in getting somebody to marry them because my father was of mixed race – African-American and American Indian of the Lenape tribe of Delaware. They finally found a Catholic priest who married them in his rectory. My mother was a wonderful woman. She was brave and defiant. She adored me and my two brothers, and we adored her. It was only when we were all grown up that we learned to appreciate what she had done for us and how much she had fought for us.

Growing up in the midst of theatre ● There was a famous theatre called the Colonial Theater on Columbus Circle near to where we lived on 63rd Street. It used to have variety shows. Then there was the Lincoln Square Cinema where they had three variety acts between the main films. I used to go to the shows with my brother on Saturday mornings for a nickel (five cents). During the summer months the performers used to sit out on the fire escapes to keep cool, and I would stare at them whenever I passed. I was always fascinated by their make-up.

On 63rd Street there was the Music Hall where Mae West created a sensation with her all-boys show, Mae West and her young men. She kept that show running for years! The men were in drag most of the time, and in those days we just thought 'Well, that's theatre!' The Music Hall was next to a fire station and a police station, and the police used to raid the place more or less every Saturday night. They'd wait for the show to finish the week – that's how crooked it was – and then, just after the performers did their finale on a Saturday night, clang-clang-clang would come the Black Marias. The police would bustle the boys out still in their dressing gowns. And, to defy the authorities, the boys would swish out, complete with long eye-lashes, lipstick and make-up. Now, this was just after the First World War, so it was frightfully shocking behaviour for most people to see. We had Saturday choir practice every week, so we would stand on the church stairs across the street watching all this going on. So, Mae West was the first great person of the theatre that I saw – but not on stage!

First stage appearance in *Runnin' Wild*, an all-black musical which opened at the Colonial Theater in October 1923 ● I went into a choir associated with the church, and the choir was hired to go into a show called *Runnin' Wild*. I was called 'the loud alto' and was given a song to introduce, which was the Charleston. Now, nobody sang the Charleston in those days, they just danced it. The chorus girls looked marvellous in their lovely costumes. I would sing the verse and chorus, make an exit, and the girls would then come on to dance it.

I was still at school when I was appearing in *Runnin' Wild*. I used to do evenings from Monday to Saturday, and Saturday matineés. My mother was proud that her daughter was singing and earning, though I was probably only making a fiver a week. When I went to my first performance, she had an old shoe which she threw down the stairs at me, for good luck. But then my father found out I was on the stage and it was terrible, really terrible. I had to go out when my father came home at the weekends. I had to go and stay with friends because my mother was frightened of what my father might do to me. You see, he adored me. I was the apple of his eye and he could not bear to think that 'Girlie' – that's what I was called – was on the stage. That upset him a great deal. He'd say: 'Girlie's on the boards. She's lost!' He thought I would become a whore or something like that. It was terrible because he started to hate me. And then, finally, he never came home. We never found out what happened to him. Sadly, that was that!

European debut ● A large number of black American entertainers, like Florence Mills and Paul Robeson, were coming to Europe and to London during the 20s and 30s. Florence Mills came here in 1926 in Lew Leslie's musical revue *Blackbirds*. After her death in late 1927, they reorganised the show with Adelaide Hall and Aida Ward as the two stars, and Bill Robinson, the famous tap dancer. I was in the choir of this new show which was called *Blackbirds of 1928* and, in 1929, Leslie moved us to the Moulin Rouge in Paris. That's how I first came to Europe.

At the time, I had a girlfriend called Henrietta and we used to go to various bars in Paris and order port. We got to know the street girls and they told us their stories. It was marvellous. Then we'd go to a restaurant and people would recognise us – 'Oh, you're from *Blackbirds*. Would you sing for us?' So we would sing a song or something, and we got to know a lot of people that way.

I returned to New York with the company, but there was nothing happening. As I had been offered a job at Boeuf sur le Toit, I decided to go back to Paris. Later I started singing at another of the smart night clubs in Paris, called Chez Florence, where all the film and Broadway stars used to go. I remember people like Gloria Swanson and Charlie Chaplin coming there. All of café society from London and elsewhere came, and I sang. It was marvellous.

Bringing 'Stormy Weather' to London in May 1933 ● I came to London via Paris, and introduced the song 'Stormy Weather' into a show called *Dark Doings* at the Leicester Square Theatre. This was then a music theatre belonging to Jack Buchanan. For the production, they created a shanty town stage set, complete with thunder rolling and lightning flashing. I would come out and sing 'Don't know why there's no sun up in the sky . . .' I don't know how I got through the song because the production was so funny. But it was a hit and I started to establish a little name for myself in the West End. Unfortunately, it was the summer of 1933, one of the hottest summers I've ever lived through, and people didn't want to be indoors, so this success only lasted about three weeks. In the August, of this same hot summer, I also had to go to rehearsals for *Nymph Errant*. This was Charles B. Cochran's show for Gertrude Lawrence, which was opening in October at the Adelphi Theatre.

Paul Robeson and *Song of Freedom* (1936) ● I met Paul Robeson in 1936. The phone rang one morning and I was livid because I'm not awake in the mornings! It was HMV saying they wanted me to come out to the studios and do a recording with Robeson! They wanted me to sing 'Ah Still Suits Me', the song which Jerome Kern wrote for the 1936 screen version of *Show Boat*. Paul sang it in the film [with Hattie McDaniel], in the scene where she is peeling potatoes with him. But the song had never been recorded.

I hadn't met Paul before. I got to the studio and there was this wonderful person. I'd seen him in concert, I'd seen him at Carnegie Hall in New York, and I'd seen him here in Birmingham in concert. And now here was this giant saying 'Hallo' and squashing me to his bosom, almost strangling me. He really didn't know his own strength. And I loved him from then on. I absolutely adored him. And so we made this record, though I actually sang very little on it.

Then, in 1936, I appeared in a film with Paul, called *Song of Freedom*. It was made at Beaconsfield Studios. That's when we really got to know each other. It was summer and during lunch we used to sit out on the lawn at the studios and talk. Paul's son, who was about eight or nine years old at that time, was going to school in Russia. And, of course, Paul being very Russian-minded, started talking politics to me, which I resented. I said 'Paul, I don't want to talk politics'. And he said – and this is what sent me wild – 'Elisabeth, you're a name, why don't you do something for your race?' And I said 'Which race? I've got black, white and red blood in me. Which one do you want me to choose?'. He just roared with laughter and asked me to forgive him. He was a wonderful understanding person.

Live from Alexandra Palace ● During 1934, I was doing a radio programme for the BBC called *Soft Lights and Sweet Music*. We were on the air more or less every week for quite a while, so we became known. There was a small group of musicians, four or five in number, and I was the singing voice. As a result I became a name up and down the country without people ever knowing what I looked like. So by the time I was asked to do television at Alexandra Palace in 1936, people knew me by name as far away as Aberdeen, but they had never seen me in the flesh.

At Alexandra Palace, you had to step over all these cables that were all

Elisabeth Welch and Paul Robeson in *Song of Freedom* (1936).

over the floor, some of them as big as water hoses like the ones you see in the streets, and some very narrow. You had to climb over a whole sea of cables just to get to the camera, and when you got to the camera, which never moved, you just stood there in front of it. The cameras were like the old-fashioned still cameras used to take pictures – the cameraman wore a black hood over his head. You didn't need make up. Everybody was white, white, white – you only had eyes and black lips. It was in black and white, of course, and you just stood there and sang your song. Then you waited until somebody said 'Cut' or 'Black out', or whatever, and moved away. It was static, nerve-racking, but amusing. And, when you had a studio with four or five artistes doing a programme, it was chaotic. I mean, we were falling over each other and trying to be quiet at the same time! But we had fun. It was wonderful.

Of course, you must also remember that everything was live. If you made a mistake, you couldn't just re-do it from scratch. And the cameras weren't that reliable – during a play or an evening of artistes in a concert-type production, you would be singing away or speaking when suddenly you'd hear 'Cut! The camera's gone'. Then we'd have to set the scene up again and make a new start. But we were all young then, and we could laugh about it.

'Auntie Beeb' and the rules of etiquette ● We used to have to worry a lot about what clothes we wore because, in those days, there was no wardrobe department. We wore our best clothes even when we were doing radio things at what we called The Big House in Portland Place. The BBC was called 'Auntie' because it had a reputation for being prim and prissy. The ladies, for example, never had plunges in their dresses – the BBC were very strict about that – and the men, or most of the men had to wear evening jackets and a black tie. Certainly, all the announcers had to dress like that. But we all kept our sense of humour.

Pauline Henriques was born in Jamaica and came to Britain with her family as a young child in 1919. A theatre-goer from an early age, Pauline visited the Old Vic every Saturday afternoon for about fifteen years with one of her older brothers.

Pauline studied acting at LAMDA (London Academy of Music and Dramatic Art) and one of her earliest experiences was understudying the London West End production of the American play *Anna Lucasta* at His Majesty's Theatre 1947-8.

In 1950 Pauline appeared as Emilia in Kenneth Tynan's Arts Council stage tour of *Othello*, which starred the African-American actor Gordon Heath. In the post-war years she made numerous radio broadcasts in programmes like *Caribbean Voices* for the BBC's West Indies service. Pauline made her first appearance in British television in Eugene O'Neill's *All God's Chillun Got Wings* with Robert Adams and Edric Connor. This was broadcast live from Alexandra Palace by the BBC in 1946. She later acted in television plays like *Halcyon Days* (1954) and John Elliot's innovative drama-documentary *A Man from the Sun* (1956).

In the late 50s Pauline retired from acting and spent the next thirty years in social work.

I always claim that I was the very first West Indian immigrant ever, but it's not actually true because there were quite a few West Indians who had come here to study and then gone back. But my family was certainly one of the first that actually came as a complete family. We came because my father had a passion for English education, which he thought was the most wonderful gift he could give his children. So he and my mother decided that they would wait until there were six of us children, when the older ones would be ready for university and the younger ones ready for school, and then we would come. So, we did and settled in a North London suburb.

We were a very unusual family in as much as the six of us were passionate about the theatre. We all took a tremendous interest in it and visited it a lot. I can remember going with one of my older brothers to the Old Vic every Saturday afternoon and queuing up. We saw play after play with all the great names. We enjoyed the experience of seeing a play on stage, and then enjoyed acting out the roles ourselves at home. We were that sort of family.

I remember seeing Paul Robeson as Othello at the Old Vic in 1930 with

Peggy Ashcroft. I always had a tremendous admiration for him because he had such a wonderful voice – there was not another like it. He also had a tremendous presence, charisma. But I was disappointed in his performance of Othello, because, although he had tremendous size and presence augmented by his gorgeous voice, he was, in my opinion, quite wooden. He carried the part with presence, but that wasn't really enough. When you are as deeply immersed in the theatre as we were, you want something different and I found lacks in Robeson's portrayal of a man torn apart by jealousy.

I had always wanted to be an actress. In fact, I spent the whole of my life acting on and off the stage, and played all the best roles that were to be had in school. My parents were used to having their six children all theatre mad and acting roles around the house all the time. But they were a little put out when I said I wanted to go into the theatre. They thought it would be nice if I studied law or went into medicine instead. They said 'Well, you know, you're not really going to do very well in the theatre because you can't sing or dance, and there's very little opportunity for straight, legitimate actresses. But if you want to take your chances, do it'. So they financed me to study at the London Academy of Music and Dramatic Art. I went there for a short course and certainly learnt how to use my voice, to project, to speak clearly and to lose my Jamaican accent. It was an extremely useful beginning. In fact, it's been extremely useful to me in my second career – social work.

But it was very hard breaking into the theatre, and I found myself playing a variety of American coloured maids. I learnt to say 'Yessum, I'sa coming with dem hors d'oeuvres you ordered!' in four or five different American accents. It was experience and I was lucky to get it, so I stuck around and did it. But I really wanted a part that would allow me to use my voice and speak clearly. I did manage to get one or two better parts as time went on.

Elisabeth Welch – early role model ● I just adored Elisabeth Welch. I thought she was the most wonderful black person ever. She had grace and beauty, and a tremendous range in her singing voice. She could also act. So, of course, I modelled myself on her and dreamed that, maybe, one day I could be her understudy. But that dream was never realised. I understudied other people, but never got to understudy Elisabeth Welch.

All God's Chillun Got Wings **(BBC, 1946)** ● After the war, when the BBC television service resumed in 1946, I appeared in a live production of Eugene O'Neill's *All God's Chillun Got Wings* at Alexandra Palace. It was the first time I had appeared in a BBC television production, and there were black and white people in the cast. There was Robert Adams who played the lead, Joyce Heron, and Connie Smith who played my mother. I think Edric

Robert Adams, Sydney Keith, Joyce Heron, Tommy Duggan, and Edric Connor in a scene from *All God's Chillun Got Wings* (BBC TV, 1946).

Connor was in it as well. It was tremendously exciting for me, partly because of the stature of Eugene O'Neill and partly because of the play itself. Although it had one or two black characters in it who were stereo-typed, it had some very strong parts for black people. Robert Adams had the opportunity to show his range of acting. And I was lucky as well, because I played his rather bluestocking sister who is very keen on putting over the black point of view, that it is important to be courageous and very proud of your blackness. I identified very strongly with that.

It was also a wonderful experience because television was in its infancy and very different from television today. We had two or three sets which we had to move between acts during the play. There were also these marks on the floor which were supposed to guide our movements, but we were rather inhibited by them. And then there were the dreadful snakes of cable all over the place, so we had to be very careful where we walked. And yet out of this chaos – and despite the static cameras, which meant we had to keep moving from one camera to another – came this magic of a well-produced play.

I think *All God's Chillun Got Wings* was a very important thing for the

BBC to do at that time. After all, it was the 40s and a very different world then for black people. I think the BBC pioneered something in giving us a play of that stature to act in.

Anna Lucasta (1947-8) ● I felt I was extremely lucky to be an understudy in *Anna Lucasta*. This was an American Negro Theatre production which had come over with the complete cast. It opened at what was His Majesty's Theatre. There was an enormous build-up for this American theatre company, and everybody was quite feverish because rumour had it that they were going to have British black understudies. So I was thrilled when I got the part of understudying Georgia Burke. She was the oldest and frailest member of the cast, but she never missed a single performance! So I was one of the few understudies who never went on stage.

Anna Lucasta had a tremendous impact on the British public and we knew almost immediately that the play was going to run. It ran for two years.

To gain stage experience, the understudies formed themselves into a small company and performed in a small theatre in Hampstead, North London ● After we had rehearsed our understudies' parts for a few weeks, we realised that we were going to have a lot of evenings with nothing to do. So I thought it would be a good idea if we – the British blacks who were the understudies – got together and did our own production. We decided to do a one-act play and chose Thornton Wilder's *The Happy Journey*, a rather unusual play about some people going on a journey in a car. We had to do quite a lot of miming, so it was an imaginative production. The cast included Errol John, Earl Cameron, a woman called Rita Williams, and myself – that was the nucleus of what we were beginning to think of as the British Black Theatre Movement. We didn't actually give ourselves a grand title. Many of us had so little experience in the theatre that we couldn't really compare ourselves with the American actors. But we had good strong voices, and decided to get experience by seeing if we could do this play and put it on as a serious production.

I booked a little theatre in Hampstead, North London, and we tried it out on a Sunday evening. We were very lucky because we had good support from the *Anna Lucasta* company. They were really wonderful. They gave us some publicity, came to the show, and got some of their friends to come as well. We also had a call boy at that time – a young boy of about sixteen called Dickie Valentine, who later became a famous singer. He wasn't actually in the play, but he did some entertaining to make it a full evening. I think we did something really important with that production. It helped to launch people by giving them the confidence to get on and take parts when

Caribbean Voices: Pauline Henriques reads short stories and poetry for BBC Radio's West Indies service (1952).

they came along. Certainly Errol John and Earl Cameron gained a lot of confidence from doing it.

Errol John ● Errol John was understudying with us in *Anna Lucasta*, and I immediately recognised his lovely personality and tremendous voice. But he was a rather shy, reserved, retiring person who found it difficult to be with a group of actors who were taking the job of acting seriously, but also enjoying it and being very joyous about it. This wasn't Errol's scene. He found it quite hard to do that. I can remember encouraging him to try and come out of his shell and to enjoy acting – because black actors have this ability to bring a sort of inner joy and vivacity to the roles that they play. I tried to encourage this in Errol. I gave him his very first opportunity in the theatre, and I was right there behind him, doing a good counselling job on him. I think it gave him a good start. He did very well for quite a time, but then things went wrong for him. He went to America and that didn't live up to his expectations. He went back to the Caribbean and that didn't live up to his expectations either. Very sadly, he just faded out of the scene and died in 1988. He hadn't been acting for quite a time. It was a very great loss, because the things he did do were very good.

Kenneth Tynan's Arts Council tour of *Othello* (1950) ● Kenneth Tynan, who at that time was very well known as a theatre critic and producer, had the idea of doing a production of *Othello* and touring it to the theatreless towns of Britain. It was a six-month tour and Tynan decided on a most original presentation of the play. First of all, he cast Gordon Heath as Othello. Gordon was a slim, sensitive American actor who was really a singer, but he had a lot to give to the theatre. We were all amazed that he had the range to play Othello, but he was, in fact, a very good and a very unusual Othello. Tynan also decided to cast *Othello* with a black Emilia, and that's where I came in.

The tour of the theatreless towns of Britain gave us tremendous experience. Apart from anything else, the staging was wonderful because the set had to be adjusted for playing in a school hall which might not have a stage at all, for a church hall which was bigger, or, if we were lucky, as we were on three or four occasions during the tour, for a full-size theatre. So the staging was always wonderfully imaginative because it had to be constantly adjusted for the different venues. It was a tremendous experience and, in a way, it changed my attitude to the theatre. After playing Emilia and speaking Shakespeare's wonderful language, I just couldn't go back to playing American coloured maids any more. I didn't want to do anything except speak language like that. That's when I began to look for a different career.

A Man from the Sun **(BBC, 1956)** ● John Elliot's drama documentary, *A Man from the Sun*, was another landmark for me. It was about working-class black people, and we were portrayed as real people, not as stereotypes. It gave a voice to black people who, unlike myself, had recently arrived in Britain. It was a very good, very lively play that had a lot of strands woven into it. It was a play for the day, right for the time, and I felt it was a very exciting thing for the BBC to do.

Gordon Heath as Othello, with Paul Rogers in *Othello* (BBC TV, 1955).

New career in social work ● I realised after I had played the part of Emilia in Kenneth Tynan's production of *Othello* that I didn't really want to play the parts that were open to me. There had not been a really tremendous advance for Negroes in the theatre in the late 50s, so I decided to train for my other love, social work. I then spent the next thirty years as a social worker. I felt it was an important, very satisfying thing for me to do, although I always loved the theatre and continued to think about it an awful lot.

I was always interested in the black movement and in what was happening with black people, and I became particularly concerned about the placing of mixed-race and black children with white families. I was worried, for example, that such children would not be able to find role models within the family, and so on. The last thing I did for television was Philip Donnellan's documentary, *The Colony*. I did the introduction for this and was able to talk about the placing of mixed-race children and some of the hazards involved.

Drama today ● I'm in a state of conflict about what is happening for black people in today's theatre and television. On the one hand, I'm delighted to see the chances they are getting, and the opportunities there are to play parts. But, unfortunately, I think a lot of the parts are still very stereotyped. They're played for laughs, and black people still don't get parts in really meaty dramas. We haven't seen anything of the same stature as *All God's Chillun Got Wings*, for example. That's what I mean about being in a state of conflict. I'm delighted to see that we're getting on, but I think we need more quality drama opportunities to show the talent we have.

There is a tremendous amount of talent amongst black people. You see flashes of it sometimes in a play. What is needed are more opportunities for full-length dramas with black actors – not just one black actor, but several. I do wish the BBC and the ITV companies would think about that. When the expression of talent becomes stereotyped, diluted, and is too often based around sitcoms and jokes, that talent is diluted and diminished.

— PEARL CONNOR —

Pearl Connor was born in Trinidad and came to Britain in the early 50s to study law at London University. As Pearl Nunez she has worked as an actress since that time, but she is, perhaps, best known for her pioneering work as an actors' agent and campaigner. In the 50s Pearl married the Trinidadian singer, actor and film-maker Edric Connor (1915-68) and in 1956 they started an agency. Originally called The Edric Connor Agency, it later became known as the Afro Asian Caribbean Agency. Through Pearl's efforts, it represented people from the Caribbean, Malaysia, India and Africa. Pearl left the Agency in 1974.

In 1963 Pearl was instrumental in establishing the Negro Theatre Workshop, one of the first black theatre workshops in Britain. Pearl and Edric launched the Workshop at London's Lyric Theatre with a production of *A Wreath for Udomo*, adapted from the novel by Peter Abrahams and featuring Earl Cameron, Edric Connor, Lloyd Reckord and Joan Hooley. The Negro Theatre Workshop's production of *The Dark Disciples*, an enactment of the Easter Story by a company of twenty-five black actors, was produced for television by the BBC in 1966.

I was a student in Trinidad when Edric left to come to England. He came from a very poor background in a village called Mayaro and had won a scholarship to do engineering in Port of Spain. He was a great researcher, even in those days as a young man. He had one of the finest collections of Trinidadian folk songs and he brought this with him to England when he came after the war. That's what attracted the BBC to him or, rather, how they were attracted to each other. It was how he started his connection with the media, and with getting himself widely known in this country. Edric always sang and he would listen to hundreds of records of opera singers, like Caruso, on his little gramophone in Trinidad. We had no real schooling in the arts at that time, but Edric was able to go to America for a short period where he had some special voice training. When he came to England he studied privately with one or two teachers, to develop his skills as a singer both in opera and in folk.

As a Trinidadian during pre-independence, Edric had a consciousness of himself and of the country from which he came. He had a strong sense of national identity which made him a pioneer of our folk arts in England. He was constantly promoting our songs, music and folklore, and trying to get people interested in our culture. After all, we were part of the Common-

Edric Connor rehearsing at Alexandra Palace for the television series *Serenade in Sepia* (1946).

wealth and this was the mother country – though I say that, more or less, with tongue-in-cheek because there wasn't much mothering at that time. But he came and made an input. He was a front man, so to speak. He had a charming personality and people liked him. He performed and loved the folk songs, and all aspects of the Caribbean. He forged ahead trying to get people, like Pauline Henriques and Robert Adams, working with him to build a structure with which to influence the British public.

Back home, Edric was a Trinidadian hero – someone we all admired. And his influence led to artistes, whom he felt needed to be presented to the British public, leaving Trinidad and going to London. He was deeply imbued with the idea of the representation of Caribbean artistes, or Afro-Caribbean artistes as we called them – because in the struggle for independence, Trinidad and Tobago was going through the same political changes as Nigeria, Ghana, Kenya, and so on. Many of the people involved in those struggles in Africa were friends of ours, and they too were involved in the idea of representing the black person in a humane and human manner. So we were involved with Africa from the word go. Our roots were in Africa.

Robert Adams with Margaretta Scott and Mary Martlew in *The Merchant of Venice* (BBC TV, 1947).

In Britain, Edric had built up such a reputation with his colleagues in the theatre, that people came to him for advice about any kind of non-European subject, or they would ask him to recommend a Caribbean, or black, or African, or Chinese, or Malayan person for a part in a film or documentary. So, for a long time Edric did this as a favour. Indeed, he spent years doing this, just sending people along. Then, when I came in, we continued, but now with the aim of establishing representation.

Establishing the agency ● Having had a legal and Caribbean cultural background, I entered the picture to put the finishing touches on Edric's ideas and to say 'Look, our people need representation. We need Equity representation. We need to know what the rates are. We need to know about repeat fees. We need to know the rights of our artistes'. So, in 1956, Edric founded the Edric Connor Agency, and when he subsequently became busy with filming abroad and his own stage and theatre work, I got more and more involved in running the agency and looking after the artistes. By 1958, when he was going to Stratford to perform at the Shakespeare Memorial

Theatre, I was running the agency myself. It was only a small set up then, and we were working from home. There was no funding to do it in a really big way. But what we had was real, true, and concentrated. Actually, we surprised ourselves when we saw what the people whom we helped could do, and what we could achieve just from a belief in our people and ourselves.

I would say that ninety per cent of the black or Afro-Asian and Oriental people who wanted to join the acting profession found their way to us — some Israelis and Anglo-Saxons as well. The people who came were looking for representation from a source where they felt at ease — and they were very much at ease with us because we had a similar background, colonialism. We had all been ruled by other people and we were now becoming ourselves.

I was working with people from all over the world and had to become very knowledgeable about a wide range of cultural experiences, not just Caribbean. For example, we had an absolutely free hand in casting Chinese actors for the play and film of *Suzy Wong* and *Flower Drum Song*. I must say we recruited quite a few from Chinese restaurants, like Freddie Mills in Soho — we were very good at doing that.

We also did a bit of drama coaching as well. We needed to do that for script reading. We worked with a number of people who had been to university and studied English language and literature, and they were able to help the artistes. We didn't have a school because nobody had money to pay a school. People more or less landed, with bags in hand, and a dream of the mother country with streets paved with gold. What they found were streets paved with good old concrete! And they had to struggle to find places to live. We got involved in the whole spectrum of the artistes' lives. There were problems like ringing up landlords and being told that there was a room available, only to be told when they got there that it had gone. It was 'No Blacks', 'No Irish', 'No dogs' — and we had to cope with that.

The agency provided a kind of backup support structure for the artistes and our home became a sort of centre. Then as we became more professional we moved into other premises. But the need of the people always remained our first priority. We struggled along for years because the pay for artistes was not a lot. We didn't have named artistes on our books, we didn't have people with great reputations, we were building reputations. And that was our pioneering work. We were breaking stones and it was very tough.

Establishing names, building reputations ● When we tried to get our artistes Equity membership, we had a lot of difficulties. To be eligible you had to have forty weeks work in the West End of London — even now, forty weeks is an impossibility! You could join a repertory company, and there was the occasional black play like *A Raisin in the Sun*, and one or two plays or musicals that had parts for a black actor, but that was about it. There were never ten parts available at any given time for black actors, and, at that stage, there were very few fully black productions to rely on. So we had to push people into whatever we could get them, like touring productions and so on.

We also decided that we needed a device to establish our artistes as professionals, so we created our own version of *Spotlight*. We produced sheets about our artistes, with their personal histories and a picture of them, and sent them around – 'This is Lloyd Reckord of Jamaica. He has performed in . . . operas and in . . . pantomimes and has done all these famous Ibsen plays'. That was how we set about building up reputations. People, like Lloyd and Barry Reckord, Bari Johnson, Carmen Munroe, Ena Cabayo, Nadia Cattouse, Ram John Holder and Yemi Ajibade, who had arrived in England were publicised through what we said about them. Fortunately, Edric had enormous clout with producers who believed that he knew what he was talking about. He also had a very good reputation as an actor and singer which was a great benefit to the business.

If he said to a director, or whoever, 'I know so-and-so and he's a good actor. Try him, give him a chance', they would always be satisfied once the person got before the cameras and had a chance. Unfortunately, if you don't have a chance, you are like many a rose born to blush unseen. And a lot of us were unseen.

We were very fortunate in having the Royal Court, and Oscar Lewenstein and George Devine who were the greatest friends black artistes ever had. They gave us Sunday nights and the Theatre Upstairs, and put a lot of effort into getting black artistes off the ground. That helped a lot because people like Johnny Sekka, for example, would not have happened without their help. He is doing very well now in America, but he started off here with us.

We always had a problem in getting material for our artistes to perform here in their own idiom. We had to fight to get plays on that people could appreciate.

The breaks ● Productions like *Hair*, *Jesus Christ Superstar* and *The Black Mikado* were a breakthrough for us and we have to thank Robert Stigwood, the producer, for his approach. At least a third of each cast was non-European or non-white. It gave people like Floella Benjamin, Joan Armatrading, Patti Boulaye and many others a great chance. All these kids went into these shows, and the only general audition criterion was that they must be able to sing and move well.

There were good and bad times, of course, but we were able to get a pianist to work with us to help teach the artistes the songs. If there was a script we'd do it as a training exercise. And we would always send people along to interviews, or to auditions, to familiarise them with that experience. You can imagine what it is like if you have never done an audition before and you get there shaking in your boots. So we propped people up, and did a great service in supporting artistes in all sorts of ways, keeping them going, helping them put on a brave face, and letting them know that anything was possible. And as I said before, shows like *Hair*, *Jesus Christ Superstar* and *The Black Mikado* were important because they gave us the opportunity to show that there were black artistes of ability and professionalism in this country.

Edric Connor's aspirations to become a programme-maker at the BBC and his activities as a film-maker ● Edric had many friends in the BBC, people who appreciated him as an artiste, but they never envisaged him as anything more. He did one of the BBC's directors courses and when he finished that he tried to make films himself.

When Trinidad became independent in 1962, Edric approached our government with a proposal to film the cricket series in the West Indies. It was a great struggle for him to get that project off the ground because people thought that he couldn't do it. It was considered an impossibility – where was he coming from, this actor wanting to make a film on cricket? Mind you, he was an expert cricketer. All Trinidadians kick balls and coconuts on the beach from the time they are tiny boys, and, since Edric came from a village by the sea, he had been knocking a ball about for years. Like his fellow West Indians C.L.R. James and Learie Constantine, he understood the game very well. But he had to fight all the way to make that film, then eventually he got the contract.

Edric filmed in Trinidad and Jamaica. The British Film Institute helped to finance the production. But there were great frustrations because he was stuck in Trinidad without enough money, and I was running to the airport picking up these films and dashing up to the BBC by car. We didn't have an express service like DHL in those days and could not afford it anyway! We even had a great struggle getting the film into Britain, and getting it shown here. It was a great struggle getting it accepted. But, with input and commitment, we succeeded. The film is now in the National Film Archive and every so often some of it gets shown.

We were then invited to Nigeria for their Independence celebrations and the government offered Edric an opportunity to make a film about the country. I returned to England, while Edric stayed out there doing his recce. He then came back to England to raise the money to make the film. I believe the British Film Institute again assisted, and the Nigerian government also put money into it. But it was an ill-fated project. When Edric went back to Nigeria to film he had a great problem – all his crew went down with conjunctivitis and he had to replace people in the middle of the production. This meant a loss of money and time.

He eventually left Nigeria in great haste and with a lot of headaches. It wasn't easy for him. He didn't have the cash flow to make things happen easily. I couldn't join him out there because I had to run the agency in London. But he managed to shoot the film and he brought it back to London to put on the finishing touches for the Nigerian government. He subsequently went back to the Caribbean to make films about the beauties of the Caribbean. He made a lot of films on that subject.

One of the films that he made was *Carnival Fantastique* about the Trinidad Carnival. We showed it at the Cameo Poly which was next door to the Regent Street Polytechnic in Central London. It was successful and ran there for six months. That was a big achievement for Edric. It was also shown at the Edinburgh Film Festival. When we compared our struggle to that of Harry Belafonte and Sidney Poitier who were making films in America, backed by people like Paul Newman, we realised that they had a similar experience to ours. But we in England were like a voice in the wilderness. There was no financial backing, and no black person, or businessman, or enterprise to help us. There wasn't funding at the level that there is now. There was only the British Film Institute and I thank them for what they did for Edric; and I'm sure he would also thank them himself if he were still here today.

The business of professional representation ● When we got into the stream of representation, people came to us because of Edric. He was considered a very big star in the sense of stardom in England. He was very well known, so when people came off the boat, they migrated straight to us. We had a great reputation for looking after people. We didn't make them rich or anything like that – we didn't have that kind of power – but we were able to take care of all the things that could be taken care of.

One of the problems we found early on with casting was that a lot of kids were being picked up at Baker Street station where they were hanging about, and they were being cast because of their behinds, or their eyes, or their faces, or how they walked, or what they did. It was a casting of extras, not necessarily of people who knew the job, or who understood the business, but people who were extremely cheap and who could provide padding for a scene. That was happening a lot and we wanted to break that system and to make production companies come to us for professional black people or Commonwealth people.

Our artistes understood what we were trying to do because we worked very closely with them. It was like a family to start with because there wasn't any money to hire professional press people – the press didn't know what we were talking about, so we had to educate them ourselves. They knew Edric, of course, and if he asked them to come and see something, they would. In our efforts to make all this work we put ourselves on the line and consequently lost two homes in the process – one because of the films, another because of the financial pressures of running the agency.

But Edric always believed that if you get something into your head, an idea, a dream, something magical could happen. I think there is some magic nowadays, but magic eluded us at that time. We were in the struggle, or what we called the struggle – fighting for recognition, fighting for people to know who we were and to accept our talent. That's where we stood then.

The American bias ● There was unfortunately, at that time, a bias about either using black Americans, or casting Caribbean actors with American accents. Even Edric, who was a brilliant actor and singer, met this problem, because the American media and the American projection was so enormous that British people were comatose under its influence. The whole gimmick was if you were American they accepted you. Black Americans had *Ebony* magazine and their own media working for them, plus the fact that there are so many millions of them in America.

But we in England did not have our own media promoting us – *West Indian Gazette* came later, *The Voice* even more recently. So we always had to wait to see if the *Daily Telegraph* or *The Guardian* would take note of what we were doing. We suffered a lot because of this bias, but we learnt early on that to be black American was an advantage. So we worked on it. A lot of our young men would go to Rome and spend a few months working on their 'American style'! And when they went for an interview they would wear tight jeans, lean up against a wall, stick their leg on the wall, throw their heads back and say 'Hi' – and it worked!

Even our writers were experiencing this kind of difficulty – for example, Errol John, when he wrote *Moon on a Rainbow Shawl*, which won him *The Observer* Award, felt that he couldn't succeed without having Americans in the cast of his stage production. This was a shock to us. When the Royal Court presented the play after he had won the award, at least three of the leads were American including Vinette Carroll. Although they were very expert, we thought 'What a loss of an opportunity. Here is a Caribbean play which we could do very well, an award-winning play which will attract attention', and yet this stereotypical practice is happening. We were very disappointed. And then, of course, Errol himself took off to America where he met another set of frustrations.

Errol John ● I think I can talk about this now. Errol became more and more frustrated about not achieving what he thought he would achieve, in not getting to where he felt he could get. He was a very versatile man, a brilliant actor and a talented writer with a fine collection of plays behind him. He had the sort of achievements which, when they happen to a white actor, mean that person receives a great deal of recognition. But that didn't happen for Errol and eventually he was brought right down to his knees, with the frustration of not getting things done. His talent was always there but the ability to project it wasn't. He virtually dropped out altogether, and we couldn't reach him, couldn't contact him. He went back to the West Indies and walked about in his native land, Trinidad, and then he came back to England. Isolated, lonely, feeling forgotten and dejected, he died alone in his bed – he was found by his landlady. It was a tragic end to one of our most talented artistes.

The Negro Theatre Workshop and their staging of *The Dark Disciples* which the BBC televised in 1966 ● The Negro Theatre Workshop came about because we had very little work coming in, and we decided to try and put together things that we could present ourselves and invite people to come and see. Carmen Munroe and Horace James put on all the Ibsen plays in St Pancras Town Hall and other similar halls that had such high stages you couldn't even see the artistes! Fortunately, The Africa Centre in London had just been established and they had an empty hall which we were able to use very cheaply. So we gathered our people together and the first really major thing we tried to do was a jazz version of the St Luke Passion called, if you please, *The Dark Disciples*!

It was Easter 1966 and there was a World Festival of Black and African Arts happening in Senegal. We took *The Dark Disciples* there and performed it very successfully in a big cathedral. We also took a play by the Nigerian playwright, Obi Egbuna, called *Wind versus Polygamy*. Earl Cameron was among the very distinguished artistes who went out to perform in that play. We made an enormous impact in Senegal, and that helped us to establish some of the people in the group professionally.

When we got back to England, we went to see Equity and talked to them about our situation – that we could not live in a vacuum, that we had to work something out regarding the forty weeks eligibility rule, and that the criteria set up for British artistes could not possibly be suitable for us, and so on. Of course, their answer was that there was no difference, that they did not accept that there was a difference between people. We couldn't agree, of course, and it has subsequently been acknowledged. There is now a black section in Equity representing black artistes and their situation. But, in those days people didn't want to see that there was a difference, that black artistes were being ignored, were not known about. And because it was impossible to become known, we couldn't get Equity membership. However, people like Horace James, Lloyd Reckord and many others subsequently became members.

The lack of quality drama and the damage done by *Love Thy Neighbour* ● We were glad to see our actors appearing in sitcoms like *Love Thy Neighbour* and *Mixed Blessings*. But at the same time, we felt cheated because we knew these programmes projected a one-sided view of us. The whole matter of 'nig nog' and 'honky' and all that rubbish in *Love Thy Neighbour*, for example, steamed us up. I mean, friends started calling each other 'nig nog' and 'honky', which we banned in our homes. We wouldn't have it. It went too far. What's more, it wasn't balanced by serious drama showing us as we really are and as we have been.

It's true that television sitcoms gave us opportunities for work, which we wanted. Everybody was glad to get in and to be working regularly. But *Love Thy Neighbour* and all the send-ups in it, really hurt us. It hurt us because we had nothing comparative in real drama to show who we really are. Our personas were being hurt, and we were being damaged in this community.

In Britain we need recognition as individuals and as people of intelligence and of character. So we are grieved by these situation comedies – they strike our children and our grandchildren, and they strike our community. The input that we could be making could be so much more meaningful, if people could only see the other side of us, how we really live.

I'm not saying that we don't have our criminals, or thieves, or cheats. And I'm not saying that drama and documentary programmes shouldn't deal with these negative aspects of life. But they must also show us doing productive things, serious things in life, because we are humane and human. We've been cheated of this kind of heritage in this society – and a lot more attention needs to be paid to giving us serious drama, serious presentations of ourselves. We have come here, we have been here a long time, and we are part of this society. These experiences need to be reflected more regularly in serious drama.

Cy Grant was born in Guyana and worked as a civil servant until 1941 when he joined the RAF as a navigator in Bomber Command. Cy was a prisoner of war in Germany for two years. After the war he studied law at Middle Temple and was called to the Bar in 1950. Deciding on a stage career instead, he played a small part in Laurence Olivier's production of the Cleopatra plays, travelling with the company to America in 1951.

His London West End stage appearances include *Cindy Ella* (1962) and, in 1965, he played Othello at the Phoenix Theatre in Leicester.

Cy's film appearances include *Sea Wife* (1957) with Richard Burton and Joan Collins, and *Shaft in Africa* (1973).

He has acted in a number of important television dramas, including John Elliot's *A Man from the Sun* (BBC, 1956), *Home of the Brave* (Granada, 1957), and John Mortimer's *The Encyclopaedist* (1961).

Cy also sang the news in calypso in the popular BBC magazine programme *Tonight* from 1957-60. He later took part in two music programmes: *Freedom Road — Songs of Negro Protest* (Associated Rediffusion, 1964) with Cleo Laine and Nadia Cattouse, and *Cindy Ella* (1966) with Cleo Laine and Elisabeth Welch. He was also one of the voices for the popular puppet series *Captain Scarlet and the Mysterons* (1967-8). From 1974-7 Cy was the Chairman and Co-founder of Drum Arts Centre, a Black Arts Centre based in London.

I was born in Guyana. My father was a Moravian minister of African descent, my mother was Eurasian – her father was English and was connected with Nelson in some way. I was brought up in a typically colonial way, singing 'Rule Britannia' and learning about English history and geography, but not knowing anything about the country I was born in. I knew as a young person in Guyana that something was wrong. I didn't feel privileged, even though my family life was very privileged –

we had servants for example. And, even as someone who was brought up to feel English and appreciate European music and Shakespeare, I felt frustrated with the colonial way of life. I knew that the colony was too small to hold me. I think that happened to lots of West Indians who had any kind of creative ability. Look at what happened to all our writers – they simply left and went to America or Britain. And history proved them right because look what happened to Guyana after independence – the country went to pieces.

My father would have liked me to go into the ministry, but I knew I had no specific calling for it, though I thought at one stage that I'd go into it because it would give me an opportunity to get a university education. But then the Second World War came and I applied for aircrew in the Royal Air Force. I was one of the first four people who joined the RAF from the colonies. They had just changed their policy towards recruiting black people, so that's how I got in. I trained as a pilot but then, half way through my training, I was switched to navigator. I didn't make anything of this at the time, because I did not realise that it was not above board. But, much later, I discovered through a friend that there were problems with the English aircrew not wanting to fly with black pilots. At one stage, I tried to get out of the RAF, but without success.

I flew on bombing missions over the Ruhr and was shot down on my third mission. I was caught by the Germans and was a prisoner of war for two years – which is a long story in itself. As a prisoner of war, I had a great deal of time to reflect on the direction of my life and on what I wanted to do with my life after I got out. I met a lot of good people because, as an officer in the RAF, you were among the cream of officers. I met all sorts of people, including writers, schoolteachers, lecturers and scientists. And, living for two years close together, I learnt a great deal and asked a lot of questions – that's where I matured, actually. I decided then, that I would study law, because I wanted to go back to the Caribbean. My ambition was to help get the British out of the West Indies.

I came back to England and stayed on in the RAF for another year or so. Around this time, they had set up a special section with the Colonial Office, a kind of liaison office to help black air servicemen who had come over to service and maintain the planes. The black servicemen were having a lot of hassles as you can imagine, and they needed people to defend them at court martials and other disputes. So that was my job for about a year, which also fitted in with my plans. When I was finally demobbed I went to study law at Middle Temple and was called to the Bar in 1950. I went on stage the following year.

Becoming an actor ● I found it very difficult settling back in Guyana, so I came back to England and tried to find a job, any job, so that I could live. The fact that I was a qualified barrister-at-law and had been an officer in the RAF didn't help me to find a job – that tells you a lot about racism in those days. Then an opportunity came along for me to act. Earl Cameron, one of the first black actors who had made it in this country, left a play which he was touring – a terrible thing called *14 Dead Street, Harlem*. I auditioned for it and got the part. I toured for a year and, in that time, I learnt how to act. Then I auditioned for the Olivier Company, which was the

Festival of Britain Company at the St James's Theatre with Laurence Olivier. It was very exciting because this was the cream of the acting profession in Britain. Just being in a company like that, although I was literally only carrying a spear and understudying a small part, I learnt a lot about stage-craft – one learns a lot by just being close to good actors.

Up to that point racism had not entered into the equation as far as the kind of parts I was playing. The first play I was in didn't have any kind of racial theme as such – there just happened to be a black guy running a club in Harlem. Racism was not the issue – it was just dealing with a certain kind of low life. But racism did come into it in other ways, because at one stage Olivier didn't want to take me to America because he feared that I might run into racism! I said 'Come on, Larry, this country is just as racist as America. And, in any case, I'd like to see it for myself'. He said 'OK' and I went to America with the company.

And, sure enough, we got to America and everywhere we turned, there were black people. This was the early 50s – I mean, half the police were black, there were black judges, and so on. There was a highly publicised court case going on at the time involving Tallulah Bankhead who was having some altercation with her maid. The English actors in the Company were all there to see the great Tallulah Bankhead and they had their eyes opened – 'Oh, there's a black judge. Ridiculous!'

In 1956, I had big billing in a BBC television play called *A Man from the Sun*, which was written and produced by John Elliot. In the following year I starred in *Home of the Brave* (Granada), a very powerful play written by Arthur Laurents and directed by Silvio Narizzano, who was one of the great directors in this country at the time. It was very powerful television, and the write-ups were really very good as well. It was broadcast live, the night after the first *Tonight* programme I did. So my career was going very well.

Singing topical calypsos on BBC TV's *Tonight* programme ● I used to sing calypsos in a club in Knightsbridge called Esmarelda's Bar. It was a very popular place where all London society used to go. Somebody – I don't recall who it was – asked me if I would be interested in singing a calypso on television. I said 'OK', and then they asked if I would like to do it every night. I said 'No way' because I wouldn't want to have to write a calypso every night of my life. I agreed to do it possibly once a week. At the time it was a nice little gimmick, but I didn't realise that it was going to develop into such a fantastic programme.

I appeared on the *Tonight* programme on and off for three years. I wasn't on continuously because they decided they would alternate me with others. For instance, I alternated with Rory and Alex McEwan, two Scottish nobility lads, who were very high-powered guys. And it worked out fine,

Cy Grant, folk singer and actor in 1960.

except that I found the pressure of trying to write a calypso every night too much. So, believe it or not, they got Bernard Levin to write the calypsos for me. In those days, Levin was considered to be a whizzkid. He was close to the news and was clever. He wrote the lyrics to my calypsos, though I changed a lot to make them scan. Sometimes I would get them only half an hour before the show. Usually we got the material about two o'clock in the afternoon, but sometimes it came late and we were still polishing it five minutes before we went on the air. It was quite a traumatic experience.

The whole thing about *Tonight* was that it was both an innovative programme and an irreverent one. The programmes were not done from Lime Grove. We had a poky little studio called Studio M in another building. And because we were away from authority, we could literally do what we liked. There was a kind of hit-and-miss feeling about the programme, which was very irreverent. And there were so many hitches – it was live television and things would go wrong, or people wouldn't turn up, or something. It was very hard work, and there was always a panic, but it was fun. It was really great excitement being part of that team. I treasured it. There were aspects about it that I didn't like, but it was great fun because we were doing something that was immediately popular. It set the scene for what television should be like.

I was a kind of stop-gap guy. My main purpose on the programme was to sing a calypso at the beginning of the show. And if something went wrong in the studio, they'd say 'Come on, Cy, sing your song', and suddenly the camera would turn on me and I would have to sing, which was great. It kept me on my toes because I had about three hundred songs in my repertoire. One of the disadvantages about it was that I could not really make a good enough arrangement. My creative thing was not as good as it should have been.

Tonight made me very popular. Everywhere I went people knew me. It sparked a lot of work for me and I started doing lots of cabaret. However, I don't think if I had asked to be an interviewer, that they would have entertained that suggestion. I don't think anyone saw me as anything other than a calypso singer, someone singing something that was very trivial and very expendable. I don't think anyone appreciated that I had anything else to offer. So while *Tonight* was great fun to do, there was a terrible price to pay. I had been an established actor in film, but nobody saw me any more as an actor, and I never got asked to play dramatic parts any more.

If *Tonight* had lasted for just six months it would have been great, maybe. But I got typecast as a calypso singer. Now, there's nothing wrong with calypsos, they are part of my tradition as a Caribbean person. They have their function and I'm very proud that I sing them. But the public saw me as just a calypso singer – people still refer to me as a calypso singer. So I paid a price for staying on the programme so long.

Freedom Road (1964), which featured protest songs of the civil rights movement, and the BBC's *Cindy Ella* (1966), a musical spoof of a well-known fairy tale ● *Freedom Road* featured the best of all the civil rights protest songs, such as 'We Shall Overcome', and it had great singers on the programme like Cleo Laine, Madeleine Bell, Pearl Prescod and Nadia Cattouse. It was a beautiful programme. We actually made a record of the sound track, but it wasn't very good. The programme was written by Elkan Allan, who I had worked with back in the 50s, when he was with the BBC World Service. I did a series of Caribbean folk songs for him, which was quite unbelievable. *Freedom Road* was made during the time of the civil rights movement in America, when the news was dominated by Martin Luther King and Malcolm X, and when the big racial upheaval was happening across America. These events politicised me. I began to read books like *The Autobiography of Malcolm X.*

The other programme, *Cindy Ella*, was a delight. It was spoofing the *Cinderella* story – set in the American South and done with such good taste. It's the only thing that redeems the absurdity of trying to do *Cinderella*. There were four of us in the cast including Cleo Laine, and we each doubled up and played about three or four roles. I played Peanuts and Prince Charming Jones. It was a delightful piece. It started out as a radio play, went to the theatre – the Garrick Theatre in London's West End – then became a television programme which was repeated twice at Christmas. It was turned into a record and a book as well.

'I moved from being a smiling, nice friendly character to someone who, by 1974, was a very angry black man. I was angry at the racism in this country from everybody. I don't think that anybody had ever really admitted to it.' (Cy Grant) ● I would say that that quote from me is a true statement – it reflects the change that I went through during the late 60s and early 70s. I was perceived as a nice, pleasant person on television – *Tonight* was that kind of programme. It was lighthearted. I was young, I was happy, I was not politically aware, and racism was not at the top of my agenda then. That came in 1968 when Enoch Powell started to open his big mouth. I was very angry when Powell made his 'rivers of blood' speech. It started to affect the quality of my life very much; people became overtly racist. Even the police started to stop you if you were driving a nice car, just to intimidate you. It was during this period that I moved from being a friendly guy, to being an angry person.

The anger was not only because of the open kind of speeches which were reported by all the press, as though they weren't racist, but also because they were putting black people in gaol. There was a black guy in this country at the time who called himself Michael X. He was gaoled for inciting racial hatred, yet they never charged Enoch Powell or any of those other people like the National Front for inciting racial hatred. Such racist double standards made me angry.

On top of that, I found that the frustration of being a black actor is that one lives in a kind of existential dilemma. If you've got to be a black actor playing only black roles, it is an existential dilemma. OK, it's nice to be seen. I used to think 'Great, you've made it'. But when you think about it, it was all just a distraction and not necessarily important in life. These things are nice and they're fun, but if as a black person you feel that that is all you've got, if you don't comment on the quality of your life, and if you cannot see where you are, then it's like being a phantom of somebody else's opera.

These things were dawning on me with the emergence of the civil rights movement in America, with Enoch Powell opening his mouth, and with the oil crisis which gripped us all in the early 70s. I was frustrated because I was an actor, but I was not getting roles because people saw me only as a calypso singer. I found a way out by specialising in concerts, but when parts came along I took them – for example, I played Othello in 1965 at the Phoenix Theatre in Leicester.

I would occasionally get a decent role to play, but I didn't get much of a choice. Our problem is that we don't normally get a choice. If we had a choice of what plays to do on television, everything would be OK for black actors. But we don't. In the end, I made that choice for myself – I said 'No, I'm not going to play certain roles, I'm not going to be in *Love Thy Neighbour*, I'm not going to deal with that kind of crap'. So I started singing seriously – I did a concert at the Queen Elizabeth Hall, basically singing songs of protest, beautiful songs with good guitar accompaniment. Then the oil crisis hit in 1973, things started to change again, and a lot of work ceased for me.

Drum, the London-based Black Arts Centre ● The decision to set up Drum came out of realising that people had always been saying how black actors didn't have enough experience, and that there was no way they could get experience because it was a chicken-and-egg situation. If there were no opportunities to gain experience, how then could they get experience. So I decided to set up a Black Arts Centre – to do workshops, to train young black actors, to give them a chance to learn their profession, to learn voice production, and so on.

At that time, around 1974, I met John Mapandero, a very ambitious young Zimbabwean who had an idea to set up a centre along with the visual arts, because he knew about African painting and sculpture. We talked about the whole concept and decided to work together. He was a very bright guy. He is now Chairman of the Arts Foundation in Zimbabwe. We worked very well together in setting up Drum.

I had the edge because I had presented a very friendly image on *Tonight*, and my image helped to open a lot of doors. We went all around the country, meeting important newspaper editors and Members of Parliament, including Merlyn Rees (who was Home Secretary at the time), architects, anyone who could help towards building a centre. And people listened to me. We were promised premises in the new Covent Garden development which had just started. We brought over a director from New York to run drama workshops. It was a very exciting and innovative project.

John Mapandero was very ambitious, very pushy, and very good. I thought we made a good team. But, unfortunately, I could not keep tabs on the operation because I had to subsidise my living. I was doing cabaret and travelling around acting. Our relationship started to become strained, especially when John started introducing people into the organisation who I did not particularly like. Eventually, sad to say, I resigned. But I'm not sorry I did so because, in a sense, I found that this was another step in my own journey, in my discovery of myself and of my own reality. I was in the process of defining myself purely in terms of being black.

It's essential for a black person to see him/herself as black. Identity is absolutely important. If you don't define yourself, someone else is going to define you. So, we have to start by defining ourselves and finding pride in ourselves, and looking at our own history and at our own culture, and seeing the things that are worthwhile.

The process of change — television today ● I believe television acts as a kind of mirror – it reflects the state of society. The beliefs, the presumptions, the culture that the society identifies with are all reflected by television. So, on that basis, we could say that things have changed, though there is still a great deal of tokenism. Until black people are truly recognised and valued within society, none of it is going to make a great change.

There are some significant changes, like the arrival of black directors who we see periodically on television. I feel that Channel 4 has done some exemplary work like *The Bandung File*. BBC2 has recently been doing some very good stuff. The *Black in Europe* series, for example, at least exposed the racism that exists in all the other major European countries. The fact that we can watch these programmes on television, as part of our normal diet, is quite extraordinary – a very big move forward. And Stuart Hall's history of the Caribbean, *Redemption Song*, was also a fine series. The fact that we now have several black newscasters is also very good. But I think we need more black hosts on ordinary mainstream programmes like chat shows, current affairs, and so on. This is happening on American television, and needs to start happening here in Britain.

Television will change when society changes. My utopian vision of television will only materialise when we have utopia here in Europe, not before.

Lloyd Reckord was born in Jamaica and came to Britain in the early 50s. He studied at the Bristol Old Vic Theatre and then joined the Old Vic Company in London. In 1958 he appeared in his brother Barry's play *Flesh to a Tiger* at the Royal Court with Cleo Laine. This was followed by leading roles on stage and in television, including the London West End production of the Ted Willis play, *Hot Summer Night*, which was also produced for television as an Armchair Theatre presentation in 1959.

His other television appearances include Eugene O'Neill's *All God's Chillun Got Wings* (1959), *Drama '61: The Day of the Fox* (1961) written by Jan Carew and starring Sammy Davis Jr, Barry Reckord's *You in Your Small Corner* (1962), *Freedom Road — Songs of Negro Protest* (1964), *The Human Jungle* (1965), *Love Story* (1967), and *Rainbow City* (1967).

Lloyd wrote and directed two experimental short films in the 60s — *Ten Bob in Winter* (1963), which was funded by the British Film Institute, and *Dream A40* (1965). He also directed television documentaries for the BBC.

In the 50s Lloyd started the Actors Theatre Company in Jamaica, and in 1968 he returned to Jamaica to live and to establish the National Theatre Trust. Since that time the National Theatre Trust has presented nearly forty plays, as well as introducing to Jamaica a festival of Cuban films in 1971 and the Harlem Dance Theatre Company in 1973. The National Theatre Trust has also introduced free theatre, and Theatre for the Schools programmes which have toured extensively throughout Jamaica.

I first came to England in the late 50s, during the so-called Angry Young Man period in British theatre when people such as John Osborne were writing plays like *Look Back in Anger*. It was around this time that I got my first break in the theatre, so I was part of that generation of radical actors, writers, producers and directors. This was also the period when many West Indians were going to England, and I thought 'Why do I want to go to England to do theatre? I've seen what English theatre and English films are like, and people like me don't appear in them'. But then I thought 'Well, theatre reflects life and, with the flood of Caribbean people going to England, sooner or later they're going to have to reflect that in drama and in films, with people who look like me'. And, sure enough, it started to happen — blacks infiltrated, got into the lives of the English, disrupted, erupted – and soon they became part of the drama.

I came to England to take part in *Flesh to a Tiger*, which was an entirely West Indian play written by my brother, Barry. It ran for the usual month at the Royal Court Theatre and starred that wonderful singer, Cleo Laine. It was directed by the bright young man of the period, Tony Richardson. It was after this that I was offered the part in Ted Willis' play, *Hot Summer Night*. This led to a series of about five or six plays in a period of just over a year. I was usually cast as a nice young West Indian in love with an English girl. I usually got beaten up by teddy boys, or quarrelled violently with the girl's parents, or some other similar situation. I must have done about six of these plays, and I was becoming rather suspicious and tired of the stereotyped role. But then it petered out.

Hot Summer Night ● *Hot Summer Night* was my first major role – my big break in the theatre. We toured it for about six weeks all over the place. I can't remember receiving any flak over the play's controversial inter-racial relationship. But I can remember one incident which occurred during one of the Saturday matinée London West End performances. It was rather pathetic. It was during the scene when I kiss Andree Melley. A frail, rather timid and very gentle voice called out from the stalls – 'I don't like to see white girls kissing niggers'. There was dead silence in the theatre, and we went on with the play. That was the only incident, but, of course, the newspapers made a big deal of it. There was a full-page picture and headline saying 'First time on London stage, Black man kisses White girl', that sort of nonsense. But I didn't mind – it gave me a little bit of publicity!

We then did a television version of the play as an Armchair Theatre presentation, which I enjoyed very much. It was nice working with Ted Kotcheff who I thought was a very interesting director. He was into Method acting, and, given my background at the Old Vic, I was anxious to learn more about the Method. After all, this was the period when Marlon Brando was having such a wild success, and all us young actors wanted to know what made him tick. I enjoyed Kotcheff because he made me think about the characters and the situation. He made us behave more naturally.

I think Kotcheff wanted a more realistic, more believable, and less melodramatic interpretation of the play than the one we did for the stage production. I enjoyed it tremendously, and I loved the intimacy created around the production. It was during this period that I was beginning to make a transition into my preference, if you like, for film and television. Soon after, however, I won a fellowship which took me to America for two years to study theatre – doing the Method for my sins!

I did all the things that young actors in England do – I went to drama school and, just like all the others around me, including English actors, kids from Yorkshire, from Ceylon (Sri Lanka), from Scotland, and so on, I went through the process of losing my 'regional' accent. We all wanted to be actors! And I suppose like everybody else I thought to myself 'I want to play Hamlet one day'. But I don't think anybody out there wanted me to play Hamlet. And so, after a spate of these plays and films in the late 50s, and especially after having gone to America and having started my own theatre company in Jamaica in 1957, I decided that I wanted to go back to Jamaica. I wanted to establish a professional theatre there, and eventually a National Theatre, doing and encouraging plays about the Caribbean. I eventually went back for good in 1968.

Edric and Pearl Connor ● During the 50s and 60s, Edric and Pearl Connor were constantly campaigning on behalf of us black artistes. They were the salt of the earth, especially Pearl who worked solidly, like all small agents, for the people she represented. But, of course, as with all small agents who represent young artistes she brought them up from nothing, only to find that after getting their first or second big break they left her and took on a bigger or more powerful agent to represent them. It's very sad. It has nothing to do with colour. It's a cruel business. We all know it's a cruel business.

But Pearl worked like a mother, and was like a guardian angel to all us young black actors. She never represented me as an agent. It just didn't work out that way because when I was in the touring company of *Anna Lucasta*, an English agent saw me and asked if I wanted to be represented by him, which I accepted. But I knew Pearl as a friend. I would go to her place and she always had something for me to eat, or whatever. She knew that young actors were always hungry, and she was wonderful. Her house was always a home for people like us. And she just worked continually, pushing black actors, quarrelling with the powers-that-be, arguing 'Why can't black actors get this sort of part?', and generally working for us.

Edric, meanwhile, was working on his acting and singing career, and trying to make films as well. It was very sad, because backing for efforts like his was unheard of in the 50s and 60s. I was very lucky to get BFI funding in the mid-60s for my short film *Ten Bob in Winter*, but Edric had a rough time and has to be admired for what he achieved despite the many obstacles.

***Ten Bob in Winter* (1963) and *Dream A40* (1965)** ● By the early 60s, my acting career wasn't really working out and I wanted to direct. I thought 'Surely, the thing to do is to direct a couple of short pieces and show them to television companies, to try to get work'. And so I wrote *Ten Bob in Winter* and applied to the BFI for funding. I was very lucky. They gave me just enough funds to cover the shooting, to buy film stock and so on. I approached professional actors because I was trying to get good people to play the roles, and they were very helpful. We completed the film and it was shown quite widely at film festivals.

Then a year later I wrote another film script called *Dream A40*, and I set about trying to raise the money to make the film. Whatever money I earned at acting went straight into this project. I remember when we reached a certain stage, when it was near completion, I showed it to a well-known film director – he has to be nameless because he asked not to be mentioned – but he gave me a couple of hundred quid to finish the film. It was all done working with friends who, sometimes, would be working as film editors at the BFI or at the BBC, or making commercials in Wardour Street. After hours, they would sneak into their cutting rooms and edit our film. That's how I made both my films.

As a young director at the time, I suppose it wasn't any more difficult for me than for anybody else. Like all young directors, it's a case of getting the little money that you need, getting the script that you want, and going and doing it. If you had a rich uncle, then your problems would be solved. But most of us didn't have a rich uncle, so it was going to your friends in the business and saying 'Look, I'm going to make this film, would you be interested?' And you would find that some young actors were ready to leap at the idea, because here was an opportunity for them to play a good part and to get some exposure. For instance, David Hemmings had appeared in one of my brother's plays, called *Skivers*, at the Royal Court. He was in the north of England doing something when I told him about the script for *Dream A40*, and he said 'Yes, I'd love to do it. Just tell me when and I'll be there'. And we're not talking about money here. Everybody understood that they were doing it for free.

Some people were not so excited when they read the script for *Dream A40*, because it had to do with a relationship between two young men which was sort of sexual. Sex wasn't brought obviously into it, but certain people were scared, I think, because of the homosexual theme. They certainly didn't dare show it. I thought the Academy Cinema in London's Oxford Street, should have shown it as a short before a feature film, because what few reviews it got were quite good. But in general, people were helpful. Even the people I rented the equipment from saw what I was trying to do and were very helpful.

Trying to break into television ● My purpose in making these two films was not to win awards. I wanted to get into television and thought this was a way to do it – a way of showing the television companies that I could direct a film. But it didn't work. I showed them the first film, then the second – because I felt that the second one was, in a way, a more ambitious effort – but they just weren't interested. I got the impression that they weren't interested at that time in hiring black directors. They fobbed me off with comments like 'Well, a film is all very well and good. But a television play, now that's different, you see, that takes a different intelligence. It takes this . . . and that . . . and so on'.

I remember going to the BBC and talking to a young director who had come in as a trainee. Originally he had been a young actor in the theatre and had worked with me as a walk-on at the Old Vic. Now, here he was, one of the BBC's latest recruits on a directors' programme. This sort of thing made me a little unhappy because I thought 'I haven't heard that so-and-so directed anything, or showed initiative by going out to make a film with his own money, which I have done twice'. And I had also produced a number of plays around town, some commercially. Yet nobody, at any time, offered me a break as a trainee director in television. Talking to people today, they tell me that it isn't much better. There are a lot more black directors working on the stage, but not many black directors working in television or films.

I eventually left Britain for good in the late 60s because I'd had enough. As I said, I wanted to start a professional theatre in Jamaica. I also wanted a fuller life in the theatre, and was very homesick. So I went back and started the National Theatre Trust. For about twelve years I slogged away doing about five plays a year. I was producing, directing, and often playing the lead as well. It was wonderful.

Carmen Munroe was born in Guyana and came to Britain in 1951. In the mid-50s she gained early acting experience with the West Indian Students' Drama Group. Carmen made her professional stage debut in 1962 in *Period of Adjustment*, and later played leading roles in London's West End in Alun Owen's *There'll Be Some Changes Made* (1969), Jean Genet's *The Blacks* (1970), and as Orinthia in George Bernard Shaw's *The Apple Cart* (1970).

Since the 70s Carmen has played a major role in the development of black theatre in Britain, appearing in plays by black writers such as Michael Abbensetts' *El Dorado*, Lorraine Hansberry's *A Raisin in the Sun*, and James Baldwin's *The Amen Corner*. She directed James Saunders' play *Alas, Poor Fred* for the Umoja Theatre, and also the British premiere of *Remembrance*, by Caribbean poet and writer Derek Walcott, in the 1987 Black Theatre Season at London's Art Theatre.

Her numerous television appearances include Armchair Theatre's *Dr Kabil* (1959), John Hopkins' *Fable* (1965), *Emergency-Ward 10* (1966), *Rainbow City* (1967) by Horace James and John Elliot, *Dr. Who* (1967), *Troubleshooters*, (1967), *Love Story* (1967), *City '68* (1968), *Mogul* (1968), *Have Bird, Will Travel* (1968), a satirical series with John Bird, written by John Bird, *The Persuaders* with Tony Curtis (1971), Barry Reckord's *In the Beautiful Caribbean* (1972), *Ted* (1972), Alfred Fagon's *Shakespeare Country* (1973), *General Hospital* (1974), *The Fosters* (1976), Michael Abbensetts' *Black Christmas* (1977), *Mixed Blessings* (1978), Horace Ové's *A Hole in Babylon* (1979), *Rumpole of the Bailey* (1983), and Caryl Phillips' *The Hope and the Glory* (1984).

Since 1989 Carmen has been making regular appearances as Shirley in Trix Worrell's Channel 4 sitcom *Desmond's*.

Coming to England in 1951 was basically a means of furthering my education. You get to a certain point in Guyana where you feel that if you want to go any further, you must go to the mother country where all the education is dished out. I took what was then called the Cambridge School Certificate, after which you go to England to college, and then to university. America was the place where you went to become rich, because the Americans who came down to Guyana always looked as if they were well off, but England was where you went to be educated.

I lived in Tooting, South London, and worked in the library in Mitcham Road, Tooting. It was fun. In the library, I was viewed as a strange character. I mean, people wondered what I was doing in a library, standing there handing out books. I was put in charge of the children's section. It was quite funny, actually. I remember the first afternoon when the children came into the library, from school, to exchange their books. One child came in, took one look at me, and ran out. Then a stream of children came in and they were all pointing, 'Look, look, look!' I felt I was making waves wherever I went, because I was a such a strange entity in this environment.

The West Indian Students' Drama Group and their performance of Eugene O'Neill's *Anna Christie* at the left-wing Unity Theatre ● The West Indian Students' Drama Group was a group of like-minded individuals, very young people who, round about 1957-8, used to meet at the West Indian Students' Centre, where a beautiful woman, the late Joan Clarke, ran classes. At that time they had what was then called London County Council drama competitions for various groups within the London area.

We did Eugene O'Neill's play, *Anna Christie*, in which I played the old woman who lives on the wharf and looks after the chaps on the boat – a very jolly, hearty sort of black lady. Anyway, we entered the competition and won. We only had to do one scene from the play, but one of the prizes was actually being able to perform the whole play at the Unity Theatre, which was left-wing socialist. It was really communist. I wasn't a communist party member, but the Unity Theatre was my introduction to this wonderful theatre atmosphere. And it was a real theatre, with a stage and a backstage! That's when I realised that I was getting closer to what I really wanted to do, and so we did the play there for a short season. It was very good for me working with people who were really struggling in theatre. In fact, quite a few well-known theatrical names started at the Unity. It was also, at this time, that I was approached by Dorothea Alexander who encouraged me to train professionally with her. I did.

Pearl Connor and her work as a pioneer campaigner for black artistes in the 50s and 60s ● I met Pearl Connor during my time at the Unity Theatre. She was a pioneer. She was wonderful. She was dynamic. Pearl was a law student at the time and she decided then that she wanted to have an agency, so that she could look after 'coloured' artistes in London. She set up her agency and it was very successful. She was such a dynamic personality that she made things happen for us. She took chances. She took risks. She pushed and she opened doors. And we learnt a lot from her life and from the way she handled situations. Pearl was the mother of us all, a great lady, and we are all very grateful to her.

Fable (1965) ● John Hopkins' television play *Fable* was a very important turning point in television for minorities because the cast was very mixed. I don't think that play would be done now. It is just so controversial, it would be too frightening for people to comprehend. It was a risky thing to do in the mid-60s. John Hopkins is a brilliant writer and he saw this reversal of the roles in the practice of apartheid. It was actually a very frightening play to be in, because suddenly you were being asked to perform the sort of acts that were performed against you in real life. Suddenly, you were put in this role of being 'master', of being really quite vicious. It was a frightening piece to do, but I thoroughly enjoyed it. I realised that it was a turning point – or not so much a turning point – an opening. There's something very new about being able to do a play like that, a hugely dramatic piece.

Round about the mid-60s and thereafter, there were quite a few opportunities for black artistes in television. There were also many very adventurous directors around at the time, who were very enterprising and innovative people. They could see the possibility of using black artistes in a very positive way, even though we, ourselves, felt that we weren't getting enough work and that we weren't being properly represented. We were few in numbers then, and there never seemed to be enough work. But it was a good time, a busy time for us, and we were able to do quite a few good pieces of television.

Sometimes I felt that I was being used. I thought they were using me because they needed to make a scene look dressed up – the 'we're going to have a black person, and it's going to be really wonderful' sort of attitude. I felt that my work was very important to me and that I would become indispensable. I had to become the person that the director really wanted, while at the same time fulfilling my own dreams of what I wanted for myself.

Looking back now, I can see that I wanted to be in a position where I was going to be asked to do lots of work. I wanted to be the person about whom the director says 'That's the person I want for this role. There is nobody else'. But, of course, that didn't always happen and then the work seemed to slowly dry up. I didn't get as much work as I thought I would. I wasn't too disappointed, however, because I didn't see myself in a situation that was divorced from what was happening to the rest of the people in the country. I knew that there would be problems for black people, and the fact that it was reflected in my area of work didn't surprise me one little bit. I mean, it was natural. I didn't think that, suddenly, people would switch on their televisions everyday and see a black person. I knew that it would take time before that came about.

So, while I was a little bit disappointed that I didn't get as much work as I had hoped, I also understood what the overall situation was. Not to understand that would have created a great deal of pain – which it did after a

Horace James and Carmen Munroe in *Rainbow City* (BBC TV, 1967).

while in any case. I came to a point when I thought 'I can't do this any longer. I'm never going to fulfil my potential as long as I'm in this job in this country'. Then, it became really hard and really frustrating, and I began to think 'Well, maybe I ought to give up'. But the real impact of that came very much later. Those were the struggling days, the days when you felt that you had to make a difference with whatever you did. Small it may have been, infrequent it may have been, but once you were there, you felt that what you were doing was going to make a difference.

Rainbow City (1967) ● John Elliot was a producer at the BBC and Horace James was a contemporary actor and a great friend of mine. We had done quite a lot of work together in the early days. Horace would adapt Chekhov and, with these little two-handers, we would go round different town halls and church halls performing.

Horace had this idea for a series about a lawyer and his wife, and the problems that would be presented to them because theirs was a racially-mixed marriage. The couple already had problems to face, so this element made it quite rich. Horace got together with John Elliot and they decided that this idea had possibilities and that it could be done.

Errol John was cast as the lawyer – Errol had seething good looks and was a great person. He had won *The Observer* Award for his play, *Moon on a*

Rainbow Shawl, which was performed at the Royal Court. Gemma Jones was cast as his wife. We went up to Birmingham to film. I don't know why Birmingham was called 'the Rainbow City' but I remember going up there and enjoying great friendships. There was a great closeness with all the people around, because we were all struggling, trying to do things and trying to make things happen. We were a great team. We did lots of lovely work, and it was rainbow city!

The late 60s and early 70s period of creative excitement with Alun Owen's *There'll Be Some Changes Made* (1969), Jean Genet's *The Blacks* (1970), and George Bernard Shaw's *The Apple Cart* (1970)
● I did three very good stage plays in the late 60s, which was very good for me. *There'll Be Some Changes Made* was something that Alun Owen had written for a special theatre group called the Park Theatre Players, which John Neville started after he had left Nottingham Playhouse. We weren't all members of the group, but I had worked with John in Nottingham and at the Fortune. This was about the fifth in a run of plays that we did, and a great play it was, with a character that I had been dying to play on stage for a long, long time.

I played a crazy girl who lives in an upstairs room, and Gemma Jones played a very proper sort of English girl who moves in downstairs. The drama centred on my character teaching this girl how to live on her own. It was a great feeling to be able to work on equal levels with such a brilliant and powerful actress as Gemma. That was something for me. I thought 'Gosh, this is the opening that I've been dying for'. We had wonderful reviews and I thought 'Oh dear, this is good, this is good. I hope this continues'.

I was then asked to do Jean Genet's *The Blacks*, which gave us black actors and actresses a great opportunity to get together and really put on what turned out to be a wonderful production. We did a tour with that – we went to the Oxford Playhouse, to Cambridge, and then we came back to the Roundhouse in London, which was really quite an exciting venue to be working in at the time.

I then played the part of Orinthia, mistress to John Neville's King Magnus, in George Bernard Shaw's *The Apple Cart*. The production was directed by Donald McWhinnie and was a huge success both on stage and with the critics. 'Following in Dame Edith's footsteps', wrote one reviewer. 'Why doesn't someone write something for this girl?', wrote B.A. Young of the *Financial Times*.

So, this was a good period for me. I had become a known actress, at least in the theatre-goers' view. This, I felt, was the reward for all the work and all the time that I had put into developing my craft. Previously to that, I might have been asked to play a role where the character was just described as 'exotic'. She wouldn't have a character name or a title, and she wouldn't have much to do – she would just be exotic. You know, 'enter exotic nurse'. I actually turned down a lot of things like that, because I didn't think that it fitted in with what I really wanted to do.

It is very painful to say 'No' when you're starving, but if you really want to make some kind of impact in your career and want to challenge yourself, you do. It's no good asking me to play 'a black woman' because I am a black woman. What is the character you want me to play? I can't 'just be'. Every time I wake up in the morning I'm a black woman. You've got to ask me to do something. And these plays did that. They really challenged me; and that's when I really came alive in this business and began looking for more challenges. I thought 'The next one's got to be bigger than the last, not necessarily a bigger part, but surely a bigger challenge'. I began to really live and to demand not only from myself, but from the people who had the work, so that they demanded something of me.

This period of rewarding work in the theatre continued into television drama during the 70s with Barry Reckord's *In The Beautiful Caribbean* (1972), *Ted* (1972), Alfred Fagon's *Shakespeare Country* (1973), and towards the end of the decade Michael Abbensetts' *Black Christmas* (1977) and Horace Ové's *A Hole in Babylon* (1979) ● The success of my theatre period in the 60s and 70s seemed to spill over into television drama. *Ted* was a story of a young man (played by Richard Morant) who has had an accident and comes to a special hospital unit to be taught how to walk again. He could only relate to one particular nurse, which I played, and it was a great relationship. It was a challenging role because I had the responsibility of this relationship, which was unique, really, for television. For a black person to be given a part where that sort of responsibility was paramount – where she alone was going to make the patient walk again – was important. Obviously, it could have been anybody – it could have been cast with a Chinese, or an African, or a white person. But I had the part, so I felt this great responsibility. I was told afterwards that I had star billing alongside Richard Morant above the opening titles. I didn't think about things like that in those days, but it was apparently something you were supposed to be really pleased about.

I then did a play for television written by the late Alfred Fagon, who was a brilliant writer. It was called *Shakespeare Country*, and was directed by Philip Saville. I was asked to play the wife of a really tormented soul whose life is falling to pieces while living in this country, Shakespeare country. Fagon played the role of the husband himself. It was a very tortured piece about a really despairing character. But, again, it was a great challenge for me to have to sustain the pain and the anguish of this woman living with this tormented man.

Creative depression in the early 70s ● Straight after *The Apple Cart*, after that frenetic period of the late 60s with three very successful plays, things started to dry up and, suddenly, I was doing nothing. I'll tell you what that does to you – you become reclused. I felt as though I was being ignored, put away, shut up somewhere. It was very painful. I couldn't keep friends with the people I had worked with for a long time, because I was probably the one who was not going to find another job as soon as them. I'd phone them and ask how they were, and they would tell me how busy they had been, doing one thing and another, and how they were about to start in something new. And then they'd ask what was happening with me – well, what was happening for me? So I never got in touch with people – I mean, people I'd worked with – because they'd always be going off to something, or they'd be busy doing things, and I was the one who didn't have a job.

I felt as though I was being excluded, so it interfered with friendships as well. It made me feel inadequate and I had nothing to talk about, except the fact that I was out of work. I'd go off and do typing in various offices, temporary work, and that sustained me financially. But there was an emptiness, a feeling that I had really come to a very, very low point in my life. I thought if I'm not going to be able to work at what I really want to do, then there's not much point even in living. That was a very, very low point. It's very painful relating it even now, because you can't go back and think how close you came to doing something really awful, without stirring up some of the actual pain of being there. But that came about – I remember it to this day, 8 February 1974, a Friday, I think – that was when I came to the lowest point I have ever been in my life, and ever will be. I'm not going back there again, because it's not a good place to be.

About a week after that, I got a call from the BBC to go and do a test for *Play School*, which I did and got. That lasted for some time, and sort of brought me out of the morass of negativity and pain. And then after *Play School* came *General Hospital*, which also cut across it because, for a period, I was doing both at the same time. And then a new joy started to bubble. I was working with people I liked, and it was fun doing *General Hospital*. There was a great atmosphere at Associated Television, the company producing the series. From the moment I walked through the gates, I knew I was in the company of friends. It was fun working there. It was good, and it saved my life.

The Fosters (1976) ● I went into *The Fosters* straight after *General Hospital*. They sort of overlapped in a way because *General Hospital* was coming to an end when I started in the new show. Humphrey Barclay, the producer, was then working for London Weekend Television and I went up for an interview. They told me that they were going to do a sitcom. I was a little bit worried about that. I thought 'A sitcom! I don't think that's me. I want to work, but I hope I don't get this job because I'm not a sitcom person'. I saw myself as a drama queen, you know what I mean? But, of course, I got the job. Then I thought 'What do I do? What's all this thing about timing and being funny, and knowing how to deliver a funny line? Oh my God, what have I let myself in for?' But then I thought, 'Another challenge. Let's go and do it'.

I think people generally enjoyed *The Fosters*. I did – it was a departure for me. I just prayed constantly that I would be able to do it with some degree of professionalism and some fun, and make it all happen, and make it all worthwhile. But I still don't think I'm a sitcom person – nobody's going to convince me otherwise.

Mixed Blessings (1978) ● *Mixed Blessings* came after *The Fosters*, but it had a different flavour. It had the makings of what could have been a good situation comedy with some hard-hitting social elements in it, but it didn't work. I don't think we were really versed in the art of making social comment without it becoming just that, and without it losing the comedy of the situation. We weren't able to do that very well then. We might be able to do it now, though – it's just a question of experience.

A Hole in Babylon (1979) ● Then came *A Hole in Babylon*, a television play based on the Spaghetti House restaurant siege which had taken place in London in 1975. It was an amazing and sad story. I was playing the mother of a young person who had really gone and messed up his life. I also knew the actual boy's family, which made me even more acutely aware of the tragedy of the situation. Apparently, when the police arrested him, they found his ticket to Africa on him – he was planning to go to Africa to study at a university. But then he got in with these guys, they did this thing, and all of a sudden his life was finished – he got a very long prison sentence.

So doing that television play was really very painful. At the same time it was encouraging to be working with a completely black team. It was the first time that I had been directed in television by a black director (Horace Ové). That was wonderful because I got on very well with Horace. It's also a joy when you turn up at a television studio and there's a black person on the boom, another black person operating the camera, and things like that. You think 'Is this really happening after all these years?' I'm grateful that I'm still here to see all this in my time. Horace directed me again in Caz Phillips's *The Record* (1984).

Carmen Munroe and Norman Beaton in *Desmond's* (Channel 4).

Desmond's and beyond ● I feel I've served my time in sitcoms, but *Desmond's* is successful because we are serious about it. We are now able to do what other series are trying to do, and that is to be about real people. We don't have to be constantly begging for acceptance, begging to be understood – that's gone, that's past. We now must live the way we really do live, and we can present that. Anyway, we're all grown up and I don't think the public wants to be told any more about how difficult life is. We all know how difficult life is, black and white.

With *Desmond's* we have successfully created a space for ourselves, where we can just be a real, honest, loving family, with problems like lots of people, and we can present that with some degree of truth and still not lose the comedy.

What needs to happen now in British television generally is to stop thinking in terms of documentaries and drama that constantly refer to the negative aspects of being black in England. I mean, that can be done but there has to be another element too. We have to advance. It's beginning to happen. There are now plays being written which offer more scope for expressing black experiences. It's probably happening more in film with the new generation of young black film writers and producers.

We have made significant inroads. We've made a difference to society, and we've made a contribution. Now I think we must grow with a new set of ideals. We must move further forward, so that we really become part of the society, and not just people who are constantly commenting on and bemoaning the fact that we are not part of society.

Thomas Baptiste was born in Guyana and came to Britain in 1950. He has worked as an actor and opera singer in Britain since then. He was an early member of Joan Littlewood's Theatre Workshop Company. In the late 60s he was a founder member of the Actors Equity Advisory Committee which campaigned on behalf of black actors in Britain.

His numerous stage roles include George in Edward Albee's *Who's Afraid of Virginia Woolf?*, Alfred P. Doolittle in George Bernard Shaw's *Pygmalion*, and Paul Robeson in *Are You Now or Have You Ever Been?*.

He has appeared in over twenty-five films including *The Ipcress File* (1965), Lionel Ngakane's *Jemima and Johnny* (1966), John Schlesinger's *Sunday Bloody Sunday* (1971), *Shaft in Africa* (1973), and Kwate Nee-Owoo and Kwesi Owusu's *Ama* which premiered at the 1991 London Film Festival.

Thomas has made numerous television appearances since the 50s including *Nightfall at Kriekville* (1961), Harold Pinter's *The Room* (1961), *Coronation Street* (1963), John Hopkins' *Fable* (1965), *Till Death Us Do Part* (1966), Alun Owen's Play for Today: *Pal* (1971), Michael Abbensetts' *Empire Road* (1978-9), Barrie Keefe's Play for Today: *King* (1984), *Drums Along the Balmoral Drive* (1986), *EastEnders* (1990), *Capital City* (1991), and *Love Hurts* (1992).

***Coronation Street* (1963)** ● In 1963, I appeared in some episodes of *Coronation Street.* I played a young bus conductor who has a feud with Len Fairclough. It was interesting because I was the first black actor to break into a major television series. So, naturally, I was a bit miffed when I wasn't invited to the thirtieth anniversary celebrations they had in 1990 for the long-running soap. It was as though I didn't exist; and, for me, it was also a corruption of history. Several years ago, I was an Equity delegate at an IBA conference and there was an interesting incident. A producer said there was a rumour going around that they were thinking of introducing a black family into *Coronation Street*. It wouldn't happen, he added, because it would mean they would have to introduce racial tensions. Obviously, that producer didn't know about the storylines from twenty-five years ago, and that things like that happened even then. The fact is, I worked on an important soap like *Coronation Street* and, years later, there's no recall, no history or acknowledgment of my work. Well, so be it.

Thomas Baptiste as bus conductor Johnny Alexander, the victim of racism when he is sacked from his job, in *Coronation Street* (Granada TV, 1963).

Fable (1965) ● John Hopkins was one of the writers on *Z Cars* and he wrote a remarkable television play about racism called *Fable*. I think what Hopkins wanted to do was to show a racist regime in reverse – what would happen if blacks took over the United Kingdom *vis-à-vis* what was happening in South Africa? In other words, blacks here would treat whites badly, in the same way as the white South Africans were treating blacks in that country. I read the script and recognised it as an extraordinary, wonderful part for a young black actor. There was a large cast of distinguished actors and I was cast as a liberal. I was flattered to be asked to do it.

But I remember having a deep gut-feeling that the play might do more harm than good, that people in England might not get the point. And I was right, because questions were asked in Parliament. I recall there was a by-election hovering in Leyton, East London, about the same time, which involved a candidate who had lost his seat a few months earlier to an openly racist candidate in Smethwick during the 1964 General Election. So people were trying to stop *Fable* from being broadcast because of its controversial racial content.

It was eventually shown and I received a lot of hate mail – which was extraordinary because I played the liberal in the story! You would have thought that I would receive sympathetic letters, but the contrary happened. I got one letter – and it's one of the few that I have kept over the years – from a man in Brighton which said 'How dare you appear on our television screens, even as a friend or a liberal. Get back to your country!' Turn over page: 'Hideous ape!' Extraordinary.

Till Death Us Do Part (1966) ● The following year I appeared in an early episode of Johnny Speight's *Till Death Us Do Part*. It was the second episode in the first series. It was a rather wonderful part, but I remember talking to the director at the time, Dennis Main-Wilson, and telling him that, although I thought the script was very funny, I felt people were going to laugh with this bigoted man, instead of at him. And there again, I was proved right. I must say, with hindsight, that those jobs always represented a dichotomy for me as a professional actor – either one did them, or one refused, in which case somebody else would have done them. Of course, I was flattered to be asked to play the parts, and I always believed that I would make a good job of them. An actor needs that kind of confidence and morale booster. That's why I did those jobs, plus the money, of course. But, nowadays, I can choose not to do a job if I think it's going to be detrimental to my career.

Actors Equity and the campaign for minority rights ● In the late 60s, a group of us black actors thought that it was time that Equity really started to protect minority actors who were getting a rough deal in the industry. We felt very strongly that Equity should urge casting directors and producers to use black actors as actors, regardless of their race, colour, or creed, and based purely upon their talent.

My feeling has always been that when people like Shakespeare and Chekhov wrote plays, or when composers wrote music, they wrote for people, not for racial groups. If you cast somebody purely on racial grounds, the logic of that must mean that, perhaps, white people shouldn't sing or play jazz because it's not indigenous to them. So casting shouldn't be on race but purely talent. Why should it be difficult to accept a black actor's performance, say, as King Lear on stage, when it might be perfectly acceptable on radio or on a disc? The answer, of course, is because you can't *see* the person in these other forms. Well, that shows some basic racism.

We felt very strongly that we had to fight this. We had several meetings and then Equity decided to form a subcommittee. After the subcommittee got off the ground, the next difficulty was trying to convince directors and

Thomas Baptiste in *King* (BBC TV 'Play for Today', 1984).

writers that they should write parts for blacks. When I say 'black', I am, of course, including Asians and Chinese, basically non-Caucasian people. Unfortunately, the attitude of some of the writers and directors was not helpful. They argued that they knew nothing about the black experience, so they couldn't, therefore, write parts for black or Indian actors. All I could think was 'Good God, you don't have to be a murderer to know about murders!' And that attitude still exists today.

It is offensive because black people pay taxes, theatres are subsidised from the national kitty, and I see no reason on earth why repertory companies shouldn't employ blacks, regardless of race, colour or creed. And it would be to the company's own good as well, because there are large pockets of people in places like Bristol, Leeds, Manchester and Birmingham – large ethnic minority communities – which should be seduced into the theatre. Having black people in more productions would enable that to happen.

It would also have another beneficial effect, in helping to lessen social tension. Young blacks who feel deprived in schools and who have no aspirations need to see people to whom they can aspire. Where are the interesting black characters in television plays? Where are the black academics, the black scientists, the black chemists, the black lawyers? You never see these sort of figures reflected in British television drama. What you see are blacks involved in antisocial activities. Or you name any situation, in a play or a documentary, and what you see is a black figure hovering in the background saying nothing. Well, it could be so, but, on a pro rata basis, it doesn't really work out in terms of numbers nationally. And this is why our committee is still fighting this issue and, who knows, we may yet succeed.

But to answer the question of whether there has been progress for black actors in television since the 60s. There has been a marginal increase in quality, but not in quantity. There are now many more black people in this country, and many more black drama students at colleges, but they aren't getting the work. So it's funny when I'm asked whether there has been progress, because my whole career seems to have been about breaking down doors. Of course, my experience is not a yardstick, but I would say that young actors today are having even more difficulty getting their careers started than I did.

I have a feeling that there hasn't been much progress, not really. People here are still cast in roles based on their race, unlike in America where you see black actors playing parts that have nothing at all to do with race or racial tension. It seems to me that people here have this idea in their heads that if you have black and white people together on screen, there has got to be some sort of racial insult or racial antagonism. It need not be so, of course, because life is not like that. People do get along irrespective of racial differences – and this simply needs to be reflected more often in television.

— ZIA MOHYEDDIN —

Zia Mohyeddin was born in Lahore, Pakistan and came to study at the Royal Academy of Dramatic Art (RADA) in 1953. His film appearances include David Lean's *Lawrence of Arabia* (1962), Basil Dearden's *Khartoum* (1966), and Peter Hall's *Work is a Four Letter Word* (1967).

In 1960 Zia appeared as Dr Aziz in the London West End stage production of Santha Rama Rau's adaptation of E.M. Forster's novel *A Passage to India*. He repeated his acclaimed performance as Dr Aziz in the New York stage production in 1962, and in the BBC TV Play of the Month version in 1965, which was directed by Waris Hussein.

His numerous other British television appearances include Paul Scott's *The Alien Sky* (1956), *Drama '61: The Day of the Fox* (1961), *Kipling* (1964), *Danger Man* (1965), *The Avengers* (1966), Armchair Theatre's *Pretty Polly* (1967) with Lynn Redgrave, *Kindly Leave the Raj* (1969), *Staying On* (1980) with Celia Johnson and Trevor Howard, Farrukh Dhondy's *Salt on a Snake's Tail* (1983) and *King of the Ghetto* (series, 1986), and Bandung Productions' *Partition* (1987). Since 1981 Zia has been a producer and presenter of Central Television's ethnic magazine programme *Here and Now*. Since 1991 he has been an Executive Producer and one of the stars of Central TV's Asian soap *Family Pride*.

I came to England via Australia. What happened was that after I finished my university degree, I got a job with the broadcasting service and shortly after that was offered a Colombo Plan Fellowship, which allowed me to go and study methods of broadcasting in Australia. Six months after being in Australia, I got attached to the radio drama department of the Australian Broadcasting Corporation. They didn't have television at the time. When my Fellowship tenure finished I was fortunate enough to be offered a contract to stay with the drama department.

It was at that time that I became aware that drama, or radio drama, really means nothing unless you know something about the theatre. For example, I was offered one or two trial productions, and every actor I came across had been in the theatre. The only theatre experience I had had was when my father, who was an amateur playwright and who had the job of producing a play each year for his university college, would write a part for me. So I realised with an intensity that I needed to learn something about the theatre.

In those days in Australia, the early 50s, everybody wanted to come to England – England was the place. It didn't matter whether you were an actor or a director, or a fishmonger, or a nurse – everyone felt that they just had to be in England. So I thought 'Oh well, I have got to go to England. But where do I go when I get there?' Everyone said RADA, but I didn't know what RADA was or how one got to RADA.

I landed in England, with £50 in my pocket which I had saved, and since someone had been kind enough to put me on a chartered flight, it meant that I didn't have to pay more than about £25 for the fare which was very fortunate.

Then I learnt that it wasn't easy to get into RADA, that you had to wait for a turn, and so on. Somebody suggested that I go to a place called pre-RADA, so I did. I went there for a couple of months, and then the time for the auditions to RADA came, and I was brazen enough to go and do my pieces. I was selected, but then I couldn't afford the fees. However, the head of RADA at the time was very kind and he waived my tutorial fees, so, in a way, it was a kind of scholarship. Incidentally, RADA in those days was a curious place – I know it isn't like this now – but, then, girls with hooped rings used to go there. It was just a finishing school. If you couldn't get into a really swish finishing school in Switzerland, you used to go to RADA.

So I went to RADA, but I can't say in all honesty that I learnt very much, because apart from the fact that the atmosphere was that of a finishing school, there were far too many students, hundreds of people in a class, so there was no opportunity to really learn anything. But because I'd been to Australia, and because I was older in years – the other students were all young teenagers – I was immediately considered to be the person who should direct. So I was given a lot of student productions to direct, which I relished very much.

The normal method when finishing drama school, in those days, was to join a repertory company, so I did a stint in a couple of reps. But it was obvious that I wasn't very good at playing the juvenile leads, because I didn't look the part. I marked time, looking for whenever a director fell ill, so I that could do a bit of directing, and playing any kind of a non-English part if and when it appeared. If a director particularly took pity on me, he'd make a part non-English, not necessarily oriental but Cypriot or Egyptian or something.

As a result of being in the repertory circuit, I eventually got my big opportunity. I was directing Noel Coward's *Hay Fever* at the Guildford Repertory Theatre when I met the director Frank Hauser, who became a great friend. I was very eager to find out what he thought of my production of the Coward play. He was putting together a stage production of E.M.

Zia Mohyeddin as Doctor Aziz in *A Passage to India* (BBC TV 'Play of the Month', 1965).

Forster's *A Passage to India*, from an adaptation by Santha Rama Rau. He asked me if I would be interested in playing the part of Dr Aziz. The idea was that we would do the play in Oxford and then see how it went from there.

I was in two minds about taking on the part because, at that time, the United Nations had, for some obscure reason, asked me to do a tour of five or six countries in the Far East, and to go to New York to do six half-hour broadcasts giving a resumé of the new cultural processes in evolution, as it were. This was during the period when countries like Indonesia, India and Pakistan, Malaysia, and numerous others, were gaining their independence. It was going to be a lucrative tour including a lot of travel. But I said 'Yes, I'd love to do the play, but how long will it run because I'm kind of committed to do this other project?' Frank just said 'We'll see shortly'. And I never looked back because the play went from one place to another, and the rest is history.

Blacking up white actors to play Asian roles in drama ● I wasn't so much offended as hurt by this common practice. What you were seeing was somebody browning or blacking up, or whatever, to play a role simply because producers would not take the trouble, or even think that it was important enough to take the trouble, to find the right (that is an Asian) actor. Admittedly, there weren't many Asian or black actors around at the time, but there were certainly some – including old mates of mine like Thomas Baptiste (who's been going forever) and other people – whom they could easily have approached. And even if they didn't want to use these people, they could have found someone from another country to play the parts.

It was somehow assumed that black and Asian actors weren't good enough. I heard this again and again, and it hurt even more when people said to me 'Oh, well, you're all right, but you know that Asians and blacks can't act – their style isn't right. Somehow when they come in front of the camera or on the stage, they're either too big or too overpowering, and they just don't mix with the style of the production, whatever the style of the production. So it's much better to have Joe Bloggs putting on reams of grease paint and trying to pretend that he's a black or Asian'. This is why some people who were not Asian, not even remotely Asian, constantly played Asian parts. And because they had specialised in playing these parts, the directors felt more comfortable using them. I don't know whether the directors felt comfortable because they knew these people, or because they couldn't cope with the real thing.

A *Passage to India* – the stage play and BBC TV's Play of the Month production (1965) ● *A Passage to India* was *the* play that made me known to the theatrical world and show business. I was also extremely fortunate in that I got to know E. M. Forster personally as well – not because he came to see the production, because everyone met him then, but because he used to invite me to his rooms in Cambridge and we would talk about everything, which was a great bonus. The two greatest people I've met in my life, whom I would describe as the absolute quintessence of gentlemanliness, are E.M. Forster and my father.

The stage production of *A Passage to India* became a huge success and we heard that it was going to America. In England, the play was a personal success for me, for Santha Rama Rau who adapted it, for E.M. Forster, for Frank Hauser who directed it, and for the Oxford Playhouse Company which had initially done it, but there were a lot of complications over the production going to America. There were lots of negotiations between the company which was to produce it on Broadway and the British company. The Americans were determined to have an American star and, for some reason, they didn't want Frank. They wanted me partly because I had received such ecstatic reviews and notices, and partly because Forster himself said he wouldn't have the play performed without me. But in the end we only had about six months run on Broadway – it wasn't the great success there that it had been in London's West End. It was said that the

Tanveer Ghani, Sudha Bhuchar, Zia Mohyeddin and Jamila Massey in *Family Pride* (Central TV, 1991).

Americans couldn't relate to the colonial tussle around which the story centres.

The BBC television production came about two or three years later and had a different cast from the stage version. The great Dame Sybil Thorndike played Mrs Moore, and I can say without hesitation that she was the best Mrs Moore ever. She was a great actress and a wonderful, exceedingly warm, humane person. The television play was directed by my dear friend Waris Hussein, whom I had known since he was a schoolboy and an undergraduate at Cambridge. In fact, he came and played one of the pukka wallahs in the court scene when we did the play in Cambridge. Soon after this, he was taken on as a trainee director at the BBC, and I watched his career develop from there, to the stage where he was now entrusted with this highly prestigious BBC Play of the Month production.

David Lean's *A Passage to India* ● There's a curious thread that runs right the way from 1960 until the time that David Lean made his film. Lean came to see me on several occasions in 1960 when we were doing the play, and on the second or third occasion he said he was very keen to make *A Passage to India* into a film. In fact, he asked me if I would talk to Forster on his behalf – other people had also asked this of me. So one day I did go to Forster's rooms at King's College, Cambridge, and, during our conversation,

Forster said the porter had been up on one or two occasions saying that a Mr Holly Rood was on the line, but that he didn't know any Mr Holly Rood, so please put him off. It was Hollywood, obviously. Forster didn't want *A Passage to India* to be made into a film and he came out with what I consider an absolutely definitive and inimitable response. He said 'Oh, I think it would be simpler to say "No" '. And he did and that was the end of that.

Forster also said to me that he was going to put in his will that *A Passage to India* should not be made into a film, because his feeling was that it would be a travesty – and how right he was. David Lean was a great director and I admired him enormously. I worked with him – my first film was *Lawrence of Arabia* – and I couldn't think of a greater, bigger, more sensitive director than David Lean. But Forster didn't want it.

And what about Alec Guinness as Professor Godbole? Guinness is a wonderful actor, a great actor. He has the capacity to look enigmatic, which he did superbly playing the part of a Hindu mystic and philosopher. But, given that they were filming in India, Lean could have picked up any number of exquisite Professor Godbole's among the talented Indian actors there. That's my feeling. As to why I wasn't cast, I don't want to suggest that there was anything personal in it, but Lean didn't want to consider me and I don't think I ever sent out a word or a feeler to him indicating my interest. But, yes, I certainly could have played that part, as could a lot of other very good actors from India. But I continue to think how right Forster was.

Rudolph Walker was born in Trinidad and came to Britain in the early 60s. He became nationally famous for his role as Bill Reynolds in the long-running sitcom *Love Thy Neighbour* (1972-5). But before that Rudolph appeared in numerous television series and single plays, including John Hopkins' controversial drama *Fable*, *The Troubleshooters*, *Adam Adamant Lives*, *Emergency-Ward 10*, *The Newcomers*, *Dr Who*, *On the Buses*, Theatre 625: *Wind versus Polygamy*, and Thirty Minute Theatre: *Thank God for UDI*.

Since the success of *Love Thy Neighbour*, for which he shared a Variety Club award as ITV Personality of the Year in 1972, Rudolph has played leading roles in several television dramas including Caryl Phillips' *The Hope and the Glory* (1984) and *The Record* (1984), *Playboy of the West Indies* (1985), *Black Silk* (BBC TV series, 1985-6), Michael Abbensetts' *Big George is Dead* (1987) directed by Henry Martin, and *Elphida* (1987) written and directed by Tunde Ikoli.

Rudolph's numerous theatre credits include Caryl Phillips' *The Shelter* and *Where There is Darkness*, *Othello* (Young Vic, 1984), and *The Fatherland* (1988)

I was fortunate enough in Trinidad to have met and worked with wonderful actors like Errol John, and the writer, Derek Walcott, who was instrumental in encouraging me to pursue a career in the theatre. I was doing something in Trinidad as an amateur actor when he encouraged me to pack my bags and come to England. I haven't really regretted it because the best sort of foundation you can get in the theatre is in England. But there is a sting in the tail because, at the end of the day, England was not as rosy as some of us in the West Indies were led to believe. Things were tough when I came here in the 60s. It was a period when we couldn't even get a room.

I was fortunate to find fantastic digs. I couldn't afford to go to full-time drama school, so I attended the City Literary Institute, which in those days had about the best drama tutors around. It was a three-year evening drama course, but after the first year, the tutors decided to put me in the third-year production group. That was encouraging. I later went on to places like the Bristol Old Vic, where I really learned my trade.

The early years and *Fable* (1965) ● In those days, Pearl Connor was particularly instrumental in getting black actors to think positively and to have a sense of pride in what we were doing. She was also instrumental in getting white producers and directors to recognise that there was a lot of talent around, but unfortunately they just didn't use it and they still don't today.

We went up and down the country doing plays in church halls and town halls. It was great because I got to rub shoulders with actors like Earl Cameron and Edric Connor. It's important to emphasise that this earlier generation of actors made an important contribution, just as we made and are continuing to make our contribution. I think one of the sad things is that there's a tendency now to criticise the older actors and to accuse them of playing certain kinds of roles, be they so-called Uncle Tom roles or whatever. What people don't understand is that what that generation was going through professionally was just a stage. We must acknowledge that they made their contribution. The youngsters are where they are today because of what actors before me, and actors like me, have been doing. I mean, I did a certain type of work in the 70s like *Love Thy Neighbour* which was extremely popular. But it's not something that I would do now, simply because the atmosphere is completely different and, as a black actor, I want to move on to other things.

I'm associated with one major, huge success in this country – *Love Thy Neighbour*. The sad thing is, nobody seems to remember that, prior to *Love Thy Neighbour*, I did a lot of interesting television drama and plays in the theatre in this country – including *Fable* (1965), which was done by the BBC and was my very first television in this country.

Fable looked at Britain in the reverse, as a black state, with the boot on the other foot. We ran the police and we were in charge of the government. The prime minister was black. I remember that when we did it – the racially-loaded Leyton by-election was happening around the same time, and the BBC refused to transmit the play because its racial content was considered too controversial. I remember Christopher Morahan, the director, ringing me and saying that, sadly, the programme was being postponed and that they had to make one or two cuts which he wasn't in favour of.

Britain seems to go in phases. In the 60s and 70s Africa was the in-thing, the emerging African states, the coups, and so on. So many of the parts I played were about Africa or about African presidents, and colonels, and coups, etcetera. One such play, *Wind versus Polygamy*, explored the theme of whether polygamy should be practised in modern African states! It was actually a prestigious play and it was fantastically well received. But then the preoccupation with Africa died and suddenly we were out of favour. So there was no continuity, no progression as far as black actors in this country were concerned. Then *Love Thy Neighbour* came up, but that was the only thing that happened in the 70s.

And what is happening now? I think that we've switched back to comedy and light entertainment and forgotten about drama! We have talented comedians like Lenny Henry, and they are being promoted. But where are our dramatic actors like Norman Beaton and Carmen Munroe? There are a lot of talented young actors and actresses around who should be promoted, but they're not.

Love Thy Neighbour (1972-5) ● *Love Thy Neighbour* came about in the usual way. I was doing a series in Birmingham called *United*. It was a football series and I did something like six episodes. Thames Television were setting up *Love Thy Neighbour* and Stuart Allen, who had worked as a floor manager on the *United* series, was now producing and directing and he obviously remembered my work. I went along for the usual audition and interviews.

Now, I actually laid down certain conditions, and one of the main things I said at the time was that I would only do the part if my character wasn't made into an Uncle Tom. They assured me that he certainly wouldn't be. So it was agreed that if the bigoted white neighbour called me something I would call him the equivalent back. If he hit me, I would hit him back. In other words, we were to be on a par. Once those conditions were met, I certainly felt happy about doing it, and, to a certain extent I enjoyed it.

What you have to remember is that *Love Thy Neighbour* was never done to solve the racial problem. It was done for pure entertainment and to make money. It so happens that it also came at the right time and in the right atmosphere. We had Enoch Powell blowing his top off, we had Alf Garnett (in *Till Death Us Do Part*) and all that, and *Love Thy Neighbour* just fitted into that period, and with what was going on. So, for four years, it was extremely popular.

One of the satisfying things for me about doing *Love Thy Neighbour* was to go into schools in Brixton, for example, and to get the reaction of the youngsters. I discovered that they had a hero for the first time on British television – suddenly there was someone who said 'Man, if you hit me I'm going to hit you back!' So there was that element which I think was important and which many people ignore. Up until then, all they ever saw on television was what we call stereotypes of black people – the black person being downtrodden, the black person carrying the spear. And now we had someone who was standing up for himself, and that had to be good for the youngsters. Another spin off is that there are a lot of young people now who are in the business as actors, because of *Love Thy Neighbour* and the exposure that I had – 'If Rudolph can do it, why the hell can't I?'.

A downturn in the late 70s ● After *Love Thy Neighbour* things became very quiet. There was no problem getting work in the theatre, if you didn't

Nina Baden-Semper and Rudolph Walker in *Love Thy Neighbour* (Thames TV, 1970s).

mind going out to the sticks to places like Birmingham to do the odd play. But television suddenly dried up. It was disappointing, especially when I took into consideration the work that I had done prior to *Love Thy Neighbour*. And then I saw how white actors, who had done far less prestigious work than me, were going from strength to strength. I started to suspect 'Is this the same thing that's raising its nasty head again?' I had seen it happen to actors before myself and now it was happening to me. So, obviously, I was down and disappointed. To crown it all, just as I was coming out of *Love Thy Neighbour*, I was given a format for a television drama series which I took to a couple of television companies. The idea involved me having my own series, but the rug was pulled from under me.

To this day I really don't know why this happened, although I have my suspicions. It certainly wasn't, well, I hope that it wasn't for lack of talent. It would have meant a hell of a lot for a black actor to finish a comedy series and to go into a quality drama series in this country. Anyway, the series was done without me and it turned out to be a big flop — so thank heavens I wasn't in it. Someone up there liked me after all!

So things became pretty quiet and that was a source of disappointment. I thought of going to America. In fact, I made several trips to Los Angeles and to Africa. I also went home to Trinidad a few times with the idea of shifting lock, stock, and barrel to one of these places. But I had a young family to consider and I thought at the time that it would be quite a wrench. Having built a name for myself in this country, it would have been very difficult to go and start all over again in the West Indies, Africa or America.

Caryl Phillips, the West Indian writer, came on the scene around this time and he, more than anyone else, was instrumental in my staying in England. He wrote a play called *The Hope and the Glory* which I did for television in 1984. It was virtually a two-hander with Maurice Denham. Then he wrote something called *The Shelter* which I also did. So Caryl was great and I thought 'Well, here is a talented young black writer whose views I respect a hell of a lot, and who is prepared to write good stuff for black actors'. But I was still apprehensive about whether things would really change — I was still battling against the odds in this country.

In 1984, Rudolph played Othello at the Young Vic. This made him the first black actor to play the role on the London stage since Errol John at the Old Vic in 1963. Several years earlier, 'the Othello controversy' had been rekindled when the BBC cast Anthony Hopkins as Othello in its 1980 television production of the play, and refused to cast a British black actor on the grounds that it didn't feel there were any black actors with the appropriate experience! ● That whole episode was particularly painful not only for me, but also for a lot of black actors in this country. The BBC bluntly refused to use any of the black actors in this country, saying that we were just not good enough. There was something rather unsavoury about that because, around the same time, the Royal Shakespeare Company was doing *Othello* with Donald Sinden blacked up for the role. The National Theatre had another *Othello* going at the time, with Paul Scofield blacked up. And then the BBC was trying to bring over the black American actor James Earl Jones to play Othello.

Yet, at the same time, the National Theatre was doing *Measure for Measure* with an all-black cast, in which I was asked to play any one of the leading roles. Now, how do you work that out? A black actor is capable of playing the lead in *Measure for Measure* and yet is not capable of playing Othello? There must be something wrong there. And, to add insult to injury, this was all happening during one of the periods when I went to America to see what was happening there. I arrived in Los Angeles and there was this headline saying 'BBC refuses to use any of their black actors, and turns down James Earl Jones because Equity refuses to sanction using an American'. And then the BBC's response saying that there are no British black actors good enough to play Othello. And there I am in America trying to sell myself as a British black actor!

Black Silk (1985-6) ● *Black Silk* was an idea given to me several years earlier by a brilliant barrister named Rudi Narayan. It was originally conceived as a stage play but I thought that it had tremendous possibilities as a television drama series. I took it to Ruth Boswell, a producer at the BBC, and she passed it on to Jonathan Powell, who was then Head of Drama. They decided to do the series, but then decided not to do any more after eight episodes. I was obviously very disappointed, though my personal feeling is that they never had any intention of doing more than just the eight one-hour episodes. I think that it was an opportunity for the BBC to put its money where its mouth is.

As far as doing something prestigious, *Black Silk* was certainly that. Everyone I've spoken to had very high praise for the series. Naturally, as a professional actor, I had personal criticisms of the series. But those were teething problems, problems which every successful series faces. I don't know why the BBC didn't do another series. I don't know why it was put out at ten o'clock in the evening and not at a peak viewing time. Those are questions which the BBC will have to answer.

Big George is Dead (1987) ● *Big George is Dead* was one of the television plays that I did in the 80s which I was very happy to be part of. It was written by Michael Abbensetts, directed by a young independent film-maker named Henry Martin, and was made for Channel 4. It was done by a black independent production company called Kuumba Productions.

One of the things that I said years ago was that I didn't particularly want to be party to the formation of so-called black companies in this country. But I've changed my position over the years, simply because I think that society has forced us to create things like black sections, and so on. It has forced us to do our own thing.

This is sad in a way, because I think that we should strive towards a

Rudolph Walker in *Black Silk* (BBC TV, 1985-6).

genuinely multiracial society. But that is not happening and, as a result, outfits like Kuumba and other black companies are forced to do their own thing. I've reached a stage now where I certainly would not refuse to be part of that development. It is sad but, perhaps at the end of the day, this is what is needed for us to gain some sort of recognition. Certainly, as a black production, *Big George is Dead* can stand up to anything that's been done by any other company, and it is something that I am very proud of.

Battling against the odds: establishing non-racial roles ● I find it very difficult to say why the powers-that-be are not prepared to promote their own home-grown talent. One of the things that frightens me a lot is the way England seems to be so many years behind America. And yet not even America has got it right as far as promoting or spending money on black talent. They will spend fifty million dollars on Stallone and only a half a million on a black talent, because they're still not sure. They don't know how to do it. So if England is many years behind America, where, then, do we stand as black actors in this country? I find that a source of worry for the young black actors and actresses who are coming up today.

Here we are in the 90s, and still the big problem is that they will only use a black actor in roles that are specifically written for 'a black character'. This means that a black actor is limited and is prevented from fully express-ing his or her skills. I had an unnerving experience a few years ago when I was cast together with my son in an episode of a television series. We were to play an ordinary family holidaying in Brighton. We signed contracts and everything, then, just before we started rehearsals, the director rang me and apologised, saying that it was all off because the writer had objected because the part wasn't written for a black family! The writer had offered to go away and write dialogue for a black family holidaying in Brighton, but can you imagine the sort of dialogue that this guy would have come up with – the black kid with the obligatory ghetto blaster saying 'Hey dad, how you doin', man? You all right?' It would have been that sort of mentality, rather than just an ordinary family, husband, wife and two kids holidaying by the seaside.

That's the sort of mentality that we have to cope with in this country. I would like to see the whole thing opened up, where a play or a television drama is cast not according to a person's colour. We should be able to switch on the television and find that ninety per cent of the roles can be played by anybody, irrespective of race or colour.

As a black actor who has been around since the 60s, I don't want to give people the impression that I go around with a chip on my shoulder. If I had a chip on my shoulder I certainly wouldn't have survived this long, because I've seen so many talented black actors fall by the wayside, even to the extent where the odd one has committed suicide. I'm talking about talented actors who have been in things which have been fantastic, who have done performances which will never be repeated – people like Errol John on stage and on television. Sadly, they haven't been lifted to star status, or whatever you want to call it.

There has been what I call progression in the media for white actors, and they have deservedly gone from strength to strength. But there isn't a single black actor who has been given the same accord. I'm not talking about light entertainment, because it seems to be very easy for the powers-that-be at the BBC and ITV to promote talented black comedians. There hasn't been one single talented black actor who has had that kind of progression or recognition in quality drama. None of us has been able to map out, to any real extent, our own careers and to go from strength to strength. But there must be something within some of us that has enabled us to survive for so long against such odds.

— JOHN ELLIOT —

John Elliot served in the RAMC in Europe, the Middle East, and South East Asia during the Second World War. He started writing and directing documentary films when the war was over. He joined the BBC in 1949, where he worked as a television writer and producer for fifteen years, except for one year spent on the staff of the United Nations in New York. He subsequently became a freelance drama and documentary writer.

His best known creations include the BBC documentary series *War in the Air* (1954), the science fiction serials *A for Andromeda* (1961) and *The Andromeda Breakthrough* (1962) which he co-wrote with Sir Fred Hoyle, the long-running 60s drama series *The Troubleshooters* (about the Mogul oil company), and the historical drama series *Fall of Eagles* which he co-wrote with his wife, Elizabeth Holford. He has also written plays for television, including several in the Play for Today series.

In 1956 John produced and wrote *A Man from the Sun* for the BBC, a drama-documentary which focused on Caribbean settlers in post-war Britain, and in 1967 he produced and co-wrote (with Trinidadian actor and writer Horace James) the BBC drama series *Rainbow City*. This featured Errol John as a Jamaican lawyer working in Birmingham.

From 1967-70 John returned to the BBC as Head of Programmes, later becoming Controller of the South and West region in Bristol. In 1959 John received an award from the Guild of Television Producers and Directors, and in 1970 he received the Shell International Television Award.

After the Second World War, I joined the BBC television service at Alexandra Palace and started making documentary films. One was the first documentary film series that the BBC had ever made, fifteen-and-a-half hours on the Second World War, which I approached as a pacifist rather than as someone making a chronicle of victory. As a result of that, I was seconded to the United Nations in New York by the BBC. When I got to New York, I found myself living and working in a multiracial society and it was absolutely indisputable that one didn't question who one was working with in terms of their race or nationality.

In 1956 when I was coming back from New York to live in England again, I went via the Bahamas and broke my flight in Nassau. I found an extraordinary sort of subculture going on there. The Bahamas had been British on the map for a long time, and it had bred a native population which believed in the myth of pre-war Britain. There was this English colonial way of life going on, which seemed like something out of an Edwardian storybook. There was this extraordinary, simple faith in England which I knew was an old, tired, grey and corrupt idea, but which the people from the West Indies were looking to as a sort of Nirvana. This was the image of England which people were being given, which the Jamaicans and other West Indians were receiving at school. And it was in sharp contrast to the more realistic and contemporary world image that I had found in people in New York and other parts of America.

A Man from the Sun (1956) ● I thought that the clash between this mythical Britain and the actual grotty real Britain, which West Indians would face when they got here, was a terribly important and exciting conflict. So when I got back to England and back to the BBC – which was still housed in curious quarters in Alexandra Palace – I said I wanted to do a programme on this subject. That was the spring of 1956 and I spent the summer researching in Brixton and in other parts of London where there were West Indian populations. I just nosed around, sinking into the background, talking and listening to people, going to parties, to church, to work, and generally being a fly-on-the-wall. I chose both West Indians and white people, because it seemed to me that the reaction of white people to coloured people in this country was extraordinarily untried.

It was virtually much the same as it is today, only much less barbed, I think. Not so many people then felt as threatened by the influx of immigrants as they do now, and it seemed to me that what was likely to happen, and what did happen in terms of the collision of cultures, had no reason to happen. Because what we could have hoped for, or got out of this new situation, was an enrichment of our lives. As soon as I saw how English life was being enriched by the people who were coming over in large numbers from the Caribbean, it seemed to me that I could say something positive. I could say this is something to be proud of, to be glad about, pleased about, something to dance and sing about, to be part of. I suppose it was rather naive, but to an extent my attitude was borne out by meeting the people who eventually became the cast of *A Man from the Sun*.

The whole race relations issue was new at the time. It was all much more innocent seeming in those days, than it has become since. The first boat loads of coloured immigrants to this country were West Indians, and unlike the previous generation who had arrived as students, they were coming *en masse* as workers. And this was having an impact which the British weren't used to. So I went round and tried to find out what everybody thought, and I

Sonny McKenzie, Gloria Simpson, Earl Cameron, Andre Dakar, and Errol John in *A Man from the Sun* (BBC TV, 1956).

turned it into a script which, in retrospect, I think is a bit verbalised. If I were doing it today, I would rely much less on words and arguments, and more on visual imagery. It was all very simple and straightforward, and was rather in the tradition of the pre-war GPO movies.

What was new was the fact that we were doing it with actors. This wedding of actors with documentary subjects is very difficult to attain. It's very hard to get a good performance out of an actor if you say 'don't act', which is virtually what you have to do with drama-documentary. But the West Indian performers we had were absolutely marvellous, because they were largely people who were in the entertainment business. They were entertainers rather than actors, or men and women in the street. They had a natural spontaneity. They also had very good language — a very direct, colourful language, which twentieth-century colloquial English has rather ceased to be. And having come from New York, where I had spent some time in a multiracial society, and where people were talking all kinds of English, I found that I wanted to experiment in other speech forms.

So it was really a verbal as well as a visual exercise, and that comes through, I think, in the script and certainly in the people. When the West Indians are talking to each other, they come alive and the film comes alive, because the people who did it knew what they were doing and made it live in a way that the inhibited English actors, at that time, could not.

When I took the idea to the BBC television service, I was very lucky because I hit them at the right time. There was an outfit in the television service at the time called the documentary section of the drama department. This dealt entirely with dramatised documentaries on subjects which were regarded as too touchy to involve the actual people concerned. So the stories were turned into semi-plays and performed by actors, and no one was offended, no one had to be 'Father Christmas' in the show.

They were done very quickly as well – I started writing the script for *A Man from the Sun* in midsummer of 1956, and we had the show live on the air by November. It was written, cast, rehearsed and recorded within that short space of time. Incidentally, it was recorded simply for archival purposes – the show was done live in the studio.

We couldn't record then, because the recording quality wasn't good enough for transmission, so the thing had to be done the evening that the public saw it. That meant there was a great demand on the writing, and an even greater demand on the people who had to act it. They had to rush from one set to another set at the other end of the studio, changing their clothes as they went along and trying to remember their opening line. But the cast were magnificent. They were as confused as I was to begin with, but we found our way around. We had pre-filmed some of it, like some of the exterior scenes of people getting off the boat and street scenes in Brixton, and so on.

Our chief actors included Errol John, Earl Cameron, Cy Grant, and Nadia Cattouse – names who have become recognised in this country since this performance. And they latched onto this curious way of doing things, so that by the time we arrived in the studio we all more or less knew what we were doing. By some kind of miracle that happens when you're doing things live, it all worked. We had a studio mixture of film, still back projection, and four cameras – that was about all we had, really. And all the sound had to be cued in off disc and things like that at the same time, so it was a complete gamble as to whether the thing would just collapse in the middle, or whether it would come safely through. We were lucky. It came safely through.

Casting *A Man from the Sun* wasn't that easy, although we knew some of the people already. For instance, Cy Grant was doing a nightly spot on the *Tonight* programme, so he was an obvious person to know. Errol John had just written *Moon on a Rainbow Shawl*, which was on at the Royal Court Theatre, so he was another obvious one. Nadia Cattouse was a well-known variety entertainer, but she had much deeper abilities than that, as she showed in *A Man from the Sun*. There was also an agency (run by Pearl Connor) which dealt almost exclusively in coloured actors and actresses. They were a great help as well. But we had to find a cast of fifty, and the number of professional or semi-professional West Indian actors in this country at that time, could have been numbered on the fingers of two or three hands.

Up until *A Man from the Sun* in 1956, there had been no real attempt to do programmes about race relations in this country – even in the documentary field there had been very little on the subject. It wasn't a major issue then, except for people who had extreme views on one side or the other. To that extent, it was controversial, but the BBC seemed less worried about controversy in those days. Certainly the BBC television service, which was in the middle of breaking away from radio and trying to present a character of its own, was less worried. And I was rather chuffed to be able to say that this was something which the sound radio hierarchy at Broadcasting House would have been frightened to put on. We weren't frightened about things like that at Alexandra Palace; and it proved to be a bit of a landmark.

***Rainbow City* (1967)** ● About ten years after *A Man from the Sun*, I was approached by the Head of Programmes for BBC Birmingham to do a series of six dramatised programmes about West Indians in this country. It involved some filming in Jamaica, and inter-cutting footage of people's home life there with their new life in England. But, of course, the subject wasn't so new in the 60s. We were now in a situation where people didn't need to be told about West Indians in this country, because there were a lot of West Indians living here. They were known, had made their own connections in this country, and were very much regarded by their neighbours as working people.

There was a very strong feeling at the time, that West Indians should be given the chance to be treated as people, in the same way that women were fighting to be considered as people. By that, I mean as people whose possibilities and talents were much greater than they had been allowed to show. And so with Errol John playing our chief character, we made him a professional man, a lawyer with a white wife, living in a racially-mixed community in Birmingham. This was different, a shift of gear from how these things had been presented before. Before, these characters would have been presented either as working people or as entertainers.

The story we chose was a six-part drama about a man who is a lawyer and very much a black man's advocate in a racially-mixed community, where there is more or less a bridge between his own people and his wife's people. I didn't have to do all the research, or even all the writing myself – because I wrote it together with Horace James, a splendid, ebullient actor and writer, who had an inside view of something which I can only see from the outside.

We wrote six scripts together but, in the rehearsals, he never stuck to

Horace James and Errol John in *Rainbow City* (BBC TV, 1967).

them. He was a marvellous ad-libber, but he usually ad-libbed to the wrong camera! Fortunately, we weren't doing it live, so we were able to edit out these lapses. The play was strongly enriched by Horace's way of talking, by the way he looked at things, by the way he laughed at things, and by the way he handled situations in life. To that extent, it was quite successful.

The marriage between the black man and white woman never struck me as a problem. I merely wrote the scenes between the racially-mixed couple as I would write any scene between a husband and wife, irrespective of race. I'd been abroad mostly in the Middle East and Asia during the war, and I had been appalled by the arrogance and condescension shown by my fellow soldiers towards anyone of a different race from themselves. I thought if I ever do anything on this subject, I'm not going to write it in a self-conscious way. If a couple are married, then just show them kissing and behaving as any normal married couple.

After the *Rainbow City* period, other preoccupations overtook the media's interest in race relations and racial discrimination. I don't think there was any great foothold in television after that period for black themes, black actors, and black performers. Those themes got mixed into the amal-gam of English cultural life in a way, which can only be good, I think. There were one or two exceptions. The chief one that came my way was

Errol John, who was not only an actor who we used in both *Rainbow City* and *A Man from the Sun*, but also a good playwright. In fact, in the mid-60s I produced a play by him for BBC TV in which he also acted, called *The Dawn*. After that I don't think there's been any significant institutional effort along those lines.

By the mid-70s, I began to feel that it was time that black writers were encouraged to write their own scripts, and not have them done by people like me who were in-house script writers. Horace James made a start, but then he went off to Trinidad and we lost him. I don't know how much of that ground has been covered in British broadcasting since.

John Hopkins went to Cambridge University before joining the BBC in 1957. Between September 1962 and December 1964 he wrote numerous episodes of the classic BBC police series *Z Cars*. One episode in particular, *A Place of Safety*, dealt specifically with a race relations situation in uncompromising terms.

His many full-length television plays include *Fable* (1965), a controversial drama exploring inter-racial relations in Britain seen as an imaginary apartheid state in which the racial roles are reversed, *Horror of Darkness* (1965), and *Beyond the Sunrise* (1969) which was about two African politicians (played by Ram John Holder and Calvin Lockhart) who are caught in a conflict of loyalties which ends in bloodshed and sacrifice.

John's most ambitious television drama, *Talking to a Stranger*, a quartet of BBC plays looking at the break-up of a family as seen in turn by the various members, was screened in 1966.

Z Cars: A Place of Safety ● *A Place of Safety* is, in a way, the best or the most completely realised episode of *Z Cars* that I wrote. The objective with all the episodes that I wrote was to set an event, or the circumstances surrounding an event, in motion. But I always thought in terms of it developing as a controlled improvisation. I would have an event, I would not know where it was going, but I would follow the characters as they reacted to and took part in the events that were happening around them. It is an uncomfortable situation because at no point in *A Place of Safety*, does anybody take a stand or give us answers to the questions being posed. They leave the questions to you, the audience, and that makes it difficult because maybe they're showing you things that you don't want to think about.

PC Fancy Smith feels that he has done something rather splendid for the Indian woman, Nana, and he expects her to say 'Thank you', so that he can feel good about himself. But she won't because he hasn't done anything except behave with normal human decency, and you don't get medals and praise for behaving normally. He felt that because she was Indian and her husband, Sadik, was black, he was being especially good. Well, in my view he wasn't. But, at the same time, I wasn't condemning him. I was not intending to show him as less than good, but only that the sequence of events follow themselves in a natural order.

What I mean is that there is a kind of writing which is very easy – and we see it all the time – where the writer presents all the questions and all the answers. But there is another kind of writing, which for me is the important kind of writing, which presents some of the questions and none of the answers. It is not my place, as a writer, to give you my answers.

Johnny Sekka gave an extraordinary performance as the tormented Sadik who loses control and attacks another man with a hatchet. There were people who felt that a man committing such an act was not the sort of person they wanted to know about. In fact, people wrote in to the programme about that. Sadik tells us in the scene in the cell, near the end of the drama, that he had done wrong and that it frightened him. He also confesses that he had discovered in himself a kind of horror, a darkness, that really scared him more than anything else that he had ever discovered about himself. He didn't know that he was capable of picking up an axe and hitting someone with it, and yet he had. And he would have tried to attack the police as well. So, there again, we're finding ourselves through the events as they unfold.

I'm not sure how I came to make Sadik's wife an Indian (played by Alaknanda Samarth). I've been thinking about that to this day. It was not a schematic choice that we would have an African husband and an Indian wife. It just seemed inevitable that this man would marry someone who understood him and who would be able to deal with him – this is the most important point in her character. As long as they were left alone, she was able to hold their life together. But the moment the outside pressure intervened and her husband attacked the man with an axe, she became helpless. And we watch her struggling to hold the centre of her life together. And the pain that she conveys, the awareness of the inevitable collapse of her life, which I find when I see Alaknanda's performance, is so moving.

In the early 60s women in our society had a pretty rough time, with very little control. It was a time when women had to accept what was happening. And Alaknanda beautifully conveyed that quality of 'Leave me alone, I'll manage'. She didn't want the police to interfere when these men were ganging up on her. She felt she could deal with it. But the inevitable interference of society in her life, ultimately destroyed her life. The final moment, when we circle the cast and look at them – the pressure of despair that we watch as we look at her face and Sadik's face and their children – is heart rending.

Then we come to Fancy Smith who is at the edge of a philosophical discovery, but happily for him he doesn't have to deal with it any more, because a small crime starts somewhere else and he has to rush off to deal with it. 'Thank God,' he says. And he's thanking God for all of us, because the problem has been taken away.

My hope in *Z Cars* was always that I could make the situation stay with you after it had finished, so that you would never be able to say 'Thank God' and then go away. It was a miracle how we commanded fifteen million viewers every week, and how twenty years later people are still watching it. We laid pain out there, and our executants, like Alaknanda Samarth and Johnny Sekka, didn't stint with what they gave.

***Fable* (1965)** ● Soon after *A Place of Safety*, I wrote a television play called *Fable* which created an imaginary situation in which black-white relations were reversed. I had read a feature article in *Time* magazine about the South African government's policy for setting up Bantustans. I had no idea that this sort of thing was happening. But the main thing that outraged me was the residential thing, the fact that if people didn't have a job, they could be shipped out to these Bantustans, even if they had been born in Johannesburg. Everybody should have the right to be wherever they want to be, though I acknowledge that it's a more complex situation than that. But I was angry and outraged. I mean, I discovered it with all the fury of someone who should have known better.

I talked to Sydney Newman, BBC Head of Drama at the time, about doing a one-off drama about that experience. And Sydney said 'Yes, well, very laudable, but how are you going to do it so that it can have an effect?' And I thought, 'Why not reverse the situation, reverse black and white?' I just thought 'I'm going to tell this story, though, obviously, I'm not going to sell it in South Africa'. I was on a roll, as they say, I had a lot of work happening and I thought 'I'll make it black and white, and I'll switch it around'.

But there is no black versus white in *Fable*, that's not what I was writing about. I was not writing about racism or apartheid as such. I was trying to get the essence of a subject race that is is ruled, exploited and violated by a ruling party. That is what *Fable* is really about.

One of the cast told me that it would not be understood, that people would say 'That's what happens if you make blacks policemen and put them in control'. Those were his words. And I said 'Oh no, that couldn't happen. Everybody will understand that it's an ironic comment'. Well, after it was shown, I got a letter from a viewer which said 'I really enjoyed that play. Boy, you showed them what would happen if they came to power, if they had the authority'. He didn't even need to specify who 'they' were. Later I was consoled by a colleague who pointed out that any executive could have told me that what I had set up was open for misunderstanding, and that it was going to be misunderstood.

As far as the BBC supporting the project, let me say, first, that working on the script was the easy bit. When I handed it in, nobody spoke to me about the problematical aspects of the story. But that's because the pro-

Eileen Atkins and Rudolph Walker in *Fable* (BBC TV, 1965).

ducer was the late James McTaggart, and the director was Christopher
Morahan, two extraordinary people who were very good friends. So I, as
writer, and subsequently the actors, were all protected by the integrity of
the people who were presenting the play. You only have to look at
Christopher's extraordinary concept – the piece is shot with such formal
control, constantly framed, matching symmetrical shots. His direction
made it possible for us to accept the horror of the situation being dramatised, because we were being conned, as it were. The baroque music was a
deliberate choice on his part, to provide a counter-balance to the awful
horrors that we were watching.

But there was anxiety within the BBC about the effect the play might
have, because the Leyton by-election, in which race was a major campaign
theme, was happening around the same time (1965). Jimmy McTaggart told
me that *Fable* was regarded as a potential problem for the BBC because if
they scheduled it at the time, it might be thought that they were taking sides
in an issue that was as potentially disastrous then, as it is today. So they
told Jimmy that *Fable* would be re-scheduled at a later date.

My concern was that, once they had taken it out of the schedule, it would
never go back in. But Jimmy – he was wonderful about it – he swore that he
would not allow them to forget it. He said to me one day 'I have to look at
myself in the mirror every morning when I shave, do you think I could face

myself if I allowed this programme to be abandoned?' I didn't think he would, but I knew that we were dealing with people who did not consider Jimmy's problems about shaving himself in the morning!

And so *Fable* was pulled, and – as often happens when clever people make decisions that they think will serve their own purposes – it caused a great deal of trouble because the papers picked it up. In those days, the press were in the habit of picking up things that I did. I had previously written several controversial episodes of *Z Cars*, for which the BBC had to make public apologies. So, because of these experiences, the press were ready to pounce again. I remember one of the tabloids doing a centre-page spread with a big picture showing a scene from the play – an act of violence against, I think, Ron Lacey, one of the white characters. Underneath this there was a brief list of my credits up to that point, and the naughty things that I had done in the past, like upsetting the public. So, in their eyes, I had obviously become totally insane, because I had written a play where there was a black ruling minority and a white slave majority, and everybody knew that it wasn't true!

When the play was finally scheduled, they actually said that it is not meant to represent a situation that could happen any time in the future, or one that has happened at any time in the past. So don't worry about it! I would have liked it if *Fable* had had a similar effect to Orson Welles' *War of the Worlds* in 1939, when everybody in America believed that Martians had landed in Upstate New York and were killing people. Obviously, it didn't have that kind of effect, but it's an interesting illustration of how wrong authority can be. In their efforts to try and avoid embarrassment, they merely drew attention to the play, which, in the end, served our purpose. I knew, of course, what I was doing, I wasn't an idiot. I knew that they would be outraged when they saw scenes like the white husband being beaten up by the black police. You have to remember that this was 1965, long before the appearance of the extraordinary films that are being made today, like *Boyz N the Hood*, which portray that kind of violence. *Fable* was fairly innocent compared to what we see today, though it was profoundly upsetting nevertheless.

Following its transmission, the reaction to *Fable* within the BBC was immensely supportive. The play got one of the biggest reactions from viewers than anything of mine before, except *Talking to a Stranger*. People kept coming up to me and saying – in incoherent praise – 'I can't believe you did that. How did you get away with it?' Everyone knew we were working for a very conservative Board of Governors at the time. I can only assume that the Governors didn't see it. But one or two people made contact with me personally, and it was very upsetting to discover that what I had tried to do could be so comprehensively misunderstood.

Once the idea for *Fable* came to me, it only took about a week of preparation before I sat down and wrote the play. I had the idea, talked to a couple of people, thought about it for three or four days while I was still writing *Z Cars*, then began writing it. And all sorts of other events from my life started to come into it, like the holocaust and the death camps, which are referred to in the course of *Fable*.

By the time we reach the climax at the end of the play, everything is happening – rape, castration, exploitative prostitution. The characters go through a living hell. I found that events which had been stored away in my mind, which I was not even aware of, started to come back. For instance, when I was about sixteen I saw a news trailer in the cinema of the first images coming out of Belsen. When I saw those images I felt as if I had walked into the concentration camp. I felt destroyed by those images. I didn't understand it at the time, I was far too young. But it was the beginning of my concern for people who are victimised and violated, and that concern has gone on all through the rest of my life. And it's there in *Fable*.

It is difficult to understand the experience of writing. It is fully realised when everything that you are, everything that you believe in, and everything that you've done, goes into the process of writing. I can usually identify the source of every word, of every line of a play of mine. I don't make up stories, I just write what has happened. Some of it, of course, is adaptation, but *Fable* is the pure expression of my feelings about people who are victimised and violated, in this case because they are black.

— JOAN HOOLEY —

Joan Hooley was born in Jamaica and came to Britain in the 50s. Her stage roles include the original production of Errol John's award-winning play *Moon on a Rainbow Shawl* at the Royal Court in 1958, Jean Genet's *The Blacks* at the Royal Court in 1962, and James Baldwin's *The Amen Corner* in 1987.

In 1964 Joan appeared in more than fifty episodes of the popular hospital soap-opera *Emergency-Ward 10* in a continuing role as an African house-surgeon called Dr Louise Mahler. She is currently working as a scriptwriter on Trix Worrell's Channel 4 sitcom *Desmond's*.

Having spent three years training to be a nurse, I came to England to do nursing. I immediately gave it up and went off to the Royal Court Theatre one day with the thought, at the back of my mind, that that was really what I wanted to do for a living. My mother wasn't at all pleased. The Royal Court took me on originally as an assistant stage manageress and I worked my way up to being a stage manageress. I was there for quite a while. Then I got into understudying various parts that came to the Royal Court – because, in those days, the stage management people had to do some understudying work as well. So we weren't doing just one job. And that's how it all started, really.

My first major roles were in Errol John's award-winning play *Moon on a Rainbow Shawl* in 1958, and Jean Genet's *The Blacks* in 1962, both of them at the Royal Court. *Moon on a Rainbow Shawl* was quite fun. In fact, I was understudying in that before taking over one of the parts. I can't remember why I had to take over, but I certainly did.

Errol John was a very productive writer and very involved in black theatre. He was one of the first black directors and writers in this country, and I remember him doing a lot of work and pushing for us to get work. He was very good. I can't remember a lot about *The Observer* Award which he received for *Moon on a Rainbow Shawl*, but he was certainly a very forceful character in black theatre at the time. *The Blacks* was great fun to do as well. To the best of my memory, it was the first stylised production of that type in England. I played the part of Bobo, and I enjoyed it.

It was around this time that theatres like the Royal Court started doing productions with black casts. Well, I think there was a need for it, really, because there was so much black talent around and we weren't getting any

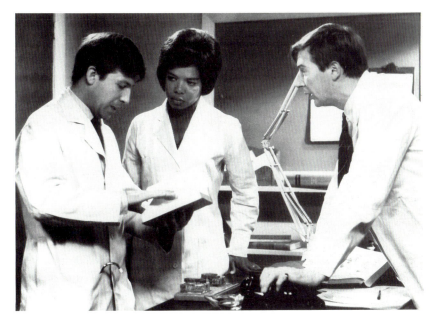

Joan Hooley with John White and John Large in *Emergency-Ward 10* (ATV, 1964).

opportunities in the theatre or in television. Then, suddenly, these plays were being commissioned by people with insight into what needed to happen to the theatre. There was a general interest in seeing what black writers had to offer, and what black talent there was to perform these works. We had this whole area in the early 60s, when there was all this commissioned work suddenly arriving on the scene, and there to be acted. It was a very productive period between 1958 and 1962. I was constantly working – very little television, but a lot of theatre.

Emergency-Ward 10 (1964) ● I was working at Theatre Royal in Stratford, when I heard that they were casting for a new television series called *Emergency-Ward 10*. I must have been one of the last persons on earth to hear about it, because all my friends were auditioning for parts and I didn't know anything about it. But as soon as I heard, I immediately rushed over to the television studios and got in by the skin of my teeth. I think they were just about to finish auditioning when I arrived, and I was amazed when I got the part. That lasted for nearly a year, fifty odd episodes, and it was great fun.

I played the part of Louise Mahler, an African doctor from a wealthy family who has come to England to train and to work as a house-doctor. She has a love affair with one of the doctors, Giles Farmer, and they had the two of us walking out together for weeks. Then there was a scene where we were supposed to kiss in a bedroom. The papers got hold of it and all the objections started to be raised. It was suggested that the kiss would be unfit for viewing at 7.30 in the evening, because there might be young people watching! The ITV authorities bandied about for several weeks. John White, who played Giles Farmer, and I had great fun speculating on what they were going to do next – whether they were going to cut it out altogether, whether we were going to end up in bed, or whatever. It was quite fun, I enjoyed doing that.

Well, we never did get our kiss in the bedroom, instead we ended up kissing in the garden quite sedately. And then Giles' family objects to him having a black fiancée, so the romance has to be broken off, much to my disgust, I hasten to add, because I was really looking forward to the character developing further and me actually getting married to Giles. But it never happened. Shortly after that, I was written out of the series – I was bitten by a snake, my body was carted off, and that was the end of Louise Mahler of *Emergency-Ward 10*. It was quite funny at the time actually – the fuss the papers made about the kiss, with headlines like 'First black and white television kiss'. And, of course, all the time I was married to a white man in real life, so we really fell about laughing.

The barren years ● In the 60s, when there was a lot of theatrical work about and I was doing *Emergency-Ward 10*, it did seem that we would have a lot of work. I didn't stop working for four years. I thought 'This is wonderful. Here I am on the road to stardom – a young, successful black actress'. But when I was written out of the series, I was obviously very sad. It seemed that they just used black actresses and actors in those days to create a problem within a programme. And when the problem was set aside or cleared up – like my character being bitten by a snake! – the writers seemed not to be able to produce the ideas to keep us in the programme. It just sort of dried up, and you were left, having been half way up the ladder, with absolutely nothing.

Suddenly, and for some unknown reason, there wasn't any work around – you'd be extremely lucky if you got two lines in a play, or managed to understudy someone, or got on television. It became very bad, and though all the black actors and actresses were very concerned, we couldn't put our finger on the problem. None of our work was being put out, and only the small theatrical companies and the independent companies managed to do any work. There was really no television or major theatrical work for about ten years.

These were barren years when black actors and actresses did what they could – stage management, bit-parts, playing extras, you name it – but we stayed with it. And that's why I'm now writing, because we need to take hold of things. I have more control writing for *Desmond's*, for instance, because I can make a statement and I'm able to suggest things to the media, and they have to do my work. I think this is a positive response to the situation – if there's no work out there for you, make it happen by writing.

Taking control through writing ● I got involved in *Desmond's* through my friendship with Carmen Munroe. Knowing her as well as I do, I thought I could write for her character in the series. So I started doing the usual thing of submitting scripts to the company that produces the series, Humphrey Barclay Productions, and luckily enough I got taken on the writing team. *Desmond's* is a very nice sitcom and I enjoy working on it.

I feel that progress is being made, for example in the portrayal of black families generally in contemporary soaps like *EastEnders*. But the writing and what black artistes are expected to do in these programmes is still very stilted. I don't think it comes across as real, and although there was briefly a black family in *Coronation Street* many years ago, they still haven't built any real relationships in it involving black people. There's still a lot of room for black people in soap-operas, well-written parts, as opposed to the airy-fairy portrayals that seem to be the norm at the moment.

I think most people are moving in the right direction, but I think more writers like myself, must make stronger points in what we're writing. It's one thing to do sitcom, but I'm also very interested in doing serious drama. I think it's up to us as writers, black writers, to say what we want, to push for our work to be produced, and to make sure that people see our work, and perform our work.

My idea of utopia, therefore, would be to see television stations showing fifty per cent black and white work, and fifty per cent something else. In other words, we need a more even distribution of the work that is available for the artistes. We're not getting a fair crack of the whip. There are not enough of us working, and that has got to change. But we, the writers, are the people who are going to make it change.

— CLEO SYLVESTRE —

Cleo Sylvestre was born in Hertfordshire. Her Trinidadian father was a Flight Commander in the RAF during the Second World War, and her mother was from Yorkshire. Cleo started her acting career as a child in the film *Johnny on the Run* (1953), directed by Lewis Gilbert for the Children's Film Foundation. She studied at Italia Conti and, after leaving school, gained acting experience in various workshops.

In 1965 she made her television debut in a production of *The Rise and Fall of the City of Mahagonny* for the BBC. This was followed by small roles in Ken Loach's pioneering drama-documentaries *Up the Junction* (1965) and *Cathy Come Home* (1966). Cleo also appeared as Cilla Christie, a factory worker, in *Coronation Street* in 1966; and in 1969 she played a leading role in the drama-documentary *Some Women* (1969), written by Tony Parker and produced by Tony Garnett. In 1970 Cleo joined the cast of the long-running soap-opera *Crossroads* in a continuing role as Melanie Harper, Meg Richardson's long-lost foster daughter.

Cleo's numerous stage appearances include Simon Gray's *Wise Child* (1967) with Alec Guinness, and the National Theatre's production of Peter Nichols' *The National Health* (1969). More recently she has appeared in David Lan's *Desire* (1990) at the Almeida Theatre in London, and in *To Kill a Mockingbird* (1991) at the Theatre Royal in York.

Although I was born outside London, I was actually brought up in London. My earliest memories are of the Euston area of London. I lived with my mum. My dad used to visit us periodically, but he was never really part of my life as such. I lived in a little street where all the kids played together. It never really dawned on me that I was a different colour from any of the other kids. I think that really started when I went to primary school. On my first day at school this little boy – whose name I shall always remember, called Johnny Haynes – came up and called me 'blackie'. Suddenly, the whole world looked different and there I was in this playground surrounded by a sea of white faces. I went home crying to my mum, saying that I didn't want to go back to school the next day because somebody called me 'blackie'. She said 'Well, you are black and so am I'. She was actually a mixture – her mum was from Yorkshire and her dad from Africa. 'And your dad is black, so of course you are. What else do you expect to be?'

After that it didn't really worry me so much, but I think subconsciously it had an effect. At school I started trying to make the kids laugh by imitating other kids or imitating the teachers, because once you made the kids laugh you were accepted. Then I started going to Conti's on Saturday mornings – I was a Conti kid and I really enjoyed it. I used to look forward to it. Then, when I was about seven – it must have been the early 50s – I appeared in a film made by a young director called Lewis Gilbert for the Children's Film Foundation. It was called *Johnny on the Run* and we went up to Scotland to film on location. It was quite a good film to be in and I was absolutely thrilled to do it. I suppose I got the acting bug from there.

After that, I never thought about doing anything else. I went on to grammar school, and somehow I didn't have the guts to mention my real ambition to go into the theatre because the school was geared to going on to university or into a teaching career. I was more or less badgered into going to teachers' training college. I was very unhappy doing that and decided to leave. I remember my ex-head calling me in and saying 'Cleopatra, why have you decided to leave college?' And I said 'Because I want to act'. And she said 'Well, there are no parts for coloured actresses in Britain'. 'Coloured' was the word in those days. What she said made me very determined and I thought 'Right, if there aren't any parts I'm going to make sure that there are'. And so I contacted a couple of agents. I also enrolled to do a course at a drama school, but while I was waiting to start I got a job, so I never actually went on to do a proper full-time course. I just kept on going to drama workshops.

Up the Junction (1965) and Cathy Come Home (1966) ● It must have been about 1965 when I went to see Ken Loach who was casting *Up the Junction*. Up until then, I used to go along and see directors, and if there were black parts at all – of which there weren't very many in those days – it was always assumed that you had either a very broad West Indian accent or an African accent. You never went up for a part which was cockney, or North Country, or anything like that, because they didn't realise that there were black people born and brought up in this country. So, when I met Ken, he was actually knocked out by the fact that I had a cockney accent, and so I got the part in *Up the Junction*. It was only a small part, but it was great fun and a pleasant change because I was just one of the factory girls and there was no big issue about me being black or anything like that.

I worked for Ken again in 1966 on *Cathy Come Home*. He tended to use the same group of actors – it was almost like a television repertory company. It was marvellous because we'd meet up as a bunch of artistes, and then we'd go off, and then we'd meet up again a few months later to work on another production with Ken. So we developed a certain sort of trust with

Cleo Sylvestre with Geraldine Sherman, Carol White, and Doreen Herrington in *Up the Junction* (BBC TV 'The Wednesday Play', 1965).

our fellow actors and with the director. It was a very exciting time working with people like Tony Garnett, Roy Battersby, Ken Trodd, writers like Jim Allen, Tony Parker, Jeremy Sandford, Nell Dunn, and, of course, Brian Trufano who was the cameraman. It was a great time and we felt that we were doing something positive, in as much as we were participating in something which had a dramatic content but was also socially very relevant to what was happening in the country at the time. It was a really exciting period.

Coronation Street (1966) ● I can't remember how I got into *Coronation Street*, but it was good to be in such a popular soap. I was a fan of the programme and watched it regularly; and now there I was, quite early on in my career, actually appearing in it. I was really knocked out. I played the part of an ordinary North Country factory girl. I can't remember how many episodes I did, but I didn't stay in for long.

It's pretty amazing that, in subsequent years, they haven't had more black people appearing in *Coronation Street*, especially as there are now lots of Northern black people. You would think that they would have had a few more in. They've had the odd storyline, but it has always been dominated by the fact that the person is black and has never involved them as just characters. I mean, the whole thing about their character depends on the fact that they're black and not because of other things. It's a shame they just can't have black people as ordinary people in it, and make no comment about their blackness at all. Because that's the way viewers will get used to seeing black people in television shows and series, and it needs to be done in order to reflect society as it is now.

Advertisements are particularly bad at this sort of thing – you very rarely ever see black people in adverts. You'd think that we weren't consumers of everyday products like the rest of society. It's quite bizarre how advertising agencies exploit the sort of cute image of black children, but are frightened of featuring black adults in mainstream advertising. I can't think of many adverts which feature black people in them.

In the early days, you never saw a black technician, maybe the odd scene-shifter but certainly not on the technical side, and definitely not in the make-up department. I mean, you would go into the make-up room and there would be a range of white make-up, and you'd start frantically mixing around trying to get some deeper colours and everything. That's all fairly organised now, but in those early days it was very unusual to see anybody black behind the scenes.

Some Women (1969) ● In 1969, I went to see Roy Battersby who was casting a television play called *Some Women*, which was based on a book by Tony Parker called *Five Women*. It was the story of different women who had been in prison, and I was up for the part of a seventeen-year-old girl who'd been in prison purely because the system had no other way of coping with her. She hadn't in fact done anything criminal at all. I think the worst thing she had done was to run away from a children's home. And there she was, this innocent young girl, in prison with all these other people.

It was a very interesting part because it was totally improvised. I was sent the book to read and, first of all, was told to memorise as much as I could about the Millie Jackson character. Then, a couple of days later, I had a phone call saying 'No, sorry, forget all that. Just read it through very quickly and you'll get a script'. So I tried to forget what I had already remembered, and then for about three weeks before we started filming I kept getting these conflicting phone calls. When we eventually got down to filming, Tony Parker started interviewing me and it was great because he would say 'Now after so-and-so, what happened to Millie?' And I would reply 'Oh, I went to another children's home in Cumberland, and then . .'. oh, sorry, no I didn't that time . . .' And so my dialogue actually came out as it would in real life. It was good without being scripted. I don't know what I'd think of my particular performance in it now, I'd probably cringe. But at the time it was a very exciting thing to do.

Then the BBC wouldn't show it for about a year, because they said that it was too much like the real thing and people would be confused about whether we were actors or not. They eventually put it out very late one night, when they thought nobody was looking. The next day I got a call – well, my agent got a phone call – from Reg Watson who was then producing *Crossroads*, inviting me to meet him to discuss joining the soap.

Crossroads (1970) ● I played Melanie Harper, Meg Richardson's long-lost adopted daughter. She was a student in France and had come back to England. I was introduced rather dramatically at the end of one of the episodes – I walked into the motel and asked for Mrs Richardson at the reception desk, and when the receptionist asked whom should she say is calling, I replied 'Tell her that it's her daughter'. And then the music came up da-da-dum . . . and the credits rolled. Now, there was never any mention of this person before in *Crossroads*. Nobody knew about this long-lost daughter, so it was quite a shock I should imagine to all the viewers suddenly having this girl arrive. And it was just me as a character, no comment was made of the fact that I was black.

The storyline developed and I ended up being a waitress in the motel and a receptionist as well. I had a lot of scenes with Susan Hanson, who played Diane – mostly comedy scenes which were great fun to do. Our storylines were just the normal sort of problems which people of that age would have had at that particular time, about boyfriends and so on. We got letters from viewers saying 'Oh, you two! We love watching your scenes. You should have your own comedy series together'.

While appearing in *Crossroads*, I was also working at the National Theatre, playing a leading role in Peter Nichols' play *The National Health*. We worked out a system so that whenever I had a free block – because we worked in blocks at the National in those days – they would write me into episodes for that particular period, which was great. So I would do the sort of classy acting at the National and then go off and do, I hope, just as classy acting in *Crossroads*. But, alas, they never had the music at the end of the episodes and the little voice saying 'Miss Cleo Sylvestre is currently appearing at the National Theatre', which I thought would have been great for all those critics of *Crossroads*.

I decided to leave *Crossroads* when they came up to me one day and said they had a storyline for me round about December – this was about June – and, suddenly, I had visions of being locked into *Crossroads* for the whole of my career. I thought 'Well, it's great. It's great money, and it's fun to do, but I really don't want to be committed to a soap for that long'. I was also not very well at the time, so I left *Crossroads* and went back to the National and to the council flats where my mum lived. All the women on the estate started to ask my mum 'What's happen to Cleo? We haven't seen her in *Crossroads* lately'. And she would say 'Oh, well, she's left. She's gone back to the National'. And they'd say 'Oh, never mind, never mind'!

I think *Crossroads* is probably the only soap that attempted to have integrated casting and to use black people. After I left they had in other people which was very good. It was great that they had made the decision to use black people in storylines where sometimes the colour thing was dominant, but where often enough it was just dealing with them in ordinary everyday situations. So *Crossroads* was a pioneer in that field, even though it came in for a lot of stick, which I don't think was totally justified.

Obviously there were times when people forgot their lines or whatever, but you have to remember that we were working under terrific pressure. When I joined *Crossroads* we were doing five shows a week – that's a lot of television to do and the turnaround was very quick. Immediately we finished one show, we got a bunch of scripts for the next and we'd be off doing them. So it's not surprising that occasionally things would go wrong. There was bound to be the odd error or the odd microphone in shot, or someone forgetting their lines.

Crossroads was like weekly repertory theatre, only for television. As far as I'm concerned, it was a great training ground. It was an invaluable experience for me because it taught me so much about working in television under pressure. What little technique I now have probably stems from having worked on *Crossroads*.

I think I was very lucky in the 60s because I got a lot of television work, and it was a huge variety, from drama through to sitcoms. At the time there were very few other black actresses who were getting this sort of work.

It's worth saying something about career structure, in as much as an actor can actually have a career structure. I know it's very difficult, perhaps not so much for women because we tend to have family concerns which are just as time-consuming and as important as our careers – I've had my children and everything, so I haven't actually dropped out, I've been looking after them. But there were lots of very good black male actors around during the early period, whose careers, if they had been white, would have led to bigger and better things. But each time they did something, and it was really good, it was like being on a treadmill – back to square one, climb your way up again, and so on. And so people like Calvin Lockhart, eventually had to go to America. I'm sure that wouldn't have happened with white actors as much, and, unfortunately, it's still happening today. You see black actors who are very good in things and you expect to see them do a follow-up, and it just doesn't happen.

— KENNY LYNCH —

Kenny Lynch was born in Stepney in the East End of London. His father was from Barbados. He entered show business as a dance band singer in the 50s. Kenny rose to fame in the early 60s as a singer and songwriter and had a succession of chart-hits including 'Up on the Roof' in 1962. Subsequently he made numerous television appearances in the 60s pop music shows including *The Beat Room*, *Thank Your Lucky Stars*, *Ready Steady Go*, *Top of the Pops*, and *Juke Box Jury*.

After 1965 Kenny wrote for and produced artistes like The Small Faces, Cilla Black, and Dusty Springfield. He also made a successful transition to 'straight' acting in drama series such as *No Hiding Place* (1966) and *Z Cars* (1968), as well as in the sitcoms *Till Death Us Do Part* (1967) and *Curry and Chips* (1969).

In 1970 Kenny was awarded an OBE for his charity work.

I was born in Stepney, East London, about nine months before World War Two started. There were eleven of us kids, plus my mum and dad – so there were thirteen of us altogether. I didn't really know my other brothers and sisters until after the war because they were evacuated to Wales. I remember they all came back speaking with Welsh accents, which was quite funny. I think you had to be a year old or something before you could be evacuated, so I was too young. I did actually go away with them the first time, with my mother, and we stayed down in Wales for three weeks. But then they brought me back, so I was in London right the way through the war.

I just remember it being a very funny time, you know. We used to go down these air-raid shelters every night, and we were bombed out of about three houses. In those days we just used to move in with the person next door, or into one of the houses that was still standing. I must have moved about four or five times. I remember it as if it happened only yesterday. I can remember watching our house get bombed as the sirens went. We walked out of the house, got about four or five hundred yards away, and this great big flame went up. My old man said to me 'That's our house. So we'll probably move in with somebody else tomorrow'. And then we'd go down the shelter and everybody would be singing – as a kid growing up, I remember it as a great fun time.

I was born in a street called Cornwall Street. There weren't any other black families in that street, and I don't remember seeing a lot of black people. I know that in the East End – places like Hackney and Poplar – there were blacks, but, as far as I can remember, I never saw that many. And I was a bit of a novelty. Being a cockney, I never had any trouble in those days, because there weren't many black people around, and the few that were around, as I said, were more a novelty than anything else. Today you hear a lot of complaints about how the Asians and West Indians are moving around the country, but in those days there was none of that going on. I didn't really think about racial prejudice until I was about sixteen. And then I became popular when I was about nineteen, so I really never suffered it very much.

My father was from Barbados and had been here since he was sixteen. He was fifty-eight when I was born, which means that he came to this country in the 1890s. He actually worked in the merchant navy, so he was in and out of home all the time. He never lost his Barbadian accent – mind you, I couldn't understand a word he was saying half the time, even though he had been here quite a long time.

I remember he talked about religion a lot, because when I first went to school during the middle of the war, they asked me what religion I was going to be and I wasn't quite sure. I went back and asked him and he said 'Well, I'm a Catholic, but don't you be a Catholic because they used to beat people up in the West Indies just to make them join the Catholic church. So you be Church of England'. So I went back and told them I was Church of England.

From boxing to show business ● I'd done a bit of boxing for about four or five years, but hadn't boxed for about six years when I joined the army in 1956. A fellow who was a champion at that time, a boy called Dave Stone, said to me 'Why don't you come in the boxing team? It's really easy. We don't wear uniforms, we wear track suits, and we get special food and that kind of thing'. I thought it was a good idea, and so for two years I was in the boxing team. I had eleven fights and got beat once, in my first fight. After coming out, I thought 'There's definitely got to be an easier way of getting a living', so I went back to singing. I became a professional dance band singer, and then I joined Bob Miller's Band at the Mecca in London. I was with the band for about six years.

I used to run a pub for a guy called Sammy McCarthy – he was a British Featherweight Champion. It was a very hard job. I used to pull up the beer in the mornings for the pensioners – pubs in those days were full of pensioners in the morning. I did this from eleven in the morning till about two in the afternoon. I used to do the barrels and all that kind of thing as well. Then I'd open up again at five o'clock and serve till about nine at night, when we had a pianist come in and I would sing about forty songs. Then I'd clear up afterwards. So I had a really full day and used to get six quid for it.

The reaction to me was very good in those days, because I was the only one around who was singing. I used to sing in all the talent competitions round the pubs when I wasn't working. I even got barred from a few because I kept winning! And then I'd go into some of the pubs and they'd tell me that I could come second tonight – you used to get £1 if you came second, and if you were with four or five of your mates you could drink all night for £1 in those days. I think a pint of beer was about sixpence or something.

I actually started song writing by accident, really. In those days, when you got a record contract the publishers used to invite you to write your own B-side, and if it was good enough you could do the A-side as well. When a company asked me to do it, I just said 'I don't write songs, that's not my game'. And they said 'Oh, you can put them on the B-side, or we can get somebody to write for you and you can put your name to it'. So I had a go. I was singing Sinatra-type songs and jazz. I was working with Ronnie Scott's Band and Don Randell and Tubby Hayes, singing a lot of jazz. I was actually singing with different kinds of bands – one night I'd be with a Dixieland Jazz band, next night I'd be with a modern jazz group. So, anyway, I wrote a song that was a kind of standard type song, and took it back to my producer who said 'Well, I don't think the kids will like this, but yes, you can stick it on the B-side'. And once I'd written one, it just took off from there.

I was singing in a lot of clubs in London's West End – places like the Star Club, Romanos, and the Flamingo – when I first got into television. I was singing one night in Romanos when Shirley Bassey came in and said 'You should make records'. So I made about three records and had a hit with the first one. It was in the top thirty. I was doing a lot of radio at the time, but I hated radio – just sitting there with a microphone in front of you didn't appeal to me – and I was really worried about ever doing television. Then I got a professional job with Alma Cogan – Sunday Concerts, they were called – in Morecambe, and while I was there we did two shows. Then she said 'Oh, I'm doing this TV special, would you like to come on it with me?' I was a bit worried about doing it, but people said 'Go on, do it, it'll be good for you'. And since I had a record coming out, they said that I could do it on the show. So that's exactly what I did. I walked onto the stage with the camera in front of me and I loved it. I was on television a lot after that, doing things like *That Was The Week That Was* and all different kinds of programmes. I took to television really well and I loved it.

I was always interested in politics, so I used to watch lots of chat shows and political shows. I watched the *Tonight* programme every night, in fact I watched it from the time it first started. I loved it and I was dying to get on it. Cy Grant used to appear on it regularly, singing calypsos – he was the most prominent black performer that one saw every night on television. I wouldn't say he was a role model, but I used to like him and always wanted to have his job, because I wanted to meet all the political people they used to have on the programme, like Adlai Stevenson. So when I was invited on it I was really pleased. But I would actually have liked to have Cy's job!

There weren't a lot of openings for black actors in films and television drama during the 60s. I played the occasional acting role in television dramas like *No Hiding Place* in 1966, and *Z Cars* in 1968, which I enjoyed. But the thing I didn't like about filming or doing television plays was that they took so bloody long to do. I never liked hanging around in studios, waiting twenty minutes just to do thirty-second shots and all that sort of thing. But I did actually want to do a full-length film and maybe go out on location or something. I thought that might be quite nice, especially if it was with somebody who liked to have a laugh like I do.

But I didn't really like acting because learning lines for me was horrific – I was never into learning lines. I've never liked doing that. So I was never a very good actor because I didn't train for it. But I had lots of laughs on the things I did because I was always working with people I loved and on programmes I liked. I actually did about fifteen films in the 60s, and I played myself in most of them. I was ad-libbing my way through them most of the time, so I wasn't doing the things that actors really do. I was just sort of being myself. And I was very lucky to work with good directors who knew me quite well. Most of the guys picked me to do bits in their films because they'd had a drink with me in the pub or something. But I don't think I would have been a serious actor.

Comedy and racial jokes: *Till Death Us Do Part* (1967) and *Curry and Chips* (1969) ● I thought Alf Garnett in *Till Death Us Do Part* was a very funny character, and I'm sure there are people like him. But I appeared on that programme because I loved Johnny Speight. I think he's a great comedy writer. Johnny was actually a neighbour of ours in East London where I grew up. I knew his family very well, but I didn't realise it was him until years later when I met him and he told me about his background. And then he asked me if I wanted to go on the programme.

I loved Alf Garnett, I still do – I even watch *In Sickness and In Health*. I'm sure there are people like him around, though I've never actually met them that bad. The point is, any character you portray on television has to go a little over the top, because people don't want to see somebody they can go next door and see. They want to see somebody who's completely different, and Alf Garnett is certainly that.

The recollection I have of *Curry and Chips* is that it was probably the happiest period of my life. We only did six episodes, but working with

Spike Milligan and Eric Sykes was a dream come true for me, and it was a very funny programme. We had a great director who would let us do what we liked, and he directed it almost like *Ready Steady Go* – the cameras were never in one place, they moved everywhere and it was really good. Everybody enjoyed themselves, and it was a really happy show.

It's only in the last couple of years that I've done programmes about black jokes and all that. There are jokes about everybody – the Irish, Poles, English, Germans, Jews – so we've got to have our turn as well. And I don't find them offensive as racial jokes. If they're funny, they're funny. I told racial jokes when I first started out. I told them not because they made people laugh, but because I thought they were funny. People who don't like black jokes have no sense of humour. Jokes are jokes, no matter who they're about.

Whenever I was working on television shows like Jimmy Tarbuck or Bruce Forsyth's thing, we'd use black jokes because I was probably the only black guy amongst twelve performers in the show. Now, this has been going on for years, not just here but in America as well with people like Stepin Fetchit and 'Rochester'. I mean, if you've got twelve people and one black guy, then the black guy is obviously going to get the brunt of the jokes. But I always thought the jokes were funny – and if there was a really funny joke about a black guy and I thought it was funny, I'd do it even though it might be aimed at me.

Because there weren't that many black performers when I first started up in television, people would laugh at these kind of jokes. But now when I do cabaret I find that people don't laugh at racial jokes any more. Most of the people around the Manchester and Liverpool area where we work have black people as neighbours, so it's just not funny telling jokes about blacks any more. It's passé. These days I tell jokes between songs, and probably do one joke with reference to a black guy or a black woman, in an act which lasts about an hour. Some performers who go out and do the stag nights base the whole of their act on Pakistanis or something. I don't find that very funny because the jokes are not that funny. They're just a way to get the audience with you, and if you have to rely on that you can't be a very good comic. All jokes, whatever they're about, are offensive if they're not funny.

There are not a lot of black jokes on television nowadays. People like Lenny Henry do different accents, and that's where the comedy comes from. Lenny won't do black jokes on television, but I like the accents he does. I think people laugh at things that are funnily said, rather than at jokes which are actually anti-black or what people say are racial jokes. Nowadays, so many people are involved with black people in their families, workplace, streets, clubs, and so on, that they feel embarrassed for blacks, more so now than they did years ago. I've just done a couple of programmes for the BBC about black comedy and everybody's up in arms about it. I was on with some people the other day who said that I shouldn't have done black jokes in the old days. What they don't realise is that we didn't have a lot of option then but to tell those kind of jokes.

Nowadays, they're saying you don't have to do it, it's racial and people don't like it. But, then, these same people are telling jokes about Tampax and all that kind of stuff. There were black performers on this programme doing these smutty jokes. Well, I prefer the black jokes myself. They make me laugh more than sick jokes. I love Jewish jokes, I was born right in the middle of London's East End with all the Jews. They never stopped making jokes about themselves, and the jokes were absolutely hilarious. Possibly that made it safe for me to make jokes about myself and about being black. Perhaps that's why I've never had problems with black jokes, never have had, never will have, and they can call me an Uncle Tom for as long as they like.

If you write jokes with a black influence in them, then you're going to get people laughing at them because of that. I don't think there's any other way that you can do it. And I think that it's going to go on exactly the same as it always has done. I can't see any way you can make jokes about black people unless they're about being black. But I don't think people are laughing that much at out-and-out racist jokes any more. And I think there will be less of them, comics will probably try to make the jokes funnier than they used to be – jokes about somebody who just happens to be black and in any situation. And if people take offence, that's their problem.

— NORMAN BEATON —

Norman Beaton was born in Guyana and came to Britain in 1960. In a career spanning more than twenty-five years he has performed in theatre, television, film and radio. He has also held a variety of influential positions on arts administration bodies and drama panels, including Artistic Director of Dark and Light Theatre and the Black Theatre of Brixton.

Norman has performed extensively in London's West End, on the fringe in London, and in most of the country's repertory theatres. His most recent theatrical credits include Derek Walcott's *Remembrance*, a Carib Theatre production for the Tricycle Theatre, and Mustapha Matura's *The Coup* at the National Theatre.

One of Norman's earliest film appearances was in Horace Ové's *Pressure* (1975), and in 1977 he starred in *Black Joy*, based on Jamal Ali's play *Dark Days and Light Nights*. He has also appeared in Nicolas Roeg's *Eureka* (1984), and in Horace Ové's *Playing Away* (1986).

Norman became the first black actor to receive a British film award when the Variety Club of Great Britain honoured him as Best Film Actor of the Year in 1977 for *Black Joy*.

Norman made his first television appearance for the BBC in *Drums Along the Avon* in 1967, and played one of his first leading roles as Grantly in William Trevor's television play *Afternoon Dancing* (1974). Major television roles followed, including *The Fosters* (1976-7), Michael Abbensetts' *Empire Road* (1978-9), *Easy Money* (1981), and *Big George is Dead* (1987).

Since 1989 Norman has been making regular appearances in Trix Worrell's Channel 4 sitcom *Desmond's*. In 1991, Norman made a guest appearance in *The Cosby Show*.

I was working at the Bristol Old Vic when the BBC invited me to come and read for a television play called *Drums Along the Avon*. I read for it and got the part. It was actually my first television drama, but it did not lead to regular television appearances afterwards. I suspect that, at the time, there wasn't a lot of black television being written, or any television that would feature black actors or actresses. So my initial break into television did not lead to anything bigger, and, even now, nearly twenty-five years later, there's not a lot.

Afternoon Dancing (1974) and Michael Abbensetts' Black Christ-

mas (1977) ● *Afternoon Dancing* and *Black Christmas* were entirely different pieces of work. *Afternoon Dancing* was written by a white man and was about these middle-aged women who would to go to places like the Odeon in the afternoons for tea and dancing. And black men would go as well, because they were quite lonely and were looking for women friends. The character I played falls in love with one of these middle-aged white women who is married, and he can't believe that she doesn't really want him, even though they have been dancing together. It was a very poignant piece of work.

Black Christmas was also a very serious work. It dealt with a young black woman – my daughter in the play – who becomes pregnant and doesn't know how to tell her mother. It was really a wonderful piece – there we were at Christmas time, Carmen Munroe played my wife and there she was, the charming mother figure, and there was this child who was finding it difficult to connect up with her problems.

I did another interesting and unusual television play at the time called *Dead Head*, which gave me the opportunity for the first time to play a real villain. It was extraordinary because my character turned out to be a villain with dreadlocks! I had to spend about five hours in the barber shop having these shoulder-length locks knitted into my own hair. Anyway, my character was an undercover agent who gets shot in the end. I thought I died absolutely wonderfully!

Sitcoms ● Was it easier to work in sitcoms than in serious drama on television during the 70s? Well, there was a television series which was a breakthrough – it was called *Love Thy Neighbour* and featured Rudolph Walker and Nina Baden-Semper. Because of that, it became clear that there were black actors who could handle a television series – Rudolph patently proved that. Then there was another series in America called *Good Times*, which Michael Grade (then Head of programmes at London Week-end Television) wanted to bring over and re-work into a British version. He also wanted a brilliant young actor, who had just come on the scene, called Lenny Henry to play in it. And that series was called *The Fosters*. I was fortunate enough to be cast as the father in this new sitcom, with Isabelle Lucas as the mother, and Carmen Munroe as a neighbour.

So, suddenly, it appeared that there were black actors who could take on these roles, and that there was an audience for such shows. We had arrived, so to speak, we were there and we were given parts. So the 70s, I think, were very good in so far as it was like the beginning of the beginning. Roles were being written for black people. It was a trickle that has not become a flood, but more like rain falling on a cliff side and a river beginning to form. I think that's what happened in the 70s as a result of these sitcoms.

The Fosters (1976-7) ● *The Fosters* was purely about a black family – and to have a black family portrayed on British television, without referring to the fact that they were black, but just dealing with the fact that they ate food, went to church, and did quite normal things – that was really quite extraordinary. That is what was different about *The Fosters*. I also believe that *Mixed Blessings*, which followed *The Fosters*, was a backwards step in the sense that it was about a mixed marriage – a black woman married to a white man, the family objections, and all that. It was trying to talk about race relations. *The Fosters* wasn't like that because it was a transfer of an American series, in which black people were just black people. That is what was wonderful about *The Fosters*.

One of the reasons why I think *The Fosters* did not continue, was because we didn't know what to do with the writing. It was American writing and in the American version of the series, the young man – the character played by Lenny Henry in the British version – was a 'street cred' guy, a street man which, of course, Lenny isn't. Lenny is just a nice guy, a lovely man, and we didn't know how to take the part that he played any further.

The Fosters really was the watershed of my career, because it led to so many things including *Empire Road*, which was really quite strange because this was written by a Guyanese playwright, Michael Abbensetts, and so it was like home time for me. I knew where I was. Unlike *The Fosters*, *Empire Road* wasn't an import, it was about our experiences here in Britain. And it was wonderful because we had great actors in it like Joe Marcell and Corinne Skinner-Carter. It really was like being home again.

Empire Road (1978-9) ● *Empire Road* really is, I suppose, the most important black soap that there has been in this country. My character, Everton Bennett, was a businessman – he was into property, had a lot of houses, and owned a supermarket – while his wife (played by Corinne) was a very upper-class sort of black woman. His son (played by Wayne Laryea) was also a businessman, and we actually went further in race relations in the sense that he was going out with an Asian girl and they got married, which was really quite bizarre, to say the least.

Empire Road took race relations into a wholly different area. Everton Bennett was a very bright, very clever man. He was like a godfather because he was always sorting out people's problems, quite reluctantly because he never wanted to get involved. But there we were, with this black man in the middle of Birmingham, sorting out black people's problem, with his sly and wonderful wit. It was, perhaps, the best thing that was written around that time, and I've got fond memories of it.

When Horace Ové came in to direct some episodes in the second series, that immediately introduced a different voice. I don't think Horace was

Norman Beaton with Joe Marcell and Corinne Skinner-Carter in *Empire Road* (BBC TV, 1978).

terribly interested in the scripts, he was more interested in the people. And so all the structures of English acting that we had been using went out the window and, suddenly, we were doing big arm movements and using West Indian language in the way that we do back home. That was a wonderful experience. So when Horace came in to direct the episodes, we had a black soap written by a black man, directed by a black man, with a black cast. It was wonderful!

Of course, Horace threw all the rules of directing television out the window, because I don't think he'd ever directed a television series before, or even a television play. So instead of leaving the stage manager to manage the set, Horace was coming out of the director's box and giving face-to-face directions on the floor. It was extraordinary. It made us realise that there was further to go in the parts. The humour was there, the comedy was there, but now we had the opportunity to take the characters and the situation a lot further, because we had a black director who understood the cultural setting and who could guide us when we were missing certain things. I think the series improved with Horace's direction.

***Empire Road* was axed after two short series, which surprised and upset many people** ● The vagaries of television production in this country, as far as black people are concerned, completely mystifies me. I don't know if they want to just give us lip-service as part of the community, or if they really are treating us as serious people. That's a conundrum which

I don't really understand how to get out of. I wrote to the BBC about their decision not to continue the series, and my father-in-law at the time (who is a white man) wrote to them as well, and they would not even give him a proper answer. They have never explained why they decided not to continue doing *Empire Road*, or why they have not repeated it. I think it's a disgrace.

I also feel strongly about the fact that *Empire Road* had a shorter run than *The Fosters*. *Empire Road* was germane to our society. It was created here by a man who actually lived and worked in Britain. *The Fosters* was a transfer that had really nothing whatsoever to do with the endemic situation of West Indians in this country. All *The Fosters* did was employ black people here, while *Empire Road* was about black people in this country.

Desmond's (1989 to the present) ● *Desmond's* is a progression from *The Fosters* in the sense that it is written by a West Indian writer, Trix Worrell, and is about real people. It's set in a barber shop and is about a barber and his family. It also shows how we (that is, black people) have moved on from being just passive, to being socially mobile people. So my character has got a son who works in a bank, and a younger son who will probably end up as a university professor. The only flaw is that the daughter is a bit scatty — I don't know why that is. But we're thinking about what she's going to do in the next two series. She is certainly going to be made less scatty and be connected with something quite interesting.

I think *Desmond's* really is where we ought to be at, if we're playing light comedy. But it is not where we ought to be, if we're talking about the seriousness of our lives. I don't really want to extrapolate too much on that here. But considering that black people have been taking care of business for a very long time — in Africa, the United States, the Caribbean, South America, all over — what we get a lot of the time instead on British television is black people who don't take care of business, and I don't like that. One of the reasons I don't like it is because I try to take care of my own business, and the images that are portrayed of most black people is of untogether people, not serious people.

There are very serious black people about, but those roles are not being written. This is either because the white man does not understand where black people are coming from and, therefore, doesn't know how to write about black people; or it's because we black people don't have the confidence in our own existence and destiny, so are not writing that kind of material for ourselves. Well, it's beyond me.

My own view is that what you've seen me in are the only roles that are available for black men in this country, and they don't really reflect our views, our understanding of life, our intelligence, or where we are coming from. In that respect, I would say that Caryl Phillips' scenario for *Playing*

Horace Ové's *Playing Away.*

Away, which Horace Ové directed for Channel 4, did get around that particular hurdle. It lived up to nearly all the expectations that black people ought to be living up to.

I think we really ought to be thinking now about where we are at. Obviously, we have to have the writers, and I don't know when we're going to find really good black dramatists. It's not that there aren't any black dramatists about – I could run you off half-a-dozen names including Derek Walcott, Mustafa Matura, Jamal Ali, Edgar White, Tunde Ikoli – they're all over the shop.

But what I find difficult to come to terms with is the absence of a heroic figure like Paul Robeson in all the work I've done. Quite recently, Malcolm Frederick produced and performed *A Splendid Summer*, by Lonne Elder, which is based on the life of Ira Aldridge, and Yvonne Brewster produced *Toussaint L'Ouverture*, by C.L.R. James, at the Riverside Studios – but these were theatrical productions. There is no writer writing on that scale, or in those grand, magnificent terms for film or television about a black figure who we all admire or aspire to be like. And I don't know when our people are going to actually start saying 'We are terrific!' and start writing something wonderful about just being us.

Horace Ové was born and brought up in Trinidad. Films were his first view of the outside world and he grew up on the best of the British, American and continental movies of the 40s and 50s. From about the age of ten he wanted to be a film director, but, at that time and place, it was very much a dream.

He came to London in 1960 and, shortly afterwards, moved to Rome where he stayed several years working as a painter and photographer. To supplement his income he worked in films as, during this period, Italy had a thriving film industry producing everything from commercial blockbusters to art cinema. This gave him his first real experience of the film world. He returned to London to study at the London School of Film Technique (now The London International Film School).

His first film, *The Art of the Needle* (1966), was made for Sidney Roseneil, the head of the Acupuncture Association, for students of acupuncture.

In 1968 Horace produced and directed *Baldwin's Nigger*, a documentary with the late James Baldwin discussing the black American experience in comparison with the West Indian experience in Britain.

Horace then made *Reggae* (1970), a documentary putting reggae music into an historical and political context. In 1972 Horace began making documentary films for the BBC. The first, *Colherne Jazz and Keskidee Blues* (1972), was about two generations of West Indians and their music. This was followed by *King Carnival* (1973), which traced the origins and influences of Carnival through Trinidad's turbulent history.

Horace's first feature fiction film, *Pressure* (1975), was funded by the British Film Institute and dealt with the timely subject of black youth in Britain. In 1975 he also directed a stage production of Wole Soyinka's play *The Swamp Dwellers*.

In 1978 he made *Skateboard Kings* for BBC TV, considered by many people as the first in-depth documentary on the Californian skateboarding craze. Horace then directed three episodes (in the second series) of Michael Abbensetts' black soap-opera *Empire Road* (1979), and in the same year he co-wrote and directed *A Hole in Babylon* for the BBC TV's Play for Today series. This drama was based on events leading up to the 1975 Spaghetti House siege in London and investigated the motives of the three protagonists. He also directed a six-part series for Thames TV, *The Latch Key Children*, from a novel by Eric Allan.

Since then Horace has directed numerous television dramas and documentaries in this country including *Shai Mala Khani/The Garland* in 1981, which he co-wrote with H.O. Nazareth; an episode of the TV adventure series *The Professionals (A Man Called Quinn)* in 1981; Farrukh Dhondy's *Good at Art* (1983); *Bacchanal/ Street Art* (1984); *The Record* (1984), written by Caryl Phillips; *Dabbawallahs* (1985); *When Love Dies* (1989), featuring Brian Bovell and Josette Simon; *After Columbus* ('The Africans') (1991) and *The Orchid House* (1991).

In 1986 Horace directed his second feature film, *Playing Away*, from a screenplay by Caryl Phillips and starring Norman Beaton. Also in 1986 Horace received the BFI's Independent Film and Television Award 'for his contribution to British film culture through his pioneering films and television programmes on issues concerning black people'. He was nominated that same year for the Grierson Award for documentary work which is innovative and socially relevant — for *Who Shall We Tell?*, his television documentary about the people of Bhopal who suffered as a result of the Union Carbide Plant gas leak of December 1984. This was first shown on Channel 4 in December 1985.

In the 60s I was trying to put together what I guess, in those days, you would have called a surrealist movie. It was called *Man Out* and was about a West Indian writer who is having a difficult time trying to write a novel and trying to live in a cold and alien environment maintaining his wife and his kids, trapped in the house, and without a job. The film takes the story up from there and is very surreal in the way that it presents itself. The writer goes for a walk one day and has a mental breakdown. He confuses reality with fantasy, which terrifies him. I actually raised some money and shot part of the film. I then approached several television companies to get completion money, but they refused.

I went to the BFI and spoke to Bruce Beresford who was fresh out of Australia, had not made a film as yet, and was in charge of film production. He looked at the material, did not understand the unconventional approach I had taken, and refused to back it. So my film stayed on the shelf. When I look at film-makers today, like Derek Jarman, David Lynch and the Coen brothers, I realise my film was way ahead of its time.

Being the first black film-maker in this country, and coming with such a strange subject, they all thought I was out of my head.

Black politics and *Baldwin's Nigger* (1968) ● The 'race problem' on British television during the 60s, I think, was looked at mainly from the white British point of view. Black people themselves had a lot to say, but nobody was listening and everybody was making up their own minds. It was the usual thing where they would have five people on television talking about 'the black problem' and no black people present to articulate their own problem. At the same time, the black struggle in America was having a great impact on black people in England. There were all kinds of demonstrations and meetings, and people were coming together and working out their own problems. One of the great meeting places in those days, where everybody met and discussed social and political issues, was the West Indian Students' Centre in London's Earl's Court. It was quite radical.

I made a film there called *Baldwin's Nigger*, with the late James Baldwin debating with West Indians and comparing the black problem in America with that of England. I remember arriving at the Centre with my camera crew to shoot the film, and even West Indians were laughing – 'What are you doing with that camera, boy? He's a film-maker!' It was obviously strange to them, at that time, to see a black man making films. But we did it and I think it helped a lot to record those moments and to start making films about ourselves. A few of us set out to do this, I must admit, with the help of a lot of white film-makers who were sympathetic, understood the problem and wanted to contribute.

Reggae (1970) ● Reggae music was played in shebeens or blues dances, as they were called at the time, where West Indians who were unemployed or who were working hard all day doing terrible dirty jobs would go at night to relax. In those days you knocked on a door and a guy would open a little hole and say 'Who are you? What you want?' And you would give your name, or say that you knew so-and-so, and he would let you in. It was sort of illegal in a way, but it was one of the ways that West Indians could escape from the daily grind and hassles, where they could sit back and have a drink and listen to calypso music, or to ska and bluebeat which were popular in those days, or listen to reggae music. I remember at the time a famous disc jockey (Tony Blackburn) saying on the radio 'We have a new record from Jamaica and I don't know what to make of it. I think it was recorded in a toilet somewhere in the Caribbean'. That made me very, very angry. So in making *Reggae*, I set out to actually educate the British public about the music and about where it was coming from.

Reggae was really an independent West Indian film because another friend of mine – Junior Lincoln, who had just started producing reggae music here through his company, Bamboo Records – actually put up all the money for me to do the film. He used all his savings and all the money he was making from records to finance the production. To our surprise the film was shown in the cinema, and then the BBC bought it and showed it on BBC2. It really took off from there and travelled all over the world. But it was a little before its time, though people still got a lot of information about the music from it. It was also the first film, I think, that actually had skinheads – because, if you recall, the whole skinhead movement had just started in this country and their main music at the time was ska and reggae, that is, black music!

So it was a very interesting time. A lot of new artistes, like Toots and the Maytals, Bob Andy and Marcia Griffiths, Desmond Dekker, had just come over and the whole thing was building. We tried to give a depth to what the music and the history of the music was all about.

King Carnival (1973) ● I came to make *King Carnival* simply because I had made *Reggae* before that. Being from Trinidad, a lot of Trinidadians said how could I go off and make a film about Jamaican culture and music, and not deal with Carnival? And they were quite right. So I went back to Trinidad and looked at the Carnival. I studied the many aspects of what makes Carnival, the many cultures that have come together to create it, the blood, sweat and tears that goes into it, everything that culminates in this one happy moment in the year. That interested me a lot. I then returned to Britain with some 8mm footage and went to the BBC's *The World About Us* programme and sold them the idea. I think because they had bought *Reggae*, strangely enough after it had been shown in the cinema, they trusted me a bit about making films, so they gave me the money to do it. However, I wanted to break away from the usual *World About Us* format which, in those days, was the white explorer travelling up the Amazon in a boat and speaking to the natives. It was that sort of ethnographic film-making which, strangely enough, they seem to be going back to again.

I set out to make a film about a people, their culture and their rhythms – to use the rhythms, and the way they see things and move, and articulate things visually and verbally – I wanted to capture that and make the film like that. Although I had a lot of problems with the production, especially with some of the people I was working with who were not too happy with it, in the end I finished the film in the way that I wanted – and it went down quite well.

Pressure (1975) ● This film was made at a time when a whole new generation was growing up in England and things were really tough for young black people – they were leaving school and couldn't get jobs, and so on. Then there were a few muggings and the newspapers really went for them and started talking about black muggers and thieves pushing over old ladies and grabbing their handbags, and things like that. But nobody was really dealing with the question of why these things were happening. I then got together with the West Indian writer, Samuel Selvon, and we decided to research the subject and to write a film script about it, which we did. Then we tried to raise the money to make the film and went to all the television companies, but they refused.

Eventually we went to the BFI. After a long time discussing the project with them – they were a bit worried about making a film which talked about black life and police brutality – they gave us the money. In fact, they started off by giving us about ten thousand pounds to make a two-hour movie with about thirty-five speaking parts, which, even in those days, was impossible to do. But we accepted the money and, with the help of other people, we actually went out to shoot the film. We shot it over a varied time, because the cast and crew were giving us their time and working for next to nothing on it. That's how *Pressure* got to be made.

After that, there was some difficulty even in the BFI which didn't want to release the film because of a few scenes about police raids and black power, and the film was actually banned for about three years. A few journalists who liked it started to write about it and sort of attacked the BFI, and then it came out and got a release. There was a very good reaction to it after that, because it was something new. It was dealing with something that was happening, and was exposing things which were being swept under the carpet at the time and which nobody was writing or talking about.

Empire Road **(1979)** ● Having established a track record as an independent film-maker, with documentaries and a feature film (*Pressure*) behind me, I was then asked to come and direct three episodes in the second series of *Empire Road*. I saw it as a challenge at first because I'd never really worked in a television studio or with television cameras and television set-ups. Peter Ansorge, who was the producer of the programme and a very pioneering young man, was trying all sorts of new things, and he thought that it was time for a black director to come and direct the series which was, after all, about black people, and to bring new ideas to it. Unfortunately, this created a lot of confusion and madness at the studios. When I got there a lot of people who were in charge were shaky because Peter had invited a West Indian with no knowledge of television production to come and do this. I thought this was nonsense, because television had bought my films and I was making films.

When I got there, I quickly decided that I did not want to work with the conventional four- or five-camera set-up because I found it a terrible system. I felt that people were spending the whole day working out where to put the cables, and nobody was thinking about getting a good set-up or a good shot. I also wanted to use one camera at times and I encouraged them to do a lot of OBs or locations in the streets. In addition to that, I wanted to use a crane and all that sort of thing. So they thought I was out of my head. But we did it, though we had a lot of fights and a lot of ups-and-downs. For example, I never liked working from the gallery, because whoever was involved in the production was also getting involved in the direction. Everybody had something to say, and I felt distant from the actors. I always want to be close to the actors, to talk to them and to deal with the problems directly, instead of speaking to them through intercoms. So I used to go down and work on the floor.

One day I was shooting a scene with Norman Beaton and there were three minutes before the end of the day's work. Norman had to open a bottle of champagne, the bottle had to pop and the champagne had to bubble out. Everybody was nervous and felt under pressure. There happened to be a very uptight woman in charge who did not like me, and when Norman opened the bottle of champagne and it did not pop, she called 'Cut!' from the gallery and the whole damn thing came to an end. Everybody stopped working and I looked around and said 'What happened?' And they said 'A certain lady upstairs said 'cut' because she thinks the time has gone and you've lost that shot because it did not work'.

That got me very angry because I knew she was being silly and stupid, because in the end the cork came off the bottle, the champagne was bubbling, and if she had any intelligence about film-making she would know that you can dub the sound later. But instead she cut in the middle of my shot. Because I was very angry and very upset I made a long speech on the floor about film-making and about the role of the writer and the director, which everybody could have thought was heavy and rude, coming from a little black boy. I remember thinking that I'd made the biggest mistake of my career, reacting like that on the set. But then everybody cheered and I was given a bottle of champagne by the crew and others in support of what I had done.

That sort of thing happened on and off all the time – people were always on my back, trying to tell me what I already knew. And half the time the people who were telling me what to do had no knowledge of film-making whatsoever. They were administrators who knew how to run things from the top, but they didn't know anything about making a film. This is still a problem today – people up there telling you how you should make films and they don't even know how to articulate the problem in film language.

I constantly had to deal with those kind of problems, and it came from my being the first West Indian director, which did and still does make people in the business nervous. There were even nasty remarks like 'Oh God, we have a West Indian director', which I had to face. It was not easy to work under those conditions, but I was determined and I got a lot of support from other people who said 'No, don't take that. Go on with what you're doing because we like it'.

When I look back, I think *Empire Road* was a very good series because it was not the usual sort of television sitcom. It wasn't really done just as a comedy or just for laughs. It was also trying to deal with real life dramas, although one could laugh at some of those situations because they were genuinely funny. That was the fun of it, trying new things and not just sitting on a couch making jokes. So I think I enjoyed doing it at the time. They didn't make it that easy for me, but that was part of the job, to fight for what I wanted.

I think *Empire Road* was well received within the black community, and also within the white community, because people hadn't seen anything like it on television before. They had seen other things but not a black family owning a shop, their problems, and the problems of the Asians, and the interaction between blacks and whites in dramatic situations. I think we got pretty close to accurately reflecting those realities.

A Hole in Babylon (1979) ● *A Hole in Babylon* really interested me because at the time of the actual Spaghetti House siege in London in 1975, the newspapers and media were saying that it was just a bunch of black hooligans who had held up the restaurant, that they had created a siege and that it was a black problem. Again, nobody tried to look into it more deeply, to find out a little more about what made these three men commit this act. When I started looking into it, I discovered that one of the men was a medical student, another was a writer, and so on. So I started thinking 'They're not hooligans, they're not even just ordinary black guys who wanted to stick up a restaurant. And even if they were black gangsters, they were still trying to pull off a coup to demonstrate their politics'. So I took an interest in the story and started to research it, and I found out a lot more about the men and their background.

The political mood at the time was that nobody wanted to admit what was going on. It was like when I made *Pressure*, nobody really wanted to admit that there was a serious problem in England – that black people were fighting for their rights under a very racist situation and that they were finding ways and means of demonstrating their feelings. I also wanted to show what created a situation which drove a bloke to wake up one morning and say 'The best thing to do, to solve this problem, is to stick up a restaurant, or a bank, or rob somebody'. And it wasn't just to get money either. It was to make a political point, to do something political with that action.

So, what I wanted to do in *A Hole in Babylon* was to tell the story of these people leading up to the siege – how they were actually trying to set up a black school to educate black children about their culture and way of life, just like Jewish schools which were in existence. How nobody would support them. How it all went wrong and why it went wrong. In other words, I wanted to explore these characters in greater depth and provide more information about their backgrounds and their objectives. I used to write and talk to the guys actually involved in the events when they were behind bars, and this enabled me to reconstruct a strong narrative of their differ-

T-Bone Wilson, Archie Pool, and Trevor Thomas in *A Hole in Babylon* (BBC TV 'Play for Today', 1979).

ent stories. Again, I tried to give a little more information about black people's situation in England, and not just make it about black gangsters or hooligans.

Although I was dramatising an actual event, I still wanted to incorporate documentary elements in the drama, to bring that reality with it. So I went out and researched all the material, like newsreel footage of the actual events. I looked at it carefully and structured the film around it, both in terms of the scripting and the direction. We incorporated this news footage into the drama. We were cross-cutting between the basement of the restaurant where the men were held up, which was scripted and played by actors, and the scene outside in the streets from where the police were speaking to them, which was news footage. So every time I cut from the scene in the basement to the police outside, it seemed as though there was a real connection which, of course, there wasn't because I was only using documentary news footage to enhance the sense of realism in the drama. We played with that structure all the way through the drama, and it worked quite well. One of the reactions from some people who saw it was that they wondered how I had managed to get certain known figures and people in government to appear in my television play!

Despite requests from American TV and university film distributors to show *A Hole in Babylon* in the US, the BBC bluntly refused the rights to do so. One BBC sales executive said: 'We are not going to sell a film abroad about a group of black hooligans'.

Playing Away (1986) ● When Caryl Phillips came to me with the idea for *Playing Away*, I was immediately interested in the way that he was using cricket as a metaphor of relations between West Indians and the English. As you well know, cricket is the one game that West Indians are very proud of and very good at, and it's the one game that they know they can beat the old masters at. So Caryl and I talked about it and researched the subject and travelled to various places. I particularly liked the idea of pointing up the ridiculousness of racism, on both sides, and exploring how it enters into people's lives and what takes place. But I also wanted to make the film genuinely funny, not in the television sitcom sense but funny in a real way. Those aspects really interested me and I was keen to get involved in making this film.

Both *Pressure* and *A Hole in Babylon* dealt with very serious hard subjects. *Playing Away* was also dealing with a serious subject, but I wanted to do it in a less intense, more humorous way. One of our strengths as West Indians is that when we get into the worst kind of situations and experiences, we still have the ability to look back and laugh at it. We can tell the most terrible jokes about ourselves and really laugh. I wanted to capture that same idea in *Playing Away*, where both black and white could look at themselves and laugh at themselves. I think it worked, I know a lot of people enjoyed it, and the film had good reviews in England, the USA and Australia. It was recently shown on British and American television.

The impact of Channel 4 ● The arrival of Channel 4 made a difference for us because of its policy of doing more interesting and more experimental television. Before that, I felt that British television was becoming increasingly flat and that the whole nation was watching programmes like *Dallas* and *Neighbours*. Increasingly, I was meeting people who did not want to take the chance to be more experimental. So Channel 4 helped to change that atmosphere, at least in the beginning when it started out. People like Jeremy Isaacs, David Rose and Peter Ansorge really kicked it off by making some very interesting films once again. But unfortunately, I think these initiatives have been lost — Channel 4 has gone back to a very flat and conventional sort of television. It is now making very dull films and dull series. That's the only way I can describe what I think is now happening.

In the beginning, Channel 4's multicultural programming policy provided space which would not otherwise exist in British television for black film-makers. But it was short-lived and I don't think it went far enough. What's more, I have always been against so-called ethnic film-making and things like that, because you end up getting 'ethnic money' and everybody looks on it as a little section of society, that we're allowing them to make these little films here and there.

But I don't think Channel 4 fully supported black independent film-making. It started in that direction in the early days, but then something happened and it petered out. I don't know what it has become now. I don't know if they really wanted to support black independent films and to help establish black production companies. Nobody has really been able to answer that question because most of the little companies that got a break during the early period of Channel 4 have now folded and disappeared. Ironically, there are now more white companies doing black things, than there are black companies doing black-related programmes. So I guess in that sense not much has changed. Maybe it happened in *The Eleventh Hour* slot, but that programme was scheduled when everybody was fast asleep in bed! So I do hope that they see this at Channel 4 and try to improve it, because I think there is a lot of good, young black talent out there that needs a break.

Of course, I'm aware that there's a problem for white film-makers as well, and that there's an even greater problem with a British film industry that has no money, no confidence and a closed door policy. The whole British film and television industry, and not just the situation of black film-makers within it, needs revitalising. We need more people with new ideas and new things to say, executives who are prepared to be a little more adventurous and not just looking at audience figures and accounts, so that, in future, you might put out ten programmes, of which six might be brilliant and the rest a mess. And why not?

The freedom to be a film-maker ● I always think of myself as a director. I know I'm black and I know I make black films, but I'm still a director and I think I have the right to make films about any subject and any people. I've always felt that, as a black film-maker, one is ghettoised, only allowed to make films and television programmes on black subjects and nothing else. The Attenborough brothers, for instance, have made films about different people and different cultures, and feature films about different things, and so have lots of other white film-makers. But it seems that black film-makers are not allowed to do this – we are only allowed to make films about blacks, and then mainly about black struggle.

People seem to like us making films about crying, and screaming about racism all the time, and those kinds of subjects. And even if we want to do a black subject from an unusual perspective, they look at us in a strange way and nobody wants to talk to us about it. But if we bring them something hard and black and angry, they say 'Yeah, yeah – let's do it!' This kind of response is limiting for a black director or for an artiste who wants to explore different ideas and who is interested in different things, irrespective of race or colour. So it's wrong to just put black film-makers in a little black bag and tie them up and throw them at the race angle.

Although we've made some impact in recent years, the emphasis has been in the area of documentary and current affairs. Drama, unfortunately, has always lagged behind. The excuse has always been that there aren't enough black writers about, which I always thought was nonsense. There may not have been a lot of black screenplay writers, but there have been quite a few very good dramatists and novelists who could have been encouraged to come and write scripts. This has never been done.

I think television has kept drama as a very special area and the people responsible for commissioning work don't trust black film people with drama productions. We are never really given an opportunity because we always get the same stupid responses like 'Well, we're not sure. There aren't enough black writers. And what about actors? Are there enough professional actors to do that sort of thing? Do they have enough knowledge of drama to be able to direct?' These are obviously silly arguments because people learn their trade from getting a break and from getting the necessary schooling to do it. As I said, I think they've put drama in a special category for themselves, and it is time that changed. There are a lot of young film-makers today who have made dramatic pieces outside television. They have proven that they can do it, so I don't see why they should be kept out any longer.

A black director or writer, born and brought up in this country, is capable of bringing new insights and a new perspective even to white dramatic pieces. And I think they should be given the opportunity to do so. Television producers and controllers are simply missing out on an experience that has yet to be fully tapped. There are enough black film-makers who can do it, and I would have thought that, after all these years, things would have changed for the better, that we would be seeing more black input in all areas of television. So I'm surprised that this hasn't actually happened. It's the old question – why?

I've recently moved to Jamaica because, in doing my last series, *The Orchid House* (1991) in the Caribbean, I felt that it was time for me to move back and to work a little more from the Caribbean and to use it as my base. That is not to say that I've given up wanting to make films in England or anywhere else, because I haven't. It's just that Jamaica is a good base for me to work from, and the Caribbean is a very interesting place where a lot is happening, and where there is still a lot more to be done. It also gives me the opportunity to try and get my things produced either in America or in England, or elsewhere.

Since I've been in the Caribbean it has been very inspiring in a lot of ways. Jamaica has a budding film and television industry, and the people working in it seem to be very serious about wanting to pull it all together. It's very exciting.

I remember when I started making films in the 60s in Britain, I could always talk about films, discuss new ideas with other film-makers, black and white, and play around with all kinds of ideas. But that atmosphere has gone. It is not anywhere in Britain now. You're more likely to find it in America, in Europe and especially in the Caribbean, where people are excited about film and television. I survive better in an environment where things are being thrown about and discussed, where new ideas are being taken seriously and not just laughed at as crazy.

Michael Abbensetts was born in Guyana. A number of his plays have been produced in London including *Sweet Talk* at the Royal Court (1973), *Alterations* (1978), *Samba* (1980), *In the Mood* (1981), *Outlaw* (1983), and *El Dorado* (1984). In the 70s and 80s he wrote several dramas for television including *The Museum Attendant* (BBC, 1973), *Inner City Blues* (Granada), *Crime and Passion* (Granada), *Black Christmas* (BBC, 1977) featuring Norman Beaton and Carmen Munroe, *Roadrunner* (Thames), *Easy Money* (BBC, 1981) featuring Norman Beaton, *Fallen Angel* (BBC), and *Big George is Dead* (Channel 4, 1987) featuring Norman Beaton and Rudolph Walker. Michael also wrote two series of *Empire Road* for the BBC in 1978-9, and the Channel 4 series *Legends* in 1987.

Sweet Talk (1973) ● Originally, I was writing short stories and trying to write books. Then I saw John Osborne's *Look Back In Anger* in Canada, of all places, and I thought that it was pretty exciting, especially at that time. It really moved me, even more than writing books. And that's when I decided to turn to playwriting. I then came to England and saw a play at the Royal Court, and I decided to try and write a play myself to fit that space. Also, I had read that Osborne's play had started there, so I thought 'OK, I'll get a play on there too'. I got an agent and he sent my play to the Royal Court, and it was put on. The play was called *Sweet Talk*.

Sweet Talk came about because I had originally written another play which had never been performed. I took this earlier, untitled play to an agent. I had read the name of this agent from a play that I liked, and she turned out to be one of the top agents in London. I just turned up at her office – which was not the normal thing to do – and we talked for a while, and she eventually took my play to read. Later on she called me and said that she liked the play – in fact, what she said was that she thought it was very good for a black writer! And I said 'What?' She tried to explain, she wasn't being racist, but if I wanted to get a first play on that would make a splash, I really had to write something a little better than that. So I decided that I would show them that I could do it.

I quit my job, went home and began to write a play about a gambler. I didn't have much experience with gamblers and gambling, but I started going to betting shops regularly. I would write in the morning and go to betting shops in the afternoon. I got so carried away that I hated Sundays, because the betting shops were closed! But after I had written the play, I quit going to betting shops and I've never been in one since. Then I found a different agent who sent the play to the Royal Court, and used it to land me my first television play which was called *The Museum Attendant*.

The Museum Attendant (1973) ● *The Museum Attendant* was directed by Stephen Frears. It was actually done in the same year as *Sweet Talk*, which was 1973. In fact, they happened in the same week, the first week of July – *Sweet Talk* opened at the Royal Court and *The Museum Attendant* was shown on BBC2. The BBC decided to create quite an elaborate set for *The Museum Attendant*, but then there was a technicians' strike, so they couldn't do the play in the studio. They found a real museum instead, so it became a television film that was shot on location.

The Museum Attendant was based on my own experience. Before I worked as a writer, I did a lot of different day jobs and one of them was a security guard at the Tower of London. During my rounds, I used to write down things that I saw in a little notebook I carried around with me. That's how I got ideas for the play. And I remember the other museum guards would see me jotting down notes and would say all kinds of nonsensical things like 'Put me down for a turkey, mate'. And I would look at them and think to myself 'One day you're going to watch this thing yourselves on television'.

Then the play was on television and one of the Head security guards called me afterwards and said 'I saw your play, I'll say no more'. And he hung up. I don't know what he thought of it. And then the Head of the museum wrote to me and said 'I'm glad to see you didn't waste all your time while you were working here!'

Black Christmas (1977) ● After that I started getting more work. I didn't find it all that difficult, actually. Mike Phillips, who wrote some critical reviews at that time and who was one of the few people who wrote about black writers, said that, basically, I was one of the few black writers who didn't have as hard a time as some did – because after *The Museum Attendant*, I wrote *Black Christmas*, and that was followed quickly by a series, *Empire Road*. I had also done some episodes of *Crown Court*. So things went on like that for a while.

Stephen Frears also directed *Black Christmas* and, again, he made it as a film shot on location for television. We found a house somewhere – it was actually a West Indian woman's house and she allowed us to film in it – so there was an authentic feel to the whole thing. It was wonderful. I really enjoyed that production.

Black Christmas, again, was based on actual experiences that I had and on people I knew about. Sometimes people would ask me why I portrayed West Indians in certain ways, and I would tell them that my characters were actually based on people I knew, that I never made up much stuff.

***Empire Road* (1978-9)** ● I came up with the idea of setting a drama series around Birmingham when we were making *Black Christmas* there. I was also fortunate enough to know Peter Ansorge, who was a producer at the BBC. He had been involved in some way with *Black Christmas* and he was interested in the idea for *Empire Road* as well. So it was a good continuation of a working relationship. We then pitched the idea to the Head of drama in Birmingham. I argued very strongly for it and stressed the point that many of the ideas were based on people I knew or on people I'd seen in the streets of Birmingham. For example, I saw a black woman running a fish and chip shop, which was something I hadn't seen in London. Later on, when the series came out, people said black people don't run fish and chip shops! But, again, I could prove that there was this woman in Birmingham who did, and that there were black people coming in and eating fish and chips served by this black woman. So I put her in the series.

I based the Everton Bennett character (played by Norman Beaton) on an uncle of mine, and he also had a friend who stammered, like the Walter character in the series (played by Joe Marcell). I wanted those two to really have a relationship that was funny, but sometimes serious as well. I wrote one episode where it was just the two of them alone, and Everton gets progressively more drunk as they talk about their lives in Britain. I would listen to my uncle and his friend talking about things, and I put a lot of that into *Empire Road*. So, once again, the material was based on real people.

I think one of the best things about *Empire Road* was that we felt we were doing something that no one else had done before. It really was a happy band of actors. It was an enjoyable experience and everybody was really excited by it. For a while, I felt I was a part of something in a way that I've never really felt again. It was wonderful.

And then when we did the second series, we brought in Horace Ové – so we had a black director, a black writer, and black actors – and that was even more special. And we added some white directors to the team, and they got involved in a way that they would not have done if it had been a one-off play. If I'm honest, it is a time that I still miss.

The demise of *Empire Road* ● I think we had problems getting a third series because the ratings for the second series, although better than for the first, were not good enough or as large as everyone had hoped they would be. But if you examine it, I think you will find that black audiences were more likely to watch ITV or BBC1, especially in those days. A lot of the black viewers just didn't watch BBC2. So many of them probably would not have watched *Empire Road*.

We also had the problem where certain sections of the white audience would say 'Oh, it's about black characters. It doesn't involve us', and they would turn over or switch off. Some of them subsequently found out that it wasn't what they expected it to be, and that it was actually entertaining for everyone. But the problem was the ratings.

It's much better, in some ways, to try and get your stuff on BBC1. But then, again, people would say 'We're in a ratings war with ITV, and we're not sure that this is going to play to the millions that we need to get'. I've actually been asked by black viewers why I had my stuff on BBC2, as if somehow I was offered the choice. It would be nice to get stuff on ITV where one might get the larger millions, but television stations won't always take that chance. When they do a black series, it is usually a sitcom. I may be wrong about this, but I don't think ITV has ever done any sort of black drama series or anything like *Empire Road*.

Easy Money (1981) and Big George Is Dead (1987) ● *Easy Money* was based a little on my own experiences. Before I started to get my plays on television, I quit my job and went on to social security. *Easy Money* is about a young man who goes on social security – the main character is, in fact, white, so it is a play basically seen through the eyes of a white character who meets and befriends a young black man (played by Norman Beaton). This young white man meets a young white woman at a pop concert but he begins to question her motives because, even though they're attracted to each other, she sometimes goes to pop concerts in the hope of meeting guys and getting recruits for rather right-wing organisations.

Then you reach a point in the drama when the two of them fall in love, though by then the man has become friendly with some black guys, so he has to make a bit of a choice. That was *Easy Money*. I remember it was quite an interesting production. It was directed by the woman who subsequently became quite rich and famous choreographing *Cats*.

After that came another film for television, *Big George Is Dead*. That, too, was an interesting experience. A young film-maker, called Henry Martin, came to me with an idea for a film. He had gone to Channel 4 with his idea and they said that if he found a writer, they would give him the money to make the film. So he got in touch with me and I liked the idea. I added things myself and wrote most of the script. And then they cast it with Norman Beaton and Rudolph Walker. It was wonderful seeing those two playing against each other. I thought Rudolph was a great actor who, in the past, had been directed to play a certain kind of role. But now he was suddenly given a tougher role in *Big George is Dead*, and was allowed to be

Norman Beaton and Rudolph Walker in *Big George is Dead* (Channel 4, 1987).

sharper. He didn't have to do a stereotypical West Indian role. He and Norman really did a good job in that piece of drama.

On the whole, I have pretty good memories of the work I've done here in England. I can't complain, really, because I was allowed to be present most of the time when my work was being filmed or staged. I was never locked out of the production process. I had heard horror stories about what can happen to writers, and had even met English writers who told me how they wrote for very successful series but were never allowed to go on the set. Well, that was never my experience – I was always present, even for some of the casting, the auditions, and for the filming, and I would actually stop a scene if something bothered me or if I thought something was wrong. And I loved it when everything was going well, like when we made *Black Christmas*. When that happens, I stand back and let them do the work. It's great.

— DESMOND WILCOX —

Desmond Wilcox has been working in television for more than thirty years. Before 1960 he had spent nine years as a foreign correspondent for the *Daily Mirror*. In 1960 he joined ITV's leading current affairs programme, *This Week*, and in 1965 he moved to the newly formed BBC2 to help establish and run the *Man Alive* series. For eight years he was Head of BBC TV's General Features Department, responsible for a wide range of documentary and current affairs programmes including *Braden's Week* and its successor *That's Life!*, as well as numerous documentary series such as *The World About Us*, *Times Remembered*, and *The Tuesday Documentary*.

He has produced and reported a number of significant television profiles on distinguished figures. He produced, wrote and narrated the BBC series *The Golden Land* on Judaism in the USA. As a BBC Senior Executive, he was particularly well-known for championing the cause of women's rights and for employing some of the most talented women directors, writers and presenters in television.

For twelve years he has run one of the leading independent film and television production companies, Wilcox Bulmer Productions, which has been responsible for producing many award-winning and highly successful documentaries. He was recently responsible for three highly acclaimed BBC series: *The Visit*, *The Marriage*, and *Black in Blue* (1990) about black recruits in the Metropolitan Police. Desmond Wilcox has received numerous awards for his work in television, including the British Academy of Film and Television Art's Richard Dimbleby Award for distinguished 'on-screen' achievement.

The civil rights explosion in the United States in the 60s was clearly what triggered any sensible journalist, documentary maker and current affairs producer in this country towards the issue. It was the time of Martin Luther King, and I feel privileged and delighted that I met him, filmed him, and produced an outside broadcast with him during that amazing march on Washington when he made his 'I have a dream' speech. My journalistic godfather, James Cameron, interviewed him. The two of them sat on tin chairs in the Lincoln Memorial, at the feet of the Abraham Lincoln statue, discussing the difficulty of protest marching and aching feet. As a practicality of passionate liberal politics, they were discussing what shoes and socks to wear, and that, it seemed to me, was quite splendid.

We had the desegregation troubles and the campaign for racial equality, the Mississippi murders and burnings, the Alabama bus boycott – all of which we were observing from this country. And we knew that after Birmingham, Alabama, it was going to be Birmingham, England, after Mississippi it was going to be Manchester. We were only a reflection, only a step behind their problems. We had to learn as best we could from what was going on over there. And we, as journalists, had a duty to signal that.

The Negro Next Door (This Week, ITV, 1965) ● Research was always the key to the programmes that I made for *This Week* and *Man Alive*. I feel there are really only two worthwhile jobs in television – the Director General of the BBC may think he's got a worthwhile job, but, frankly, the researcher and the producer are the only two functions that make sense in terms of the gratification you get from doing what you do on the screen.

So, we sent an excellent researcher to Leeds – to those *Coronation Street*-like back-to-back terraced houses, in which there were an increasing number of black and, at that time, just a few Asian families. These are streets that traditionally offer a northern welcome – a cup of tea, a front door never closed, an availability for gossip and warmth. And it was quite clear that black families in those streets were not getting treated this way. It was also clear that the prejudice was ill-formed and rather ignorant, because the white families weren't quite sure what it was they resented. They weren't quite clear why they felt disturbed, but they were articulate and open people.

In those early days on *This Week*, and subsequently the whole ethos of *Man Alive*, we were always determined that it shouldn't be politicians, or television presenters, or boring pontificators who would tell us what black or white people thought about an issue. It should be the people themselves. So the researcher's brief was to go out and find them. Our skill, if you like, and certainly our ambition, was to be as mobile as possible, with equipment as light as possible, to be as unobtrusive as possible. We were never so-called 'fly on the wall', that is an idiotic invention of the tabloid press which doesn't exist. When we move into somebody's house they have to take the furniture out to make way for the film crew, so they know we are there! But at least we can relax them in such a way that they will become themselves again.

Reporting bigotry and intolerance ● I think our main worry during those years, while making films about issues of prejudice, intolerance and hatred, was that we had to use the media to produce more information and to reduce prejudice and bigotry, and dispel intolerance. The danger, however, was that we might do the reverse, by allowing the expression of bigotry. We might actually end up recruiting bigots! The only programme I've ever refused to do was a biography of Mosley. He stood for everything that I found despairing and hateful, and I felt I couldn't do that documentary. So I was very cautious about issues concerning race. With all the documentaries that I did for *This Week* and *Man Alive*, I was very concerned not to give too much ventilation to what, these days, would be called the National Front attitude. I didn't want the result of what I was doing to be the reverse of my ambition.

Man Alive (BBC TV) ● My partner, Bill Morton, and I were invited by David Attenborough to join the brand new BBC2 channel, and to run a new documentary series. The programme *Man Alive* was started by Chris Brasher who caretakered it for the first six weeks while we wriggled out of our contracts with *This Week* on ITV. We then turned it into what we had always intended it to be – a programme that threw light on areas in life that were grey, unilluminated, even dark. It was to be a programme that did without pontificators, politicians, and professional presenters like myself in vision. The programme would use us as reporters, to extract information by way of interviews or to produce information by way of narration. But mostly, it was to be a programme which went into the backyards of our own domestic circumstances or other circumstances abroad, and allowed the people themselves to speak.

   Man Alive was meant to be the programme which was a forum for ordinary voices, which allowed, for example, people who were homeless to describe their own condition rather than having a politician say how horrible it was; which allowed people who were suffering from educational deprivation to talk about what they felt they needed and what their ambitions were; which allowed people who were unemployed to talk about it and to talk about it in their own terms, in their own language. In the early days of *Man Alive* some of my bosses at the BBC, I have to confess, would suggest that we put up sub-titles when ordinary British people were speaking about their circumstances, and that was only Yorkshire! You can imagine how they reacted when I went to Glasgow for a programme. Fortunately, that feels like a century away, although it wasn't very long ago actually that we were battering down the walls of the television establishment mythology about whether ordinary people could articulate their own condition. We were determined that *Man Alive* would pioneer a new approach and be in the forefront of proving that ordinary people could and should articulate their own circumstances.

Go Back Where You Come From (Man Alive, 1968) ● 'Go Back Where You Come From' is one of the more horrid labels that has entered the

English language and, indeed, entered it because of Enoch Powell. He claims today that much of what he said in those days about 'rivers of blood', and about race and immigrants, has been misunderstood, distorted and misapplied. That may be so, but the fact of the matter is that he was the man with the match and he did touch the blue fuse paper. He did blow the issue wide open – and the results were appalling. It allowed a screaming level of prejudice to enter our society, and even produced, to the shame of those who talked about it, suggestions from the politicians for a Ministry of Repatriation to send West Indians back to the West Indies, with some kind of pay-off, some kind of 'colour redundancy' – a cheque for having a black skin, which would send a person back to Trinidad, Jamaica, Barbados or wherever.

We decided that we would find some people who actually wanted to go back to where they came from, because they couldn't bear the level of intolerance and prejudice and discomfort any longer, or because they couldn't bear the discrimination in terms of jobs, education and housing that they were facing in this country. And we followed them back.

The funny thing about it was that when we were watching the rushes of them back in the West Indies, all of us wanted to go there with them, because it was obviously a so much happier place. It was a so much nicer place, where people had no sense of prejudice, where there was no intolerance. If you were white in Barbados, nobody gave a damn. You were just living in Barbados. The problem was that there was no work there. The economy of the West Indies was already in a pretty rocky state and people were, therefore, returning to a kind of economic disaster, but a happy land where there was no prejudice. We decided to look at what they would return to, and dispel the racist myth that way, hopefully.

The idea of having one of these Goebbels-type ministries, where we would do the South African thing and inspect people by their skins and give them a cheque and a boat ticket, was appalling. It's sort of reverse slavery. It seemed to me incredible that the society in which I lived, where we had fought two World Wars and the Korean War for various freedoms, was actually proposing these things.

Effects and reactions ● I don't know what any of the programmes I've made about race have succeeded in doing. I was only one journalist, one documentary maker, with my partner, my producers, and my team doing what we could, and what we felt it was necessary to do. We weren't always liked by our bosses for doing what we did. We made waves. But it's the job of good documentary makers, of good journalists to make waves. They may never get to be Director Generals, but they'll be better journalists for it.

I think there's a tendency among those who are prejudiced in our society to write me off as some kind of liberal causist. It's a bit like patting the vicar on the head when he comes round for a contribution to the church. A lot of documentary makers and journalists who deal with these issues are thought to be mildly eccentric and far too gentle to be real.

In the early days, the prejudice against what we were doing was considerable. I think there was probably a feeling of latent unease among my bosses, but I met no great resistance. Nobody ever told me not to do a programme about a racial issue. But there was a huge reaction from the viewers who used to go into the BBC duty log by the score with their vile and racist telephone calls like 'Tell that nigger-lover Wilcox to get his team off the screen. What's he doing favouring these black bastards?' That sort of thing was a very common reaction, but I became very used to it. It was something I learned to put up with, and it reinforced what I was doing. Even print journalists in those days, would rather patronisingly review the *Man Alive* programmes that were about racial issues.

I think a lot of people suspected that we were doing it because we thought it was the professional liberal thing to do. But in our hearts, they believed, we were the same as them – that we were prejudiced, frightened, disturbed, our jobs felt threatened, our women felt threatened, and so on and so forth. I don't think they realised that a lot of us who travelled round the world didn't feel at all threatened, that we wanted integration, miscegenation, and other cultures to be allowed to exist as other cultures. I didn't want black people coming to this country to be turned into versions of white people. I enjoy life today in which Asian and African, and West Indian and Indian cultures exist as their own cultures in our society. That concept is more acceptable today than it was two decades or so ago. The prejudice now has died down a lot, but it's still there.

Mixed Marriages (Man Alive, 1968) ● Mixed marriages were becoming increasingly common. As more and more immigrants, black and Asian people came to live in our society, it was inevitable that the younger members of those families and our society would mix, meet socially, fall in love, and want to marry. But there was a lot of emotive nonsense, a lot of white tribal mythology, fearsome mythology about mixed marriages – about what dreadful things would lie ahead for the children of such marriages, what prejudices would await them. And, as ever, it seemed to me that the proper job of a reasonable documentary maker was to go into an area where there was prejudice, where there was the need for information, education and enlightenment, in order to find out what the truth of the matter was. And we did that.

The worst prejudice we came across in making the film *Mixed Marriages*, was from the *Radio Times*, the BBC's very own publication. They wanted to feature it on the cover, because they thought it would be an emotive selling photograph. I agreed with them and thought that it was a jolly good idea – it would help pump up the viewing figures for my programme and, therefore, help the purpose of the programme even more. And so we produced, from a wedding, a picture of a man and his brand new wife kissing in their bridal kit. The *Radio Times* said 'But they're kissing!' And I said 'Yes. That's what people do when they get married. The vicar says "You're now man and wife" and "you can kiss the bride".' And they said, 'Yes, yes, but one of them is black!' And I said 'Well, yes, that's right, that's what this programme is about – it's about black and white marriages, and they too are going to kiss'. And the *Radio Times* wouldn't use it. They thought that it would be inflammatory and wrong.

I'm afraid I was not known for my restraint in writing memos within the BBC – which is another reason why I never became Director General! – and I treated myself to some pretty inflammatory memos on this occasion. But I was unable to dent the worst prejudice of all, which was the BBC's very own publication, the *Radio Times*, refusing to put on its front page a picture of a black person kissing a white person at the moment of their marriage.

I did think that going into a mixed marriage was a worrying thing for people to do because they lived in a prejudiced world, a world that was more ignorant and more prejudiced then than I think it is now – although it's still much too prejudiced now, violently prejudiced. But people who do nice things, like falling in love, tend not to be terribly sensible about the long-term future. The same applies to ordinary people, not just to mixed marriages. Do you think sensibly enough about children? About education? About mortgages? About where you're going to live? About your relationships with your in-laws? There are all sorts of responsible things we should think about when we get married; and if you're entering a mixed marriage, there are even more responsible things you should think about.

I wasn't setting out to be a campaigner or a causist in particular. But by ventilating the issues that might lie ahead for these couples, I was going to make other people think of them in real terms. I was putting facts where otherwise taboos, lies, mythology and ignorant cat-calling noises might be.

Black in Blue (BBC, 1990) ● We were able to do the *Black in Blue* series because a very wise Irish policeman in the Metropolitan Police, now the Chief Constable of the Ulster Police, knew that there was too much prejudice in his ranks. He was a very senior man and he persuaded the Met to let us in and do the series. Fourteen per cent of Greater London's population are black, or Asian, or drawn from the ethnic minorities, yet Greater London's police force has less than two per cent of its membership drawn from the same stock. Three years after we did that series, the

WPC Julie Paul in *Black in Blue: Raw Recruits* (BBC TV, 1990).

relationship remains the same – fourteen per cent population, two per cent police. Of the seven ethnic minority police officers we filmed, two quit while we were filming them over a two-year period, and one has quit since. That's a nearly fifty per cent dropout, which is a bigger dropout rate than among white recruits, and it's a dropout for reasons that we ought to be ashamed of.

At the top of the Metropolitan Police are leaders who want to make it right, who are not prejudiced, who are determined to drive their force, and call it a service, into the twenty-first century. At the bottom are the people they need to recruit – the young blacks, Asians, Greeks, Italians and Poles – in order to give themselves a fully mixed police force. But in the middle, there is a hard core of people who, I'm afraid, have to die. We have to let them retire and go to some graveyard for the bigoted and the prejudiced. There must be some such place, rather like when elephants go somewhere to die, so should racists.

The Metropolitan Police Force has too many people like that in the middle ranks. They're concealed, they've learned to be clever, they know it's not on to speak as overtly as they might have done ten years ago. There are too many older policemen who nurse prejudices for which we cannot blame them because they grew up with those attitudes – those prejudices were part of the society, of the education, and of the family life that they took with them into the police force. That's what I learnt from making *Black in Blue*. It will get better, but it's going to take a long time.

Broadcasting today ● I think the management of the broadcasting companies, including the BBC, is significantly more enlightened now on these issues than it was twenty or thirty years ago. That's not to say that they were deeply prejudiced then – they were just deeply nervous. Most establishments are nervous about new things, about explosive issues, about difficulties created by programme-makers who want to fly in the face of the majority prejudice of the viewer. The majority of the viewers didn't want us to make programmes about black issues. The majority of the viewers didn't want to be told that they were intolerant and prejudiced, and they made waves and reacted, and, of course, the establishment in the BBC and in the independent broadcasting companies found that uncomfortable.

These days, however, the leaders of these companies and the BBC will quite deliberately reach for hard-hitting programmes. They will commission independents like myself, to do series like *Black in Blue*. When I suggested *Black in Blue* to the BBC they snapped it up. There was no hesitation. The only discussion was 'Good heavens, why didn't we think of it sooner?' It is a good thing that we've become strong in that way, but there are other problems ahead. It's no good them saying 'Well, that's enough' because it isn't enough. There aren't enough black people being employed by the BBC in significant positions. That's understood by the BBC and they're dealing with it as best they can.

— TREVOR PHILLIPS —

Trevor Phillips was born in London to parents who had emigrated from Guyana. He was President of the National Union of Students for two years before joining London Weekend Television in 1980 as a researcher on *Skin*. For Channel 4 Trevor produced LWT's *Black on Black* (1982-5), and from 1985-6 he produced *Club Mix* and *The Making of Britain*.

In 1986 Trevor moved to Thames Television as a reporter on *This Week*. He returned to LWT in 1987 as presenter and editor of *The London Programme*. In 1988 he was promoted to LWT's editor of regional programmes while continuing as presenter of *The London Programme* and as anchor of *Eyewitness*.

Trevor has won a number of awards for his work, including the Royal Television Society's Regional Current Affairs award for *The London Programme*, and the 1985 Prized Pieces International Video and Film Competition award for Top Public Affairs/News Program organised by the National Black Programming Consortium in Columbus, Ohio (USA). This was for an edition of *Black on Black* which included items on black sections in the Labour Party, Paul Robeson, and music from Afrika Bambaata and Little Willie Littlefield.

My entry into television was pretty unremarkable. Like a thousand other people I replied to an advertisement in the paper which said 'Features and current affairs researchers', but I had no idea what that actually meant. I had graduated as a chemist from Imperial College and had done some research, but I knew that I was not going to spend the rest of my life looking through a spectro-photometer or thinking about excitation energies of particles! So I just looked through the newspaper and the advert said 'People who are interested in current affairs should apply for this job at London Weekend Television'.

I applied and was interviewed for a programme called *Skin*, which was a regional programme about black and Asian people in the London area, and astonishingly they gave me the job. I took it like a shot because my alternative was to go and be a trainee plant manager in Middlesbrough, which seemed a fate worse than death. That was in 1980.

When I replied to the advertisement, I thought that what I was going for was general current affairs. The programme that I was really interested in was a religious programme that LWT produced at the time called *Credo*. But

LWT's recruitment system worked in such a way that all the producers got to see all the applications. One or two thousand people were applying for these jobs, and if you were a producer who got to an applicant you wanted you just snatched the person out of the pile, so the other people didn't see him or her. In this particular case, the producers of *Skin* looked out for all the black applicants, and as they knew about me they took my application out. Nobody else saw me, they interviewed me for *Skin* and that's how I got the job. At the time it didn't really mean very much to me – *Skin*, *Credo*, blacks, Asians, religion – it was just working in television, so I took the job.

Skin ● I certainly wasn't disappointed in joining *Skin*, if only because I'd been a student for seven or eight years and getting the job tripled my income overnight. Very shortly afterwards I was quite pleased to be on that series, because I've never had any qualms about working in areas which address the black experience. I don't have any negative feelings or embarrassments about that, or feelings that, in some way, one is being marginalised in doing that. The issues, the questions and the stories inter-ested me, and I had some knowledge to bring to them.

The way that LWT came to make *Skin* was really part of a much wider policy. John Birt, who was then running factual programmes at LWT, took the view that all television audiences were, in some senses, minorities. In other words, there are very few television programmes which are actually watched by a majority of people. There were some minorities, he believed, which were somehow ignored – the elderly, the young, teenagers particu-larly at the time, the ethnic minorities, and also sexual orientation, that is, gay people. And because these people are amongst our viewers, and because we are performing a public service, then we have to perform a public service for them too. So what we need to do is make sure our programme schedule reflects their interests as well.

Now, you can't do that simply by saying 'Let's make the odd *Weekend World* or *World In Action* which addresses black people' – because you know, as a black person, that you could sit there from one end of the year to the other in those circumstances and never see a black face or anything that addresses your experiences as a black person. Having done a short series called *Babylon*, which was about young black people, LWT set up the London Minorities Unit which began to make programmes for these groups of people – blacks and Asians, and a programme called *Old Times*, for the elderly, and that's really how it came about. *Skin* was the most important of those minority programmes because it addressed the biggest and, in a sense, the most significant minority grouping in the London region.

Explaining blacks to whites ● *Skin* was a series of half-hour documen-

taries. I think we made about twenty-six each year, which were described
as for and about the black and Asian communities in London. That is to say,
their aim was to address questions that affected the black and Asian minorities, but not necessarily just for those people, but for the whole of the
viewing audience in London and the South East. That gave rise to a peculiar
sort of tension because what we were doing all the time, to some extent, was
explaining blacks to whites.

We had a formula for the programmes in which we would start with the
hook – you'd say something like 'There's been a spate of racial attacks'.
And then you'd say 'This programme is about racial attacks and what we
should do about them'. Then you would have a little section in which you
would say 'Black people regard racial attacks in this way', and you'd have
to explain something about black attitudes, which for a black person would
be immediately self-evident. If we were making it for a black audience we
would never have that in a programme, but because we were also making it
for a wider audience we had to explain certain things. Occasionally this led
to bizarre moments where you would have to translate bits of dialect for the
white audience. So there was always a bit of a tension.

The second thing that *Skin* did was to drive us, to some extent, into
constantly making programmes about racism, about the relationship between blacks and whites. I think that was a problem for *Skin* because it
meant that the agenda for *Skin* was constantly about conflict between the
races. But we had to do that because the programmes had to be of interest to
both blacks and whites, and the dominant characteristic of the relationship
between blacks and whites at that time was one of conflict. So that gave the
series a slightly unhappy whining feel.

Two communities collapsed into one ● *Skin* dealt with the experiences
of both blacks and Asians in a single programme. There was a problem with
that structure in two senses. The first was a practical problem – we only had
one Asian researcher on the team, so he often had the burden of trying to
find our way into what was then, and to some extent still is, a rather closed
community that was rather suspicious of television. But the bigger problem,
I think, was that it meant that the overall tone of the series was always
somehow saying that blacks and Asians only really mattered in relation to
whites, that the only thing that really mattered to both communities was
their relationship with the majority community.

What this meant, of course, was that we were always going on about
discrimination, always talking about racism. There's nothing wrong with
doing those things as such, but if you're making twenty-six half-hour programmes, then you really ought to be able to say that the experience of
being black or Asian in a capital city is a bit more than waking up every

morning and thinking 'Who's going to discriminate against me today? What job am I not going to get?' – because life isn't like that for people.

A training ground? ● I don't think when they started *Skin* that LWT thought of it as a training ground for journalists, who would then get Channel 4 commissions. They were really thinking about what they had to do to serve the community in the capital. In retrospect, I would say that the *Skin* team on the last series I worked on was the equal of any journalistic team that I've worked with. So, to describe it as a training ground would not do it justice. On the other hand, of course, everybody wants to move on, and the problem with programmes like *Skin* is that, to some extent, they are professionally narrow. You're going back to the same sources all the time and doing the same stories again and again. If the series had continued, it would have needed new blood, new people. But in so far as it brought into television people who were not from journalistic backgrounds, it was fantastically successful.

Channel 4 began broadcasting in November 1982. There were high expectations following the appointment of the first ever Commissioning Editor for Multicultural Programmes (Sue Woodford). But this was soon followed by controversy when she commissioned LWT to produce two new flagship programmes for ethnic minorities – *Black on Black* and *Eastern Eye* – which replaced *Skin*. ● To be honest, I had no real sense of a serious controversy about LWT getting the commissions to make these black programmes. The basic point was, 'Who could make them?' You couldn't just give them to somebody who hadn't been in the business, or who didn't actually know how to make long-running series. What people often forget is that *Black on Black* and *Eastern Eye* were big shows – we were making forty hours of television a year. That was more than *World in Action* or *This Week* was making. So it was one of the biggest strands of any kind in television.

Anybody who knows anything about television knows that to churn out that amount of television week after week, especially multi-item format programmes, takes an immense amount of back up. It takes a big company to turn it out. Amongst the big companies, the BBC had not done anything like this, nor had any of the other companies in the ITV network, with the exception to some extent of Central Television. But we had made two series of long documentaries with big teams at LWT. We had experienced people and we were a big television company.

Had I been the Commissioning Editor of Multicultural Programmes at Channel 4, that's where I would have gone as well – because the most important thing at the beginning of Channel 4's existence was that if we were going to put black programmes on television, they had to be made on time and they had to fill a regular slot. We couldn't have a situation where the time wasn't being filled because the production company didn't have enough people, or because the cost accountant had got it wrong and they'd run out of money. That's why the commission went to a big company like LWT – because it had a track record and had made good programmes. A lot of the people who were complaining hadn't – what they had was a lot of ideology and not much television.

The format for *Black on Black* and *Eastern Eye* ● When I sat down with Samir Shah, who was the producer of *Eastern Eye*, and Jane Hewland, who was our joint Executive Producer, to think what these programmes that we wanted to make for Channel 4 were about, the dominant consideration in my mind was that the programmes had to be about our community's experience speaking in its own terms. They were not about explaining 'us' to white people. They were not primarily about our conflict or our relationship with white people. They were about our lives, part of which was to do with relationships with other people, but a lot more was to do with the things we were interested in, such as our art, music, the places we came from, where our ancestors came from, and so on.

That was a dominant consideration, which immediately meant that two things followed. The first thing was that we couldn't any longer collapse the people from the Indian sub-continent with the people from the Caribbean and from Africa. I come from Guyana for example, where the population is actually half Indian, but even so, we are light years culturally from the people who come from the Indian sub-continent. Our traditions are quite different and, in many ways, we are actually closer to the majority community here, the white community, than to the Indian community in things like the books we read, the history we have, and so on. So collapsing blacks and Asians together could not be done. It would have led us off into a completely wrong direction, in which we would constantly be thinking of blacks and Asian only in terms of their relationship with whites.

The other thing we had to decide was that if we were going to cover the black experience with any kind of breadth, we couldn't just say that we were going to have twenty single-subject shows. We had to be current and we had to cover a lot of ground, from the serious to the light in each show. Inevitably, that meant a magazine programme which is live or near live – so that we could pick up both on what was happening and, at the same time, cover a whole lot of different things.

The studio audience in *Black on Black* ● I chose to have a studio audience for a very specific reason. I had never seen a television programme in this country which brought together a lot of black people in the studio. Now, I think it was true at the time – and is still true – that, to some extent, people in this country are afraid of seeing a lot of black people together. They think we're going to riot, or eat somebody, or something! So my purpose was twofold – to show that, as a group of people, we could behave like everybody else, and to give the viewer a sense of solidarity with a community, which one presenter in a show would not have done. The actual visual representation of our community with an audience that had young and old people listening, some interested in serious stuff, some interested in light, reflected, as people watched television, the black community as we experienced it, and that's why I chose it.

From a production point of view, it also gave the studio a kind of warmth and life that other people envied. I have to say that when we started *Black on Black*, the studio audience concept had gone out of fashion in television programmes generally. But I think the success and the value of the studio audience to our show, helped to bring that back for a lot of other factual programmes.

Studio audience encounter with Lord Trefgarne ● What happened in the first programme was that we had a group of health workers who were black, and for the first time they were talking about industrial action, and Lord Trefgarne, who was the Minister of State, came in to answer questions. The health workers got infuriated, as people do, and they reacted in a way that I recognise to be a West Indian reaction. Interestingly enough, Lord Trefgarne himself wasn't tremendously alarmed by it. He was a little bit unsettled, but he realised that there wasn't any kind of malice. But some people watching the programme, because they're predisposed to think that a lot of black people together and getting too passionate, must mean petrol bombs in the streets next, got very alarmed by what they saw. We had quite a lot of reaction from people phoning in.

I think there was a bit of uneasiness inside Channel 4 and LWT as well. This was expressed as the feeling that, perhaps, we hadn't planned the studio properly, that we hadn't been professional enough. I think that might be true. Today, I might be able to plan and work the studio in a way that wouldn't get rid of the passion, but would make it less incoherent and more intelligible to the viewer.

Editorial control ● As we went through the series, I think it would be fair to say that *Black on Black* became more my show, and I think Samir Shah would say the same for *Eastern Eye*. You must remember that when we started I had been in television for only eighteen months. I had never done a studio show, never been trained as a director, and I didn't actually know a lot about the production of television. So the opportunity to take advice and to lean on our Executive Producer (Jane Hewland), who happened to be white, was incredibly valuable. The relationship with her was rather important because, ideally, what we wanted to happen was for her to underpin us with television production skills, while we kept the intellectual and journalistic perspective that I and the black team would bring to the programme.

Of course, it's never as simple as that. The technique often limits your options journalistically or creatively, and there is always a bit of a tension. But I have to say that I rate Jane Hewland's television skills very highly, and it's no accident that she subsequently won a BAFTA award for innovation with *Network 7*. She knows how to make television and that was tremendously useful to us. As the series went on, she was able to back off, and to put more control both in terms of the perspective and the intelligence of the series, as well as the production of it, in our hands.

So, by the time we got to the third series of *Black on Black* I had to take responsibility for whatever happened. There wasn't any kind of white puppet-master pulling my strings. I think some people would like to say 'Oh, it wasn't really Trevor's fault'. But that, in a sense, would be a dereliction of duty and would belittle my role. I wouldn't have done the job for as long as I did if I didn't feel that I was in control of the programme. So I think certainly by the third series the choices that were made, the stories that were chosen, the way they were done, the way the programmes were constructed, the choice of presenters, and so on, were all mine.

The target audience ● My view about the audience was very simple – we made *Black on Black* for a black family audience. I even had them imagined, rather like my own family, sitting on the sofa watching the programme every Tuesday night – and I knew what levers I wanted to pull for dad, for mum, and for the kids if they were still up that late! So there was never any question in my mind about who the audience was. But that didn't mean it had to be exclusive. There were things which white audiences would want to see on *Black on Black* – for example, they liked black music too. It wasn't just us who bought soul music records. But I always thought of them as an over-the-shoulder audience; they were looking through the window at what we were doing. They were welcome to, as long as they understood who the primary audience was in the case of *Black on Black*.

'Moves' – a televisual griot ● There was one critical element in *Black on Black* which came out of my own experience, which I had always wanted and had invented, and that was the regular item done by Victor Romero Evans called 'Moves'. He represented a kind of African and West Indian

Victor Romero Evans as 'Moves' in *Black on Black* (Channel 4/LWT, 1982-5).

tradition of the person who, through song or comedy, talks about the day's news, whether in the village or in the country. That is something which is still very strong in our culture, and I wanted it in the show.

The problem with it was that we had to make a choice – was it really going to be our thing, or was it going to be intelligible to everybody? In the end we decided that it had to be directed at the black audience with the language firmly within our tradition. So 'Moves' mostly spoke in dialect. We tried to make it intelligible, but it wasn't always intelligible to a white audience. In the end, it actually didn't matter because what happened was that viewers learnt some Jamaican patois, so that was OK. And that was, I think, a tremendously important touchstone that told people who this programme was for, and we never compromised on what 'Moves' was about. He did his stuff in his own language, in his own way, and in our own tradition.

The pitfalls of ghettoisation ● People have asked 'Is this a ghetto?' In relation to *Black on Black*, the answer is that it could have become a ghetto – black programme-makers could have got stuck there, people could have said the only place we want to deal with questions about the Third World, or about the black community, are there rather than on the news or on some other magazine programme. My view was both personal and as producer. As a producer, I felt that after the third series things had changed to some extent. The context and the atmosphere had changed in that it seemed inappropriate to continue trying to pack the whole of the black experience into a show that had a single format, because it was always a rather uneasy compromise.

There was something rather peculiar about putting very serious issues into that framework, and then we couldn't always go all out as we would like for the entertainment spectacular. So my view was that we really needed to separate the two. We needed a journalistic programme and a separate entertainment programme. There was also the personal element. *Black on Black* was my first producing job. I had done it for three years. It had become reasonably successful, and now I wanted to learn to do other things. So, in that sense, it could have become a ghetto for me personally. It didn't because they killed it.

The demise of *Black on Black* ● Channel 4's decision not to re-commission *Black on Black* was not in itself a major national tragedy. What I think was a problem and a disaster was the decision to take away a flagship, a rock solid black programme that was there, week in and week out, which people knew and could find in their week's schedule. What that did was to take away one of the things that black people don't have in this country, an institution. We were building an institution which people could constantly refer to, similar to the way they refer to their church, for instance – 'Did you see *Black on Black* last night? Did you see Beverly Anderson? What do you think about her?' These are some of the ways in which we define ourselves. So I think it was a tremendous mistake to kill off the slot.

In my view, what they should have done was to have more than one show. They should have taken the journalistic element of *Black on Black* and made it into a programme; and they should have taken the entertainment element and made that into another programme. Both programmes would have the same philosophy, that they would be addressing themselves directly at a black audience, in its language, and with the same priorities, week in and week out, at least thirty weeks of the year. People would then know that these programmes are part of the television landscape.

Instead, what they've done at Channel 4 is to produce a series of different programmes of varying quality, which appear ten weeks at a time. Some of them are very good, some not so good. You never quite know where they are, you never quite know who they're for, and there are no points in a schedule to which you can latch on to and say 'Hey, that's ours. This reflects our experience. This is what we, as black people, share'. I think what they've done is a terrific mistake and, indeed, the BBC is making the same mistake right now, because instead of changing *Ebony*, they've killed it.

Black broadcasters and the future of television ● The role I would like to see black broadcasters and black audiences playing in television is really twofold. I would like to see a flagship black programme or programmes – one dealing with the arts and another dealing with current affairs or factual material. And I would like these to be part of the television landscape, constantly recording, monitoring, and reflecting the black experience for everybody who wants to see it. Though these programmes would be targeted primarily at black viewers, everybody could be part of it, and the first thing that these programmes would say is 'We are part of Britain's national life'.

The other thing I'd like to see is a really thriving group of black programme-makers and journalists working in television – sometimes working in black programmes, sometimes working in so-called mainstream programmes. I don't think there should be people who feel that they have to escape from a ghetto. I have done programmes in the recent past which are both supposedly mainstream and marginal, and I think we have to be able to do both and bring both perspectives to television.

So, ideally, what we want to do is bring some of the people who are great journalists and great dramatists who are outside of television, into television and give them a place, both as black voices but also as British voices. The two are not exclusive, but they can do two different things, whether it's in a black programme or in a BBC Play for Today, *Panorama*, *World in Action* or *The London Programme*.

People like me are always being told to be careful about being seen as only concerned with black questions and ghettoising myself, and so forth. Unfortunately, a lot of young black people are misled by this, and they think that doing black programmes, or things about blacks, is somehow second-rate. Of course, nobody says that about Woody Allen who makes Jewish movies, because the Jewish experience is somehow seen as generally acceptable and universal.

The problem is not to do with us ghettoising ourselves, it's to do with people thinking that our experience is second-rate. If we abandon black programme-making and pretend that we don't want to have separate black programmes, then we're also saying that we think our experience is second-rate, not worth preserving, not worth having in its clear and separate form. And that's really why I think we need to battle for television slots that are about black programme-makers speaking to black audiences.

Samir Shah joined London Weekend Television in 1979 as a reporter on *Skin*. From there he went on to work on most of LWT's output as a researcher/reporter, then producer/director. He helped to set up and produced LWT's *Eastern Eye* (1982-5) for Channel 4 Television. He was then the editor of *Credo* and later *The London Programme*.

Samir joined the BBC in 1987, where he is in charge of BBC TV's current affairs output. This includes programmes such as *Panorama*, *Question Time*, *On the Record*, *Assignment*, *Public Eye*, and *The Money Programme*. In addition, he is responsible for ad hoc programming – series and specials – in current affairs. He is part of the senior management of BBC's News and Current Affairs Directorate.

My entry to television was pretty straightforward. I had just finished my doctoral thesis and was languishing in the Home Office, when I saw a block advert in *The Guardian* for researchers at London Weekend Television. I thought 'This looks interesting, it's more research'. So I applied for a couple of jobs, one for *The London Programme* and one for a programme that turned out to be *Skin*. I was interviewed for both and got a final interview for *The London Programme*, which was hard work – the interview lasted for two hours. It was actually worse than my doctoral final. In the end, I was offered a job on *Skin*, the programme for minorities, which I happily accepted.

Criticisms of Channel 4's decision to commission London Weekend Television to provide programmes for Asian and Afro-Caribbean viewers – *Eastern Eye* and *Black on Black* ● I have to be cynical about those criticisms because most of them came from companies which had failed to get the commission. I think the history of Channel 4 is a history of criticism of programmes by people who've failed to get a bit. So I wasn't terribly upset, or worried, or concerned about the criticisms. What it did show, however, was that there was quite a big constituency of programme-makers in that area, and that we had to be better than them.

London Weekend Television's track record in minority programme-making was pretty good, starting from *Babylon* and going through to the *Skin* programme. We had to build on this and deliver a product that would be watched and enjoyed by people. In a way *Skin* had no opposition, but it was pretty clear by the time *Eastern Eye* and *Black on Black* came along that there were a growing number of alternative places to make such programmes.

The notion that programmes for or about black people should only be made by black people, or made in institutions run solely by black people, relates to a very deep question about the nature of the programme-making that you want to engage in. I don't think from LWT's point of view, nor from my own point of view, were we interested in making programmes that were propagandising for black people or for Asians. One of the great criticisms I got about *Eastern Eye* was that it wasn't on the side of the Asian community.

The point is, I had come from a tradition previous to *Eastern Eye*, where I'd worked on *Weekend World* and had learnt skills of analysis and impartiality. And I think one of the great things about the LWT tradition was that it did not treat any group of people in any way other than with the highest standards of journalism.

This meant that we approached subjects from the point of view of a journalistic endeavour – there were heroes and villains, and we reported on both sides. We didn't just do the heroes. We didn't pretend that there weren't warts in the Asian community. But this didn't go down terribly well with a whole section of what I call 'the campaigning propaganda side'. I think if you want a campaigning programme or a propaganda programme, then you should commission an organisation that is about that kind of journalism. If you commission London Weekend Television, you commission journalism of the sort that is across the board – it's not so much white or black. I also think you can easily commission programmes from white people who are campaigning on behalf of blacks. It's a question of what kind of journalism you want.

Some people argue that the distinction between propaganda and news value is a white establishment distinction. But the point about Afro-Caribbean and Asian programmes is that they should be challenging even the agenda of what constitutes news. My own interest is not to make programmes that just propagandise or campaign for any particular community, whether they're to do with social workers, or with Asians, or whatever. We can make such programmes, but I don't think that's journalism. That is a different kind of programme which may have its place, but, in my view, it's not what we need for Asians or for black people.

A new remit for minority programming ● Trevor Phillips and I were instrumental in coming up with the ideas for *Eastern Eye* and *Black on Black*. We had both worked on *Skin* and one of the feelings we had about that programme, the reaction we had when we went out into the different groups of people in England, was that *Skin* tended to focus only on problems, on defining black and Asian people in terms of their antagonistic relationship with white people, such as discrimination and police harassment. So what was bringing blacks and Asian people together was the fact they were non-white, which is a very negative definition of these groups. And what I discovered was that the Asian community was much richer than that. They had a much greater experience than that of discrimination or hassles with the immigration authorities, and so on. What they really wanted was a programme that reflected a wider range of activities. And Trevor was finding the same thing in relation to the Caribbean community.

So we decided to create a programme that had a wider brief – which is why it was a magazine programme. We wanted it to reflect not just hard stories about the experiences that people faced in Britain, but also stories about their own communities in the sub-continent. We also wanted to cover cultural and social lightweight stories, which, in the context of *Eastern Eye*, meant a lot to do with Indian films and film stars which was a very important part of Asian life. Trevor and I decided that what we needed was a programme aimed at our respective communities, but which also had a wider brief. The fact that these communities were not white was obviously a part of their experience, but there were other aspects too.

In terms of editorial control, the relationship I had with Jane Hewland, my Executive Producer, was in many ways more open and more relaxed than the relationship with my colleagues working on other programmes. Partly, this was because we were delving in an area that Jane and others didn't know very much about, so, in the end, we were keepers of the information. On the whole we were left very much to our own devices. Jane was obviously our Executive Producer and she was our editorial chief, but she very rarely exercised control in any way that I would particularly disagree with. In fact, I think that happened far more on programmes like *The London Programme* and *Weekend World*, than it did with us, and certainly far more in my current job at the BBC.

But *Eastern Eye* was quite a draining show – week in and week out, finding programmes, finding stories – and it needed tremendous energy and enthusiasm. After three years, I felt, for my own personal development, that I wanted to move on to a wider canvas. *Eastern Eye* still had tremendous interest, and we were still getting a lot of reaction from people, but I personally wanted to move on, do other things, and let other people carry on with the programme. I wanted to develop my television skills and my programme-making skills in other areas. And there were now enough good people working on *Eastern Eye* for them to take over.

The demise of *Eastern Eye* and *Black on Black* ● From the moment that Farrukh Dhondy took over as Commissioning Editor for Multicultural

Programmes at Channel 4, there were bound to be changes. *Eastern Eye* and *Black on Black* took up a lot of his budget and he is not a man who would just rubber stamp his predecessor's ideas. So, inevitably, he had to take programmes away. I think he has come up with rather an interesting strategy of separating out the programmes, which might be the right thing to do. For three years we had established a magazine programme, putting hard stories next to soft items, and that, perhaps, started to feel a bit uncomfortable. So it was probably better to develop new forms. I always think it's interesting to try new forms, and there's nothing wrong with changing something after three years. And *The Bandung File*, which replaced the journalistic strand of *Eastern Eye* and *Black on Black*, had some tremendous successes – the most recent being the coverage of the BCCI scandal, which I thought was terrific and showed what that kind of journalism can achieve. They have done some pretty good journalism over the years.

Farrukh's interest is quite heavyweight and serious, and he has tended to put the lightweight items back in Sunday morning slots. I think it would have been better to suggest that the Asian and black communities aren't just interested in heavyweight stories, and to have some lighter stuff in the weekday evening slots as well, maybe done in different ways. But he has done a tremendous amount in ethnic programming at Channel 4 – there's been drama, hard journalism, light stories – and I think that it has flowered under him. We've now got a much wider range of programming in different places. So I think it has been a positive development.

The importance of 'ethnic' programming ● I think that there will always be a need for ethnic programming on television, as long as there is such a thing as Afro-Caribbean or Asian. As long as those terms have meaning, then there will be the need for programmes that address the content of that meaning. But I think that there is a real problem over this business of ghettoisation. It is really specialist programming of the sort that addresses a particular interest group. It is like the television equivalent of a regional newspaper. There are regional programmes for Yorkshire people, and regional newspapers for Yorkshire people.

Well, you can equally have programmes for the Asian people for example. Asians have a different set of news values, interests, agenda, and they need programmes that reflect that. It is not reasonable to expect network programmes, addressing the national community, to have that set of values. On the other hand, because Asians have a different set of values, they shouldn't be ignored. So it seems to me that there will always be a need for programmes aimed separately at Asian and at Afro-Caribbean viewers – until the difference between Afro-Caribbeans and Asians becomes the same as the difference between the Angles and the Saxons.

I don't know what my effect on television has been, but I do think that the entry of black and Asian people into television generally has had a terrific effect. When I look at some of the people who've come into television through ethnic programming, and I see where they now work, I think that what we've got is a range of imaginative programming, original programming, and I wonder if it would have happened had it come from other groups of people. Programmes like *Network 7*, *7 Sport*, and *Good Sport*, are all run by somebody who worked for me on *Eastern Eye* – and they are all very interesting and very different, and you can't pin them down in any simple direct way. I think that what you have are people who've come into television with a different perspective, a different way of looking at things, and I think we've ended up getting programmes that are different, original, and distinct from the ordinary – that is, distinct from the stuff that we have become used to seeing since the 60s.

New initiatives at the BBC ● My move to the BBC was the classic phone call out of the blue. Ironically, I had just finished my first year as editor of *The London Programme*, the programme I'd first applied for when I went into television. John Birt, who had just joined the BBC as the Deputy Director General, rang me up one Saturday afternoon and invited me over for a drink. After a long chat he told me all about the changes he was making at the BBC, in particular how he was bringing news and current affairs in television and radio together into one big organisation and was now re-staffing it. By this time I had twigged that he was going to offer me some kind of job, and, as he went through the hierarchy down to the programmes, I was speculating which particular programme he might offer me the editorship of. Suddenly he went back up the hierarchy again and asked me if I would like to run the current affairs department. I thought about it for two seconds before saying 'yes'!

One of the most important things about television and its relationship to black and Asian people is not only its representation of the people on the screen, but also the number of people who work behind the camera. I believe very strongly that the programmes we get on screen reflect the kind of people who make them. By and large the BBC is run by white middle-class males, and we get that kind of television. So it is terribly important that we change the social mix of the people who work in the BBC.

With John Birt leading it, the BBC has now taken that on board rather strongly, because John has always been very keen on this. We have a new and younger group of people running television at the BBC and they are very committed. The first thing that the BBC has done strategically is to set targets to ensure that, by the end of this decade, there will be a certain proportion of black and Asian men and women in grades across the board, from the bottom right up to the top. That is a really important managerial objective set by the Board of Governors, and we are all enjoined to make it happen.

Now, in order to try and achieve those targets, a lot of practice has taken place, a lot of ad hoc and specific schemes to recruit black reporters and black production people. There have been lots of training workshops – for example, Jonathan Powell (the Controller of BBC1) has set up comedy training workshops to try and encourage new people in that area. There are a lot of one-off schemes being run in different bits of the BBC, in an effort to bring about the changes that are required.

We're also doing a number of other managerial things like instituting fair selection procedures. The gatekeepers, the people who recruit – editors, managing editors, supervisors, and so on – all need to go through training about how to recruit. Put crudely, the problem for women in the BBC is that they don't get promoted. There's no recruitment problem. We get a lot of women coming in, but they tail off as you go higher up the grades. The problem for black and Asian people, on the other hand, is not lack of promotion but a lack of recruitment – we don't get black and Asian people in the first place.

One of the most important things about trying to meet the targets the BBC has set for the recruitment of black people, is to address the problems faced by those people who sit on boards recruiting them, the managers across the departments. And what is really important in trying to get managers to break through their preconceptions and their value systems, is to get them to go through a variety of different training systems in order for them to understand themselves better. Then they will be able to pick the best people for the job, rather than people who they think they are used to, or feel comfortable with. Inevitably, if there is a board full of white males, they're going to feel more comfortable with a white male than with others, and they're not going to see the skills and abilities which are manifest in a black person, whether male or female.

What we need to do, and what we have started to do is to put the managers through training. They need training. They need to know how to conduct interviews, phrase questions, get the best out of people. They need to establish more clearly in their minds what the real criteria are that are needed to pick the right person, rather than criteria which are implicit in their heads and not explicitly stated. I've put all my editors and managing editors through training schemes, equal opportunities schemes, fair selection schemes, and that's only the first stage. We now have to monitor it and see what kind of output and outcome there is from this kind of process. If it's not working, we will do it again, and we will keep on doing it until we recruit the right group of people.

So, there are a lot of initiatives now under way at the BBC, but the key thing is that we have an objective which we have to meet. That applies across the board, including my own department in current affairs. I've set up a system which tries to ensure that we go to a wider range of 'experts' who we quite often use in journalism. But what we need to do is to get information, so we've started to collect information on people who are Afro-Caribbean and Asian, who can speak not on Afro-Caribbean or Asian issues, but on any general subject, the economy, the health service, or whatever. That is also beginning to have an effect.

The most telling thing, of course, is on-screen presence. We need to have more black and Asian people on-screen in television, because that is what sends the signal to the world outside, that this is a place for black and Asian people to work. We haven't gone very far on that – we need to go further. Where there is great improvement is in the sort of youth programming area that Janet Street-Porter does, where I think you get quite a good sense of a multicultural, racially-mixed department. We need to get that sense throughout all the departments in the BBC.

The BBC is a very white institution. At practically all the meetings I attend, I'm the only non-white face present. There are 28,000 people employed in the BBC, and there will be statistics shortly showing how many non-white people there are. Obviously, like all large institutions, we tend to get most of the non-white faces down in the canteen, and that's not good enough. Changes have to be made everywhere, right up to Board level. I'm relatively new to the BBC, so all I can say is that I feel that the current set of ideas and initiatives which have been put in place, show that there is real commitment from executives like John Birt and Jonathan Powell to bring about the necessary changes. This group of people are really keen on bringing about change, and I hope it will happen.

— FARRUKH DHONDY —

Farrukh Dhondy was born in Poona, India and studied at Pembroke College, Cambridge (1964-7) and Leicester University (1967-9). Between 1969 and 1980 he taught in Inner London schools, was a member of the *Race Today* Collective, and published several books of stories before entering television as a writer. In 1983 he adapted some of his short stories for the BBC including *Good at Art*, *The Bride*, *Salt on a Snake's Tail*, and *Come to Mecca*, which was recognised as the first complete drama series devoted to a British-Asian background. He also wrote the four-part drama serial *King of the Ghetto* for the BBC in 1986.

Farrukh co-wrote (with Mustapha Matura) the Channel 4 sitcom *No Problem!* (1983-5); and he wrote the monologues for 'Moves', a short fortnightly commentary for the actor Victor Romero Evans which was featured on Channel 4's *Black on Black*.

In 1985 he wrote the first series of the sitcom *Tandoori Nights* for Channel 4. Since 1984 Farrukh has been the Commissioning Editor for Multicultural Programmes at Channel 4.

I never intended to get involved in television. I didn't grow up with that ambition. I went through my childhood and my teens without ever having seen a television set and not quite knowing what it was. American comics, literature and magazines acquainted me with the fact that there was such a phenomenon, but I'd never seen it. I saw television when I first turned up in London. I stayed in a rooming house for a day before going up to Cambridge, and there it happened to be. *Top of the Pops* was on and The Supremes were singing 'Baby, Where Did Our Love Go', and I thought 'This is terrific!' I watched and listened to all of it. And then I saw how British people were hooked on television, and I knew then that here was a new language, a new way of hooking people onto something. But it didn't cross my mind that I ever wanted to work for it or that I ever could work for it.

We didn't have television in our rooms at university, of course, so one had to make an effort to go to a junior common room to watch it. I was very selective about how much time I'd give to this box — I remember I watched *Talking to a Stranger* and *The Wars of the Roses*. I definitely did not watch *The Forsyte Saga* at the time, I picked up on that much later. At that time, I didn't make a distinction between trash television and so-called quality television. I didn't know then what values to put on these things. But I don't think there was any cultural snobbery in how I consumed television.

By the time I got to Cambridge, I had been like any good, middle-class Indian – I had already thought about why India was poor, why one saw beggars on the streets, and why there was a disparity in caste and class. One is brought up in India to believe all manner of nationalistic truths and untruths – for instance, the nationhood of India itself. But you get to know that there are all sorts of people in India and that the economy is not quite right. And any thinking person begins to wonder whether there should be a balance between religion, the sort of superstition and the traditions that are all around you on the one hand, and a sense of rationality on the other. And so you come to a kind of crude popular Marxism.

That's where I was at the time. And I remember joining the Communist Youth League in India, partly to defy my parents, and partly because I thought that solutions had to be implemented which, living the kind of bourgeois existence they lived, they would not understand. Not that I didn't live a bourgeois existence myself – I applied for a scholarship to Cambridge, for God's sake!

But when I got to Britain, the distinguishing factor was not black politics at all. I wasn't aware that there was going to be friction between blacks and whites. I knew about the American civil rights movement because we read all about it in India. In that sense, India is not starved of world news. Of course, at that time there wasn't a militant Black Panther movement or anything like that. But while there was a lot of friction between blacks and whites in the United States, I didn't think that it would be replicated in Britain at all. In fact, it hasn't been. But those were the politics that entered my head at the time.

Then one day in 1964, the year that Harold Wilson's Labour party won the General Election, I went with a group of Indian friends to protest against Peter Griffiths, the Tory candidate for Smethwick, who had been invited to speak at the Cambridge Union. Griffiths was the first parliamentary candidate to make racial politics the central issue in Britain and actually win. Mosley had tried it before but he got an extremely derisory vote. Nobody followed him and he went into the wilderness. Then Griffiths came along. He had made some racist slogans popular, and we went to protest at his presence. I don't know whether we thought we would stop him from speaking or what, but we stood there and barracked him. Anglia Television were there of course, and the first faces they wanted to see in the crowd were the Asian faces, so there I was on camera for the first time. I went around Cambridge for a few days as 'The man who had been on television'.

After university, I lived and worked in London but I still didn't own a television set. Television wasn't part of the furniture of my early homes in Britain. I used to watch television at other people's houses – this was the late 60s, early 70s. We used to make an occasion of going to a person's house where there was a television set and watching particular things. I watched quite a lot but selectively. Television only really began to affect my life as it were, when it offered to pay me to write for it. Then I thought 'I must catch up on everything. I must know how this thing is done. I don't want to do a bad job. I want my work to be new. I want it to be fresh. I want to be the greatest writer television has known; and so forth'.

I always wanted to write, so after university, I became a schoolteacher and wrote books at the same time. I wrote a book called *East End at Your Feet*, which was a set of short stories about Indian kids in London's East End, in Leicester, in the Midlands, and so on. I had been asked to write the book, it was not something I touted around to publishers. A kind of multicultural audience existed before the advent of multicultural literature, so publishers went out looking for authors to write the books. Macmillan published my book.

At some point the book got into trouble. What happened was that it was being used in schools and the National Front ran a demonstration and a picket outside a school in South East London. I heard about it and legged it over to the school to try and get some publicity out of it, which would help boost the sales of my book. Because of the attention it got, the book came to the notice of a BBC producer at Pebble Mill. He called me and we discussed the idea of adapting the stories for television. I said 'OK,' although I didn't know what a television play looked like. I said 'If you show me a script, I could imitate that'. And that's how I got into writing for television.

I was then asked by Charlie Hanson to write a play for what was going to become the Black Theatre Co-operative. He was working with Victor Romero Evans, Trevor Laird, and several other people and they asked me to join the gang. Mustafa Matura had written their first play and they wanted me to write something for them, so I wrote a play called *Mama Dragon*. Arising out of the two or three plays that we did as the Black Theatre Co-operative, we drafted a constitution and formed ourselves into a sort of organisation so that we could get money from people for productions.

When we produced those stage plays, Humphrey Barclay came along from London Weekend Television and said that he had seen our work and that he would like the group and the writers to come up with a situation comedy. He gave us the money to run workshops – and we got into the workshops extremely enthusiastically. That's how Mustafa and I wrote *No Problem!*, the successful situation comedy of the early 80s. That went into two or three series. By then, I was being asked to write individual plays as well, for Central Television, for the BBC schools programmes, and so on.

Front row: Judith Jacob, Chris Tummings, Angela Wynter; Back row: Janet Kay, Victor Romero Evans and Malcolm Frederick in *No Problem!* (Channel 4, 1983-5).

No Problem! ● I think what was behind *No Problem!* was my feeling, and Sue Woodford's feeling – she was the first Commissioning Editor for Multi-cultural Programmes at Channel 4, and commissioned it, and Humphrey Barclay's feeling, perhaps – that the best service that could be done for black television, at that time, would be to try and join in the highest traditions of mainstream television output. So, if we were going to produce a situation comedy, we shouldn't try and turn it into complaints program-ming. We should make it as situation comedy, and the function of situation comedy is to make people laugh.

Now, I can take the criticism that *No Problem!* did not make some people laugh, but I know that it actually made a lot of people laugh, that they watched it for that reason, and that as a result it became a fairly popular programme over three series. In fact, it was killed off when I took over from Sue Woodford as Commissioning Editor of Multicultural Programmes at Channel 4.

Apart from not making some people laugh, *No Problem!* got on the wrong side of what I would call 'the nascent bureaucratic black middle-class which lives off a grievance industry'. When you give these people some-thing that is quite innocuous, that should make people laugh, they find it unfunny and switch it off, which is fair enough. But, unfortunately they don't stop at switching off, they believe it's something to campaign about as well. If black television ever becomes the norm in Britain, and does the whole range of television output including current affairs, situation comedy, drama, chat shows, and so on – in other words, lives up to the great traditions of television, as well as the mediocre television traditions – these professional protesters will be out of a job and the grievance industry will collapse!

King of the Ghetto (1986) ● Before *King of the Ghetto*, I had written six plays called *Come to Mecca* for the BBC, and then I co-wrote *No Problem!* for Channel 4. I was also writing a character called 'Moves' for Victor Romero Evans, but I didn't sign my name to it because it would have spoiled the joke. To have a streetwise West Indian character making political monologues and then to reveal that it was actually written by a Parsee from Poona would have ruined the joke for the population that watched *Black on Black*, on which 'Moves' featured every week. I also wrote *The Empress and the Munshi* for Central Television, and a couple of plays for BBC TV's *Scene*. So I was doing a lot of things and was quite used to being called up. At one time I felt I was flavour of the year – although that faded eventually.

King of the Ghetto came out of the experience I had working as an 'agitator' in the East End of London. I used to write for a magazine called *Race Today*, which was edited at the time by Darcus Howe. It was a very radical magazine with a radical message. One day we got a phone call from some people who I think misunderstood the function of the magazine. They were Bangladeshis and they said that they wanted to speak to somebody about a problem they were having, because they needed our help. They had been sold a dud house on an East London housing estate, and there were six Bangladeshi men living in this house at the time. They produced a document which they believed was proof that they had bought the house for £600 and that they were the rightful owners of it. Now, you couldn't buy a house for £600 even in those days in London's broken-down East End, but they had given the £600 to a guy called 'Sammy', and 'Sammy' of course worked for somebody else. Obviously, they had been deceived into parting with their cash.

The house was actually owned by the Greater London Council, who promptly ordered them to move off because they were squatters. That's when they wanted our help. We got to be friends with them, because we said that we would take up their case. We started writing stories about it in *Race Today* which attracted the attention of the national press. And with the help of other squatters, white squatters, we turned that into a squatters movement – it became the Bengali Housing Action Group.

One of the very prominent members of that group was a white squatter who used to break down a lot of doors, put in toilets which were destroyed by the GLC, and just open up estates. With his help we succeeded in opening up about two estates in six or seven streets. We just opened the place up and said to people 'Form your own kind of street committee and get in here. Bring your furniture, it's now your house! If you have any trouble, call us – we know solicitors, we know the squatting law, we are in contact with the police and we will tell them where to get off'. And that's how we started a very thriving Bangladeshi squatters movement. You can imagine the nest of stories that grew out of there – and that's where *King of the Ghetto* came from.

King of the Ghetto got a damn good reaction from the press. But towards the fourth episode, there was a picket of exactly twenty-four Bangladeshi young persons outside BBC TV Centre in White City. It's interesting to have your plays picketed. I wasn't surprised in the least that they had mounted such a picket. I kind of knew who they were too – they were part of the industry, or at least their leaders were part of the industry that gets money from local government agencies to protect the image of young Asians, or Bengalis, or whatever.

They were project people – their project was not to get houses, or to stop the exploitation of one person by another that goes on in the Asian community. Their project was to protect the image of Asians from the likes of me. So I wasn't surprised, because I grew up in India and in India many people believe that the constitution gives them the right to flattery. Well, I don't believe that. I also believe that all good writing starts with observation, and the more accurate your observation the more of a service you are doing to the development of observation and of the literary life in your own community.

Protecting the image of a community is, in a sense, an absurd enterprise. However, it has developed into a pseudo-science nowadays, with people saying things like 'Let's have positive images'. When Mrs Thatcher wanted a positive image of her government, she didn't ask a novelist or a television writer to do it, she hired Saatchi and Saatchi. But we now have people who are posing as writers and protectors of the community's image and they are no better than public relations salespersons. There's no harm in that as such. If indeed there is a need for such a function, they ought to be paid handsomely for it. But, in my view, it is not the function of creative writing or film-making to engage in that sort of activity.

Becoming Commissioning Editor of Multicultural Programmes at Channel 4 and axing *Black on Black* and *Eastern Eye* ● When I took over as Commissioning Editor for Multicultural Programmes at Channel 4 in

1984, my first act was not, as some people seem to think, to axe *Black on Black* and *Eastern Eye*. I actually continued to run both programmes for a year and I attended most of the recordings of them, to see what was going down. I discussed with the extremely eminent producers, Trevor Phillips and Samir Shah, what was going into the programmes and why. So not only did the two programmes run for a year of my tenancy at Channel 4, but they were also better funded and were championed by me.

The second notion that *Black on Black* and *Eastern Eye* were extremely popular programmes, is not true. The viewing figures had actually been steadily falling from a peak that Sue Woodford had managed to achieve when she was the commissioning editor. However, the viewing figures didn't influence me so much, because I had other ambitions for my commissioning programme, so to speak. Channel 4 is an editorial channel, more so than any other television channel, and a commissioning editor's role is not, to put it very bluntly, representative but interpretive. Parliament says that we ought to do three things − we should make programmes which other people are not making, we should satisfy minority viewing, and we should do things that are innovative.

Those three injunctions leave you, especially as a multicultural editor, with a tremendous amount of scope for interpretation. I had to take on that interpretive role with a vengeance, and my interpretation was that we ought to get out of the catch-all 'show your presence in Britain' type magazine programme, and to start doing things that would count as current affairs, music, culture, comedy, drama and so on − and by so doing, try and live up to the best traditions of television. A lot of intellection goes into the production of the extremely high quality news that we still get from ITV and BBC. I thought that it was time we began doing that, rather than presenting a box which says 'Here are the blacks, there are still problems surrounding their presence', and so on.

The second reason for cancelling *Black on Black* and *Eastern Eye* was that I felt that it was time to alter the whole basis of commissioning the Channel's flagship black-related programmes. My predecessor, Sue Woodford, had no choice but to use a company like London Weekend Television to produce such demanding programmes in the multicultural strand, and of course LWT had a fair amount of experience of programme-making in that area with *Skin*, for instance. But I felt that it was my job, as the second commissioning editor, to try and build the black independent sector; and the only way I could do that was by taking the money away from LWT and giving it to somebody else, or giving it to lots of other people.

So, instead of *Black on Black* and *Eastern Eye*, I commissioned about six programmes. I commissioned about thirty-one companies in my first year, only one of them very well known. The rest of them got to be very successful production companies that went on to make series of all sorts. My strategy was intended to make an inroad into black independent production.

The Bandung File ● There was (and still is) a popular perception that any letterhead wallah can write a proposal, send it off, and they'll get a Channel 4 commission, or should get a commission. I didn't see that as the criteria for commissioning programmes. I thought one had to have current affairs of a slightly new sort, possibly polemical and certainly something that would draw the attention of the general public. And I think we succeeded in doing that with *The Bandung File*.

The Bandung File did something extremely necessary. As I said earlier, the commissioning editor's role is essentially interpretive, and one of my interpretations of what was happening in the Asian and black communities through the 70s and the beginning of the 80s, was that we were getting a lot of radical, polemical thinking. The conservative thought that arose from the Asian and black communities was not worth looking at because it wasn't original. It was parody, it was imitation, and it was easily made fun of. But in the radical thought that existed, I had to single out the different strands, and being an interpretative commissioning editor I had to see which was the best strand to represent on television. In other words, I had to decide what would best serve the community now, and what in years to come would look as though it provided continuity and added a foundation.

One of the strands I could have chosen, and it was offered to me by people who thought they were journalistically sound, was a kind of boiled nationalism – in which everything that Britain did was wrong, and everything that blacks did was right; where there would be no investigation, and where there would be only 'positive' images, celebration, and so on. I didn't understand it and the very notion repulsed me. I thought 'Yes, there ought to be polemic to an extent, there ought to be committed programming, but it ought to take a much more informed world view'.

So when the proposal for *The Bandung File* came to me, I thought 'Fine, this is how we shall progress'. Actually, the producers initially offered me documentaries and not *The Bandung File*. So the first thing that they did to limber up, as it were, was to create a multicultural team of people with an established record in political journalism and television production. They got together and made seven documentaries which were quite startling in their impact, because nothing like them had been done before for television.

I think *The Bandung File* established itself solidly as a radical current affairs programme. But then there came a time when all good things had to come to an end and I thought, again, that two criteria applied – the removal of *Bandung File* and the utilising of the limited amount of funds and slots I had towards something else. I've now got a programme called *The Black Bag*. This has a number of companies working for it — about eight or ten companies get commissions to work on this programme.

The Black Bag tries to fulfil a very specific purpose — namely, to instigate investigative journalism which is fearless, to breed real investigative journalists, rather than people looking for racism in every corner of British society. Again, we want to get away from grievance programming, though if there is a grievance and it can be well substantiated in investigation, fine, let's go for it if it's important. But that's a judgment which current affairs editors always have to make.

The current state of drama ● To my mind, there are basically two inhibitions to the progress of black television drama. First, drama is extremely expensive to do and very few black fictional programmes pull in the kind of audiences that one gets for straightforward white soap operas or mainstream white drama. And because drama is expensive, television companies tend to think ten times before they do it. So there is that very basic material reason why black television drama has not progressed.

The second reason has to do with the emergence of writers. No population, old or new to a country, can live without generating an imaginative output. It always will and it always does. But successive generations of black writers, I believe, to put it very simply, have been discouraged from producing imaginative work because of a kind of political mafiaism. Belief gets around that the only thing you ought to write about is something that will help race relations, or something that will 'represent' somebody. The critical criteria you place on yourself, therefore, becomes a kind of Stalinism of the mind. They try and police you, and you are then supposed to write in relation to ghetto criteria, which pleases other people.

These criteria mythologise Asians and blacks, the disabled, homosexuals, and so on. And when that becomes the norm we get two things — a politically inhibiting factor, and the encouragement of fashionable yobbery. By fashionable yobbery, I mean that such people try to impress the world with an image, and it is the sort of image which is not exploratory of the human spirit or of the potential drama of lives as they are lived. It is exploitative of how people can sell themselves — by the costume they wear, by the posturing they adopt and, I'm sorry to say, by the use of the well worn cliché of living in the dilemma of two cultures. Whenever I see those kinds of scripts I won't commission them.

There's an argument which says that the people who control the institutions of communication don't want fictional drama from a black perspective, and that they have no feel for black lives. I think that is absolute nonsense. I don't believe that anybody, consciously or unconsciously within television institutions, is picking on black drama and not commissioning. In fact, quite the opposite is happening. I believe that as soon as a person shows that he or she can string two sentences together, they will be snapped up as a potential BBC, Channel 4, ITV writer. Whether there are funds available for producers to bring that to fruition, I don't know.

I've seen a lot of nonsensical black drama being produced, with just the criteria that I've attacked. And the reason for this is because the liberal intelligentsia of Britain have noticed, and rightly noticed, that the cultural products of Britain have been restricted in large measure to a sort of middle-class output. Now they want to compensate for that with a vengeance, and the vengeance leans towards recruiting working class writers. The most obvious working class writer today is not your miner from Nottingham, nor somebody who can write yet another version of *The Ragged Trousered Philanthropist*, but the black writer, because there is a kind of liveliness, energy and anger in black writing – and people who commission things want that. They are paying lots of money for anger.

Ethnic provision in television ● Channel 4 began the trend of institutionalising so-called ethnic provision in broadcasting, and the ITV companies have, to some small extent, taken up this policy. But the BBC, to a very large extent, has picked up the idea that they ought to have separate ethnic departments, with their own budgets and with their own autonomy. I believe that for now this is absolutely correct. I believe there ought to be that autonomy, and I believe very seriously that the multicultural budget of Channel 4 ought to be trebled or quadrupled. And I am not simply saying that to expand my empire. I think there is a lot more to be done.

It is sometimes said that having a multicultural department stops other commissioning editors from even looking at proposals coming from the so-called black and ethnic sector. This is absolutely not the case. I think, in fact, quite the opposite happens. A healthy competition starts to grow – 'Can we in the drama department, or in current affairs, or in alternative film and video, do something better than what Farrukh can produce from India, Africa, and the black sector? Can our section make an even better feature film than *Salaam Bombay!*? Let's try and outdo the multicultural department and show them up'.

Those sort of criteria get a lot of investment – just look at the expansion of black programming at the BBC for instance. I don't think that would have happened without the existence of Channel 4's special multicultural department with it's own budgets. There wouldn't have been the competition and the emulation. For once, the notion of market economy is correct, that competition produces more quantity. I don't know about the quality, however, that's for you to judge.

— MIKE PHILLIPS —

Mike Phillips was born in Guyana and emigrated to join his family in Britain in 1956. Mike is the older brother of Trevor Phillips. After graduating from the University of London with a degree in English, Mike worked in a variety of jobs, including factory worker, garage mechanic and post office telephonist, before returning to college to study for an MA in Political Behaviour at Essex University and for a Post-Graduate Teaching Certificate at Goldsmiths' College. He subsequently worked as an outreach teacher in West London, started a hostel for homeless black youths in Notting Hill, and spent two years in Manchester as a Community Worker.

Mike also worked as a freelance writer, contributing to various publications including *The Guardian*, and joined the BBC World Service as a radio journalist. He edited *West Indian World* and worked as an Education Officer for BBC Further Education Television. From there he went to work for Diverse Productions which produced *The Friday Alternative* at the start of Channel 4 in 1982. He left to become a Senior Lecturer in Journalism and Media Studies at the Polytechnic of Central London. Mike was a founder member of the Black Media Workers' Association which was formed in 1980.

Apart from journalism, Mike has also published many books including *Community Work and Racism* (1982), *Smell of the Coast* (1987), a collection of short stories, three novels — *Blood Rights* (1989), *The Late Candidate* (1990), which won the Crime Writer's Association Silver Dagger Award, and *Boyz N the Hood* (1991) — and *Notting Hill in the 1960s* (1991), a photographic memoir. His next book, *Point of Darkness*, is due to be published in 1992.

In 1990 Mike adapted *Blood Rights* for BBC TV. He has also adapted *The Late Candidate* for Carlton Television as a two-hour film, to be broadcast in 1993.

The Black Media Workers' Association (BMWA) started up from a conversation between myself, Diane Abbott, Julian Henriques, Parminder Vir and Belkis Belgani. We met quite often, and at the first meeting there was also another guy called Glen Noble. We talked about the situation of black workers in the media and what we hoped for. Then we decided to form an association. This was 1980-1. We formed it as a sort of talking shop, a discussion group. Then it went through a progression which black organisations in this country have gone through in the past. It went from just five friends talking about it, to a series

of meetings which became more and more acrimonious, and then organisational chaos, and then it broke up.

BMWA was a professional association with a register of black media
workers in this country. It was part of a whole organisational network of
ideas which was designed to attract grants, for example. In a sense, it got
out of control. I think it should have been a different kind of organisation,
but we were slightly obsessed with the notion of creating a sort of pseudo-
political forum. I suppose it broke up because there wasn't quite the same
need for it any more. A number of things that we wanted to happen happened. And certainly the arrival of Channel 4 in 1982 changed the terms.
In the beginning there were only a few of us working in the media. But when
BMWA broke up lots of people were working in different parts of the media
and wanted different things.

Writing fiction ● I've long wanted to write fiction. I wrote a short story
when I was sixteen and thought then that I wanted to be writer. I've felt the
same ever since. I had written a play for the NUS (National Union of
Students) Drama Festival and it was quite well received. And I thought
'Yeah, I'm going to be a playwright'. So I wrote two or three plays, but
nobody was interested. After a period of about two years doing odd jobs, I
decided that I wanted to do something different, that I wanted a grip on life
which I couldn't have by sitting in my room writing plays and having them
rejected.

I eventually emerged as a journalistic writer, and that went on for quite a
long time. Then when I came to teach at the Polytechnic of Central London,
I took advantage of the fact that we had fairly long holidays and began
writing short stories during the holidays. *Blood Rights* came out of that – I
wrote it during one of my summer holidays. It was accepted for publication
fairly immediately. A couple of weeks after that, someone at the BBC rang
me and said that they heard that I had a book which was going to be
published next year, and that they wanted to have a look at it. A week after
that, they rang me up again and said they would like to commission a
television drama series of it.

Blood Rights **– the novel and the screenplay** ● When it came to writing
the screenplay for *Blood Rights*, I was at a loss because I didn't have any
real models. When I wrote the book, one of the things I was thinking of was
the American detective novel of the 30s and 40s. That had been part of my
reading for a long time, and those things tended to be translated to the
screen in the thriller film genre – James Cagney, Edward G. Robinson,
Alan Ladd – I loved most of those films. At the back of my mind I had
something that would look like that. I wasn't a great deal concerned about

Brian Bovell and Akim Mogaji in *Blood Rights* (BBC TV, 1990).

writing a black drama, as it were. That emerged as it got to the screen. I think, in a odd way, I was fairly naive about what would happen. I kept thinking 'OK, a detective thriller that says something about society, and I can turn it into a series, and that's how people will look at it, because that's how I want them to see it'. But what began to emerge was something a little different to that.

The main difference between what I had written in the novel and what emerged in the screenplay, is that when I wrote the novel I knew exactly what the shape of the detective thriller was. I was working in that genre and

I was faithfully reproducing a great many of the classic features of the detective novel. But when the production people at the BBC read the novel, partly because they didn't know anything about detective novels, or weren't particularly interested in that structure, they didn't see what I was aiming for. What they saw instead was a multiracial drama set in Britain. So I think the main difference that emerges between the television screenplay and the novel, is that there's a different kind of concentration on the way the characters interact with society, and on the way they interact with each other. The television version became something more involved with ideas about multiracialism and discrimination, than I had thought of in the novel.

It was a disappointment because I had in mind a much starker story. *Blood Rights* is structured around a mythical notion — what you've got is a heritage that is denied, somebody coming back to claim that heritage, and the confusion, and the pain, and the difficulties that ensue. It isn't about young delinquents or criminals, although those people do feature in it. It is a triangle in time and a triangle between characters. The way in which the story was constructed by television made it a fairly average domestic thriller. This obscured the strengths of the original conception of the story and the relevance of the myth.

Once I'd thought about it, I saw that myth as the situation of the black community — this is our heritage, we're partly fathered by this country, we return to claim a heritage, and we're denied. There are also a number of complex things going on within that which underpin the story. But the television version itself was simply, in popular terms, a thriller.

A question of identity ● The identity of the people in the novel is a kind of metaphor. What I was writing about has a lot to do with my own experience. Who am I? I'm an immigrant; I came here; I've been through a number of things; I went to university; I worked in garages; I washed dishes; I was into politics; I ran a self-help project; I was down fighting in the streets in Manchester and Birmingham; I had my troubles. In other words, I have been through the entire spectrum of the black community. And when I sat down to write the book, all those things were going through my head.

One of my crucial experiences, one of the things that made a difference to me, and which I was still struggling to understand, had to do with the actual identity of the black community. Another part of my identity is I come from the Caribbean. Although we talk continually about the Caribbean as African, it is actually a mongrelised area, both genetically and culturally. Show me one black person who is, as it were, of pure African descent, and I'll eat the bugger! Now, if you come from the Caribbean, one of the crucial areas of your heritage is precisely this genetic and cultural mixture. And one of the things that I saw in Britain, was the way that the black community here had started to become a mixed race community. Again, there is that sort of genetic mixture and adaptability which is characteristic of the Caribbean. But one of the things that happens in the black community is a kind of blindness about that. We've instead invoked an ideological notion which is linked to Africa and which is problematical.

Lots of people, when they think and talk about us and our identity, simply do not have the slightest idea of what we actually are. And one of the things we actually are, is a mixed race community. And I'm not just simply talking about a particular group, but throughout our whole identity – culturally, genetically, socially – we're mixed in a way that we don't seem to understand. I wanted to use the character of a mixed race boy and his situation in *Blood Rights*, to open up that can of beans and to talk about the black community in precisely those terms. That is, the sense in which an important part of our heritage, what we are, has to do with the parentage of the English culture and, if you like, an English genetic heritage. So, in a sense, it is true that the mixed race boy in the book is a metaphor for the situation of the black community and the theme of reclaiming a heritage which is being denied.

'Negative' images? ● I can't take seriously the notion that one is doing a disservice to black people by writing about all the different sorts of black people in our community. I write about black people who do wonderful things, but I also write about black people who do very nasty things as well. I think that if you're any kind of artist, you have to deal with the whole spectrum of human experience. The notion of sitting down consciously to write about black saints is a ludicrous one. I do not believe that I present the black community as uniquely criminal, or whatever. Criminal elements exist within the black community, as they exist among white people. But to say that because everybody thinks black people are criminals, you shouldn't write about black criminals, that is like asking me to operate within a racist context, and I refuse to do that. I am not going to spend my entire life looking over my shoulder to see what white people think.

We actually have to deal with the whole spectrum of black experience, because that is the only way we will begin to sort out what our real identity is, as opposed to some illusion of us being sort of 'noble Africans', somehow lost here in the developed world, in the belly of the beast! We have to understand who we are, rather than setting up a pretence, reading Eldridge Cleaver or something, and applying all those notions to our lives. There has been too much of that already. I think that the idea that you must somehow exemplify a liberal notion of black life when you write, is actually part of a racist context which demands that you go around making sure that people don't think there's anything less than saintly about black life. That is nonsense.

I don't have to question what the effect would be on black creativity, if people actually chose to work under those constraints, because we've seen the effects on black creativity for a long time now. The kind of opportunities that have been opened to us have always guided us away from the realm of ideas, from examining our individual notions about the nature of our collective lives and our collective identities. The most harmless and most acceptable things we can do have been to do with dancing and singing – and not just these, but the whole notion of black life has been fundamentally ghettoised. So, for instance, we're supposed to write in dialect in order to sound like a real black person. Real black language, nation language.

One of the interesting things about that is that we've probably got 165 different dialects in the Caribbean. A BBC Radio drama producer recently played me a tape of a play written in 'Black Caribbean dialect'. It was actually written by an African girl who'd only ever heard the kind of street language that comes from Bob Marley record albums. The dialect in which the play was written would have been incomprehensible even in the Caribbean, but it was presented to me as the real Caribbean dialect – 'Here is a real black writer because this person is writing in this kind of street slang'.

It's amazing how many of us who have no idea what our dialects are, pushed this notion of blackness as exemplified in a kind of corrupt slang, which they call dialect. That's the kind of thing that happens when we begin trying to impose unreal limits on individual creativity and vision. It doesn't happen to whites – you can't tell white writers that they should stick to writing about the working class or about the middle class or whatever, because somehow that would represent them in a way that other people would find distasteful. They would only tell you to push off and add 'I'm an individual artist' – and he or she would be quite right too. So why should I accept any less?

Black characters in contemporary drama ● There's a kind of flattening out of identity in the representation of black characters in contemporary drama. There are usually about two or three different types of black people. The way black characters are represented in Alan Bleasdale's *GBH*, for example, is very much in line with the way that any English playwright or screenwriter represents black characters. Black people are always acted upon. They're always reacting. They never ever have any sense of the initiative, and their lives are always totally bonded by the issue of discrimination. They're always confined by the responses of white people. So, if you look at anything that any white writer has written for the screen, what you see is a series of white reactions, and the space that they outline is where the black person is. The black person doesn't exist. It's like the English philosopher Bishop Berkeley's tag line – 'To be is to be perceived'.

White people look at black people in that way – you don't exist unless they're looking at you. And the screen writing that we see, with black characters, always has that sense of those black people only existing in terms of white people's perception of what they're about, how they might react, and how they live. They hardly ever break out of that. It is a relationship not between people, but between perceptions of that black person. And that black person is always reacting to those white perceptions – if a black person is perceived as awkward, difficult or whatever, it's in terms of white perceptions of what that might mean.

So, to come back to *GBH*. We always see the people in Liverpool reacting to the various manipulations of the Michael Murray figure, who wants to do something for black people, and the issue is whether they appreciate it or not. The secret service wants to manipulate people and the issue is whether they'll respond or not. There is a dramatic incident where this guy gets out of the van, he sees a group of black youths coming up the road, and says 'They're the ones who have been causing all the trouble'. And, of course, the youths immediately converge on the van and beat up everyone in sight – they're that stupid, they just need this guy to say that.

Now, I was in Liverpool at the time of the uprisings in 1981. I know a lot of people there, and one thing they're not is stupid. The riots didn't happen because people were being manipulated. They happened as the result of specific conditions and attitudes. And the way that black people are written about really upsets me, especially in Liverpool, because Liverpool is probably the longest serving and the most authentic black community in Britain, and it happens to be mostly mixed race as well. It's a community that has been so badly treated. The problems of the black community in Liverpool are continually subsumed, obscured and disguised in the rigid British notion of class, the working class. There's something more than working class going on there, that's why those people are stuck in Liverpool 8. And it really upsets me that none of those playwrights has ever taken the trouble to actually take on the objective conditions under which black people live in Liverpool. And that certainly includes Alan Bleasdale.

Channel 4 and so-called ethnic minority programming ● I'm not sure what Channel 4's broadcasting policy is towards ethnic minorities. Speaking as a viewer, it is true that I see a number of documentaries about the Third World. It seems to me that they tend to go for the notion that somehow we belong to the Third World, and that what they're doing is exploring the culture, the films, and the customs of Third World people. And what's supposed to make it interesting or relevant to black people in this country, is that it's actually being done by black people, or being done in a more authentic and respectful way.

From my point of view, it's a barren and banal sort of policy. And I feel very strongly about it because one of the things that we argued about before the setting up of Channel 4 was that the coverage of Third World affairs ought to be better, that Third World concerns ought to be injected more precisely and strongly into the current affairs and news agenda. I'm disappointed, and have been disappointed for some time, by the sense in which those things are ghettoised into what amounts to travel documentaries. It's very interesting to see a documentary about corruption in Pakistan or about politics in Trinidad for example. But as a black person living in this country, trying to construct a life or another identity for myself and my children, it is not particularly useful. I would like to see a policy that is directed more towards talking about what we are, giving us the sense to emerge from what I call the kind of dumbness that is imposed on us.

One of the things that happens continually is that we aren't able to speak to each other across a broad front. I imagine that there is a ground swell of ideas, attitudes, and concerns among young black people in certain directions, which simply don't emerge on television or in the programming schedules. I'm thinking about the fact that such a huge proportion of the black community here is mixed race for instance. We don't talk about the implications of that and there is nothing, I suspect, within ethnic minority programming to enable that to happen. There is no possibility of dealing with that question, apart from some sort of ridiculous crisis-laden discussion with a hundred people shouting at each other in the studio. We don't have the possibility of dealing with those things, because it isn't part of the way that the white people who are in control want to represent the black community.

An increasing gap has been developing in the representation of black experiences in ethnic minority programming – between the sense of black people as media images on the one hand, and a sense of black people as real people on the other. I'm sure what they're trying to approach is the sense of black people as real people, but, ironically, what has happened is that black people are being presented more and more as 'ethnic', as 'Third World', as 'alien' to the concerns of people in this country. So if you actually want to get a sense of what your life is like as a black person, you are left high and dry, because there is nothing that makes any sense in that strand of programming. I think it's a great pity because an opportunity has been lost.

A Utopian vision ● I don't think that what I want to see on television in terms of media representation is in anyway utopian. The only reason it sounds at all utopian is because we live in a racist context, in which we're treated as groups and as images. What I want to see is more freedom being given to individual artistes in the black community to control the images they offer. I want to see more space provided, so that every time a black person does something, he or she doesn't have to stand or fall entirely on that one thing. I want to see, if you like, an area in which things can be tried and pursued, in the same way that whites are able to do.

What we desperately need is not representation, not the voice of groups, but the voices of individuals. What I want is more room for individuals and less, if you like, of the politicisation of an artistic vision. That isn't to say that the artistic vision of individuals won't be politically relevant. That's not the point. The point is to get out from under the caricature and the sense that what we must do is to continue to reflect a pre-existing image that was established within a racist context.

— TRIX WORRELL —

Trix Worrell was born in St Lucia and came to Britain when he was five. As a teenager he joined the Albany Youth Theatre in Deptford, South East London, then run by director Martin Stellman. Trix has been writing and directing the Channel 4 sitcom *Desmond's* since 1989, and has also written various other projects for film and television.

A graduate of the National Film and Television School, Trix won Channel 4's Debut '84 New Writers competition for his play *Mohicans*, which was subsequently produced by Channel 4 as *Like a Mohican* and shown in 1985.

In 1989 Trix co-authored (with Martin Stellman) the feature film *For Queen and Country* which starred Denzil Washington, and in 1990 he acted as Executive Producer on the science fiction film *Hardware*. Through his own company, Writers Ink, Trix is developing a range of ideas, treatments and comedies for film and television.

I started writing because there weren't many parts for black actors, and the parts that were available weren't particularly good. I was an actor originally and whenever I got parts to read, I used to think 'My god, I can write better than this. How come we're not getting enough good roles?' Some friends of mine just said 'Why the hell don't you start writing, then?' So I did. I got a group of friends together to do my first play, which was called *School's Out*, which ended up at the Royal Court. That was in 1980. Then we formed our own theatre company called The Ordinary Basement Youth Theatre, which no longer exists. I wrote and directed and became a bit of a megalomaniac, but it was actually a real training ground in terms of my writing. I was also a trainee on the Arts Council's theatre directors course at the Albany Theatre in Deptford, South London, and I was assisting on various other professional plays.

Eventually, when I left the Albany, we had professional actors within our production, so I directed several professional shows as well. But then I got to a stage where I felt that I had had enough of theatre, because it has its limitations and I wanted to go beyond the proscenium arch. So I applied to the National Film and Television School and got in, initially as a producer before changing to the writer/director's course. I then wrote a film called *For Queen and Country* with Martin Stellman, and then went into television to write *Desmond's*. That's how I started writing.

For Queen and Country (1989) ● *For Queen and Country* was based on the actual experience of a black veteran of the Falklands War who subsequently couldn't get a British passport. When Britain changed the Nationality Act in 1981, it affected me and an awful lot of other people, including the likes of Irwin Eversley, the person on whom we based the film. The Act meant that they could now redefine you as a black person. It also meant that you had to pay for the privilege of being a British citizen, when, in many ways, they should be paying us. That's my personal conviction, because we've done an awful lot for Britain. So the passion and the power to write the play were all there.

Irwin's case was particularly interesting because it represented a black man in uniform, and I always think there is something incongruous about black people in uniform. I still question that image. I also question images of Linford Christie swathed in the Union Jack and what that represents. Uniforms always represent the army or fighting for a particular cause – and in this particular case it was the Falklands War – and it just seemed such a trifling thing to be fighting for. Here you have this black man who is willing to lay down his life for this country, who is actually killing people in the name of the cause – he stopped counting when he got to thirteen. Then after that experience, he was told he was no longer British, that he would have to apply for citizenship, and that it would cost him £200. I mean, it speaks volumes.

I think Martin Stellman did an honourable job in directing the film. The great thing was that he co-wrote the script with me, so we were fighting the battles together in order to get the money. Martin stuck very true to the script. I think eighty per cent of what is written is actually up there on the screen. But that's because he was the co-writer and director of the piece, and we sat down and had a shared vision of how we wanted to make the film. All too often you hand over your screenplay to someone, get a pat on the back and are told to go away.

Obviously, you can never have complete control over how a film is made, as we found with the casting of an American, Denzil Washington, in the lead role. There is a marriage between creativity and money and, unfortunately, the two really don't mix, though one feeds the other. So in terms of Denzil, what they needed was a black actor who would put bums on seats. But, in all honesty, I wasn't happy with the decision to use an American actor. I wanted to use a black English actor to portray what is ostensibly a black English story and struggle. I felt that to bring in an American was a real cop-out. Having said that, and in all justice to Denzil, I think he did an amazing job.

For Queen And Country was critically well received in this country. But there was a major problem from a political standpoint, in the sense that it made certain people in important places very nervous. A classic example was when we had a journalist from the *Sunday Times* who wanted to interview me about the film. He knew very little about the new Nationality Act, so he phoned the Home Office to get more information. When he said who he was and told them that he was doing an article on me and the film, they said 'Yes, we know all about Trix Worrell, thank you very much' and put the phone down on him.

To be totally honest with you, I think there were some rumblings upstairs, because we had a distribution deal which was going to go nationwide with UIP – and you can't get bigger than that, really, over here. But then in the second week into *For Queen And Country* it got pulled and the film wasn't exhibited nationally. Interestingly, it was then released on video by Sony, and there was something in the region of £750,000 worth of business done on it. So, yes, I'm bitterly disappointed that it actually didn't get a chance to be shown nationwide.

Desmond's (1989 to the present) ● After *For Queen And Country*, which took some two-and-a-half years out of my life, I got a phone call from my agent saying that Humphrey Barclay and Farrukh Dhondy were looking for a new comedy series and that they were interested in meeting me. At the time, I didn't have the vaguest idea of any comedy I wanted to write. I'd never written comedy before, though I had written satirical material for the theatre. I was very nervous about entering sitcom territory. Anyway, I was on my way to meet Humphrey on the bus when I spotted a barber shop – the bus must have pulled up at a set of traffic lights and it was about nine o'clock in the morning. All these school girls were coming past and I saw these guys, three barbers, with their faces pressed up against the shop window, ogling.

I remember it so vividly, because the barber shop around the corner from where I was brought up in Peckham (South East London) was like that. And that's how the idea for *Desmond's* came to me. I sold it to Humphrey as a verbal pitch there and then, and he bought it. Then we had to sit down and really examine the kind of images that we would be creating in *Desmond's* – because we wanted to make sure that they were positive. We didn't want to rely on the cheap kind of racial jokes, so to speak. We wanted to say something positive about black families and, more importantly, about migrant families within this country and what it is to be black in England. That's how we set about creating *Desmond's*.

The funny thing is, before I had actually made up my mind whether to pursue this or not, even though Humphrey had bought the idea and had said he wanted to do it, a lot of my friends were urging me not to do it. They thought I would be letting the side down by going into sitcom territory, or

Justin Pickett, Kim Walker, Norman Beaton, Carmen Munroe and Geff Francis in Trix Worrell's popular sitcom *Desmond's* (Channel 4).

what they regarded as cliché territory. But the more people told me not to do it, the more determined I was to do it. I thought 'Well, at the end of the day if I don't do it, somebody else will. So why not me?'

Interesting characters in *Desmond's* ● In everything I've written, I have tried to highlight the fact that there are a number of different islands in the Caribbean, and that we're not all Jamaican! One needs to emphasise this even today. Initially, the idea was for the characters in *Desmond's* to be St Lucian – which is probably a bit too close to home. My mum and dad would have probably jumped up and down about it. But the way things eventually fell into place made it more Guyanese in the end – Norman Beaton, Carmen Munroe and, indeed, Ram John Holder, who plays Porkpie, are all Guyanese. So I thought we might as well go with the strengths of that situation.

Michael, the son, is a reflection of my generation and my type of friends who were driven educationally to do their A-levels and to go to university, and so on. I made him a bit of a protagonist, mainly to add more colour, really, for want of a better word, and to enhance the dramatic situation. And the African character, Matthew – the reason I had him in initially was that I remembered when I was a kid at school, there were always conflicts between Africans and West Indians, and it was 'mega' in Peckham, I can tell you. It was really a question of misunderstanding between the two communities. But because there are a large number of Africans in South East London, I felt that it was truer to form to have an African in the series. And also the whole joke about Matthew being an eternal student, that is true, in the sense that there are a lot of Africans who are eternal students because of their political circumstances or whatever.

I also thought that having an ongoing African character in the series would add an interesting dynamic between Afro-Caribbean or West Indian and African cultures – by actually showing the similarities or, indeed, the disparities between the two and how far down the road we, as Caribbean peoples, have gone from our original cultures. It was nice to discover a lot about that subject and to do some research into it, and to actually get to present it in television drama.

Re-vamping *Desmond's* ● I've now started directing some episodes of *Desmond's*, which I see as a natural progression. I always wanted to write and direct. So now we're coming to the fourth series I'm directing a lot more, and we've also brought in new writers, which is good – ninety per cent of them are women, which is also very good because we felt that *Desmond's* was a bit top heavy with men.

They also want me to do much more with the Shirley character (played by Carmen Munroe), like exploring the idea of the middle-aged West Indian woman in London and the dilemma she has about either going back to the Caribbean or staying here. Actually, Shirley has made up her mind to stay. We all know that about her, but what will she do with herself? So that's interesting to start looking into now. Hopefully, we'll bring on board a black producer at some stage as well. I would also like to see more black people behind the camera, but there is a very great shortage of black camera people. So, positive steps are being taken to improve the quality of *Desmond's* both in terms of its content and its production set-up.

Desmond's is incredibly popular in the Caribbean. It's also doing very well in America where it is shown on Black Entertainment Television, the black cable network. I went to the South London barber shop on which I based *Desmond's* to get my hair cut, and they told me that six black Americans from Chicago came over recently to take photographs of the shop because of *Desmond's*. So it's something that has really gone beyond my wildest dreams. Initially, I thought that I was going to get savaged for this one; then, at the end of the first series, I thought that it had grown and was getting better. If more writers come on board, I think it will get better still.

The strangest thing is that since *Desmond's*, I've been getting phone calls asking me to write sitcoms for other stations. Why on earth didn't they commission stuff before? Why have they waited for *Desmond's* to come along? Other black sitcoms have proved popular in the past, so it's not a question of television companies not having the statistics. We should be examining the black experience in England and we should be seeing that experience incorporated much more in television output. But I don't think that will happen for a long time, because there are people in power who would like to keep it that way.

British broadcasting and multicultural programming ● I personally think that British broadcasting is a stuffy little establishment that needs its backside kicked. For me, the main problems still are that black production can only be done via comedy, or you only see black faces via singing and dancing, for instance. We have the likes of Trevor McDonald in terms of news and current affairs. But we should be breaking it open now, and we should certainly have more black television drama. It's about time that we actually had more actors doing drama and showing off their skills, because I think there's a serious amount of talent out there, and I'm talking to some of them now.

As for having special multicultural commissioning sections in broadcasting companies, I think this effectively lets everybody else off the hook. At the end of the day, it seems to me that there's always this 'one-only' mentality which says that it's OK to have one black show, but if there's more than one then there's a problem. It's like it is OK to see one black man walking down a road, but if there are two or more, people start to think they might try to mug somebody. So now we have a Multicultural Commissioning Editor, the attitude is we have taken care of the black problem in terms of access to mainstream broadcasting, and we can just put everything into that slot, ghettoise it, marginalise it. This attitude, which is all too common in the broadcasting industry, says in effect that black people haven't many stories to tell which are universal stories. This is frankly not true.

Charlie Hanson has worked extensively as a theatre director at the Royal Court, The National Theatre, the ICA, Riverside Studios, and Sheffield's Crucible Theatre. He is a co-founder of the Black Theatre Co-operative. His television production credits include three series of Channel 4's sitcom, *No Problem!* (1982-5) which he co-devised and produced, *Party at the Palace* (1984), the first ever British independent entry at the Golden Rose of Montreux TV Festival, producer of *The Management* (1987), written by and starring Hale and Pace, co-producer and one of the directors of the Channel 4 sitcom *Desmond's* (from 1989), one of the directors of the BBC comedy series *Birds of a Feather* (from 1990), producer and director of the BBC TV's *The Real McCoy* (from 1990), and producer of *The 291 Club* for LWT (from 1991).

In 1978, I was working with the Trinidadian playwright Mustafa Matura at the Royal Court and we got on well. I was offered another play of his to direct called *Welcome Home, Jacko*. We touted it around various theatres, but everyone turned it down. I was sure that it was going to be a success, but the problem was that theatres didn't really know how to read the script. It was written with a sort of London Trinidadian patois in mind, and needed a cast of young black teenagers. Theatres in those days, of course, didn't really know any young black actors, nor had they experienced any. So they didn't know how to read the play, and they didn't know where to find a cast.

So it was out of frustration, really, that we formed the Black Theatre Co-operative, to put on *Welcome Home, Jacko*, and the success of that led us to tour for a year. We then wanted to work together again and do another production, so one of the actors, Victor Romero Evans, and I went in search of Farrukh Dhondy. We had read one of his books, and we got him to write for us. It escalated from there. It was a working relationship that we all liked and wanted to continue. For most of us, it was the first time that we were actually being paid to do what we wanted to do and also touring the world. That was an advantage, we actually enjoyed travelling around Europe and experiencing things.

The main thing I noticed through that experience was that theatres that purported to do new work by new writers really didn't know how to read scripts by black writers because they didn't have that experience. Of course, I didn't really know how any better than them, but because I was working with young black actors, I could tell if a piece would work and I've learnt from them ever since, really.

No Problem! **(1982-5)** ● The Black Theatre Co-operative worked for about five years, putting on new plays in various theatres around London and building up a fairly loyal young black audience, including young people still at school and teenagers – in other words, the kind of people who hadn't been to the theatre before. And amongst that audience were people from other theatres and a few liberal executives from television companies, like Humphrey Barclay, who was then Head of Comedy at London Weekend Television. Unbeknown to us Humphrey had seen all of our productions and he recognised a nucleus of talent working together. He rang up one day and said that he was coming to the show and wanted to meet us afterwards. He more or less offered us the opportunity to create a situation comedy for LWT. They had been trying for years to put something on screen with black actors by black writers but had failed. Perhaps we could do it?

Well, that invitation led us to do workshops on devising characters – it was a collaborative group effort. We had not really worked in a television studio before, so we learnt a lot and had a lot of fun. But then because the series was going on for three years, we found it quite a difficult show to do because of it being comedy. I think it started to delve into stupidness in the second series, and we started to disagree among ourselves about what we should be doing with it.

The other problem was that it was the only black show on television at the time. What I've realised, especially since coming back to do *Desmond's* and *The Real McCoy*, is that when you're the only black show on television and you're a comedy show, there is a responsibility both for the performers and for what is being said in the piece. The actors in *No Problem!* certainly came under a lot of pressure. We took a lot of stick from the black press, and became aware that, because there was nothing else happening, everybody expected something from this one show. They all wanted to be represented in it, wanted to see 'positive images'. Black situation comedy comes under the microscope far more than any other situation comedy on television. Nobody discusses *Birds of a Feather*, for example, which I'm also working on at the moment, to the same lengths as they discuss *Desmond's*. So there is this added pressure on black situation comedy.

The Real McCoy **(from 1990)** ● *The Real McCoy* came about after a series of coincidences, really. I was working with Curtis and Ishmael and we were doing *The 291 Club* at the Hackney Empire. We had proposed that show to the BBC, but they weren't particularly interested in it. They came

Richard Curtis and Ishmael Thomas in *The Real McCoy* (BBC TV, 1990).

to see Curtis and Ishmael perform anyway, and then they had a meeting with me literally to see whether there were other young black comedians out there that I would want to do a television sketch show with. They more or less said they would like me to do that. And because it was an opportunity I took it, and it all happened very quickly.

What I liked about it was the opportunity to do a sketch show which would also open the way for a lot of new writers to come in and almost serve an apprenticeship, because they would only have to write a few minutes at a time. What I didn't realise was that it is probably harder to write two-minute sketches and be funny, than it is to write a narrative story and be funny. We had people who could develop good characters, but who found it quite hard to make their sketches really short, succinct, funny and sharp. We didn't get it right and now I actually want to do another series of *The Real McCoy*, because I realise how difficult it is to do that kind of show.

Any new comedy has to come from people who have got something to say. Obviously, we have had *The Young Ones* and *The Comic Strip* people who came after the Oxbridge bunch, if you like – that generation comprising *Footlights* at Cambridge and *The Revues* at Oxford. I think what you will see now is young black comedians who are expressing themselves and who have something to say. While that exists, there will be quite a few more of them coming onto the screen, I'm sure, in other series. But I hope it won't rely on *The Real McCoy* to develop all that talent. I just hope that there will be other shows for people to perform in.

Avoiding ghettoisation ● There is still the problem of black comedy programmes being ghettoised. Certainly when *No Problem!* was on, and I think now that *Desmond's* is on, it would be difficult to get another black comedy on because commissioning editors would argue that their budget is going into *Desmond's*. I think this is wrong because television companies don't actually judge comedy on this basis. They simply say 'Let's have another comedy' and they do it. I think once you have a success like *Desmond's*, it ought to be financed out of the mainstream light entertainment budget and not be part of the multicultural budget. This would then enable the multicultural department to use its limited resources to develop other, perhaps newer and more interesting black-related projects.

One of the things that appealed to me about doing *The Real McCoy* for the BBC was that it was for the Head of Comedy, that is, someone who has been producing *Bread* and all kinds of other comedies, who didn't have a particular multicultural axe to grind and who wasn't looking for that particular perspective. He actually came because he thought Curtis and Ishmael were funny and he wanted to do a show with them. Of course, it's taken a different turn for Curtis and Ishmael since that initial meeting, but the whole initiative was extremely important for the development of black television comedy.

I think the most acute gap in terms of black representation in British broadcasting is in the area of producers, directors, production managers, and stage management. If you're working as an independent, as I do with *The 291 Club*, you can actually have an all-black production team working on a black show. But, ironically, you can't have that when you go into an institution like the BBC to do a black show. When I went to the first meeting for *The Real McCoy*, for example, it was quite clear that there was no black person in the entertainment department of the BBC at any level, not one, and I pointed out how ironic it was to have a group of white people sitting around discussing a new black show.

The BBC have now agreed to advertise various training posts and so on, but I think they've got a long way to go yet. They tend to get one person in each department and, of course, that person leaves because s/he is then looked upon as the spokesperson for the black community within entertainment or drama. Most of the black people I know who have gone into the BBC don't want to be the sole person having to face all that. They would much rather have a few colleagues and people around with whom to talk about all kinds of things, and not just have to represent the black issues within a department. So, until you get dozens of black people just working normally in a television department, it's going to be quite difficult to effect real changes.

The BBC have said that they want to change things, but I think they're encumbered by the way they go about doing it. It is easier for independents because we can just pick freelance people for individual productions. But the BBC have obviously got stuck in their ways, as to how they develop talent. I think that's the main problem, particularly with writers and in the drama area. I was at another one of these talks about this same subject, when an Executive Producer from *EastEnders* spoke about how difficult it was to find black writers and how expensive the whole process would be if they went out to look for black writers.

I realised that it wasn't to do with expense or with the difficulty, it was just to do with a lack of knowledge about where to go to find the talent. That's why I don't think change has happened in drama at the BBC, or anywhere else for that matter. It has happened in comedy to a small extent, and in news and current affairs because of individuals like Trevor Phillips, Sharon Ali, and Samir Shah, all of whom started their careers in a particular department at LWT, before branching out. What would make all the difference, would be to have people in the organisation who know where to go to find the talent. But, as I said, there's a long way to go in that area still.

The main problem is that there are too many executives and too large an administration of people who do not mix in the right places. They don't go out to look for the right talent. I don't think it's fear. It's just ignorance and leading sheltered lives, basically. That's what it comes down to. There are one or two exceptions to the rule – Humphrey Barclay actively went out looking for talent, and I know that Michael Grade, when he was at LWT, backed him up. What we really need in the different institutions are people at the top who act, and not just make speeches and talk about figures and percentages. We need people to go out and do something about it. When I see those people going to black plays, then I'll believe some of what they're saying.

Judith Jacob was born in London and, while still at school, started working with the Anna Scher Theatre. At the age of seventeen she joined the cast of the BBC series *Angels* as Nurse Beverley Slater, a role she played for three years.

Judith played many leading roles for the Black Theatre Co-operative and, along with other members of the company, devised *No Problem!*, the Channel 4 sitcom which ran for three series from 1983-5. On 5 June 1986, Judith joined the cast of the popular BBC soap opera *EastEnders* as health visitor Carmel.

Since leaving the series in 1989, she has made several stage appearances, including *Twelfth Night* (as Maria) with the Birmingham Repertory Company. In 1991 Judith toured in Mustapha Matura's play *Meetings*.

I was very fortunate, in that I was one of those people who went to Anna Scher's Theatre. I decided I wanted to be an actress when I was about nine years old, but I didn't know how I was going to do it. A friend at school told me about the Anna Scher Theatre, so I went there and had my first audition for a thing called *Jumping Bean Bag*. It was actually called *Slag Bag* initially, but because it was for BBC TV they had to change the title! I was fourteen and I applied for my Equity card because I was told I had to. I didn't understand it, my mother didn't understand it, I couldn't explain it, but we got it nevertheless. And that was my entrance into the business. I then started auditioning for other jobs.

Angels (1980-2) ● *Angels* was my first major acting job and I had to leave school to do it. I was in the middle of my A-levels at the time. Both my maths teacher and my English teacher were not keen on me leaving. My maths teacher was black and she was very good at making sure that her black students studied. My English teacher was married to a black man and she had the same sort of attitude about her black students. She wanted to make sure that they progressed. So neither of them was keen about me leaving school. They thought I should go to university and take up acting there. Anyway, I left school at seventeen to do *Angels*, and that was the beginning of my acting career.

When I got the part in *Angels*, my main thing was 'I'm now on the path to being what I want to be'. I had never watched *Angels* and assumed that no young person ever watched it. Then I got on the bus one day and a bunch of school kids stared at me, and I started to get paranoid. When that happened, I got off the bus and bawled my eyes out. I went to meet my young man and told him about all these people staring at me and how I didn't know why they were doing this to me. That was my reaction.

I don't think I was aware that I was breaking any barriers as a black person, because at seventeen I don't think I was very aware at all. I had no historical background to myself. I listened to reggae music, and reggae music was very instrumental in telling people what was going on. But I was living in a little cocoon. I was OK, so I didn't notice anything.

The Black Theatre Co-operative ● It wasn't until I had left *Angels*, after three years in the show, that my attitude changed. I left *Angels* because I didn't want to be there any more. And then Trevor Laird, who was directing a production for the Black Theatre Co-operative called *Trojans*, asked me if I would join it, which I did. There was another actor in that, Archie Pool, who was so wonderful to me. We were having interviews and I was asked what sort of parts I wanted to play, and I said 'All the classics – any of Shakespeare, Brecht – I want to do all of them'. And Archie sat there and said 'Well, you know, I would like to do any of the African classics'. I didn't even know that there were African classics. He gave me some books to read, including one called *Destruction of the Black Civilisation* by William Chancellor – that was the first black book I had read and it was an amazing eye-opener for me. And so that to me was just wonderful. It was my first black theatre production, and Archie was there as my guiding torch, feeding me books. If I had questions, he'd feed me books and he gave me a lot of inspiration.

The Black Theatre Co-operative was really important for my development, because I was with people who were aware of their culture and were willing to share it, and I met people who shared it with me, Archie Pool being the main person. And because I enjoyed reading, I was able to take these books, read them, move on, and still keep reading them. So I started my whole re-education a bit late, but at least it happened from my point of view.

No Problem! **(1983-5)** ● *No Problem!* came about because Humphrey Barclay, who was then Head of Light Entertainment at London Weekend Television, approached the Black Theatre Co-operative about devising a comedy series. Up until then, I don't think there had been a comedy series written by black writers. There were just black actors employed in them. So we workshopped for four weeks and, at the end of that period, we produced three ideas that we thought were good. *No Problem!* was our personal

Judith Jacob in *No Problem!* (Channel 4, 1983-5).

favourite, the writers had another favourite. Humphrey and ourselves
agreed on the *No Problem!* subject and that's what we worked on. So the
first series was mainly workshopped ideas, things that we had already
developed when we were working it out. It was brilliant working on *No
Problem!* because it was our ideas, our writers, and we were working with
friends. We also had control over what was going on up to a degree, which is
something you never have as an actor. Normally, you come in, you're

employed, you do your lines, and you go home. But on *No Problem!*, we came in, looked at the script, looked at the set, and could say 'Rubbish, ain't having that . . . Move that . . . Take that out . . . Oh, that's nice . . .'

In retrospect, I think *No Problem!* was probably more successful than we realised at the time. We were young people then putting our ideas down. It reflected on black people because we were black people, and our whole approach to our lives is from that perspective. But, at the same time, we could afford to take our humour in different directions from the norm. And because of that, I think the humour in *No Problem!* was probably advanced for its day. We were dealing with things in a way that was often different from how most black people were used to seeing things. If they watched it now, they'd go 'Yeah!'. But at the time I kept getting a lot of aggravation about being a black woman on a motorcycle for example. Even if there are only two black women on a motorcycle in real life, there's nothing wrong in representing black women on a motorcycle in a piece of fiction. But people were all saying that it was not realistic. This shows how even we can pigeonhole ourselves sometimes.

EastEnders (1986-9) ● I was working on another production with the Black Theatre Co-operative called *Waiting for Hannibal*, when Julia Smith (who was then a producer at the BBC) approached me and asked if I would be interested in doing *EastEnders*. Julia had produced *Angels* – she and Tony Holland (who was also part of the *EastEnders* team) produced and wrote it, so they knew me. They also knew that I had a nine-month-old daughter and said that they could work around it. So I went and did a couple of episodes, and then dropped out for a bit, because I was doing a play at the time and I couldn't really do any more. A year later they asked me if I would come in as a regular, which I did. It was pretty easy, really.

I came in as a health visitor. All I knew at that time, was that I was going to be looking after Pauline Fowler and Mary, the punk rocker. And then they decided to give my character some sort of love interest, so they linked me with Kelvin, who was the only other youngish black person in the show for me to have a relationship with. It was sort of the young boy/older woman situation. They didn't really develop it, but it was there. Then I had a brother, Darren – they discussed with me the idea for this character and how they wanted him to be sort of a wide boy, in comparison to the Leslie Grantham 'Dirty Den' character. Gary MacDonald came in to do that and he played the part brilliantly. I thought he was wonderful in it.

There were criticisms about the Darren character, because in people's eyes it was a black person playing a negative part. I can agree with that to the extent that that is probably how the majority of black men are seen on television. But from *EastEnders*' point of view, it was the first time that they had portrayed a black person from that perspective. Up until then, there had only been very good black people in the series. So Darren came in and I had this conflict with him because of his way of living; and, at the same time, I was dealing with all the problems of a health worker. All these things gave my character a new and interesting dimension.

Then we discussed my future with *EastEnders* because originally I was only intending to stay for two years, and I had said that I would leave after that. But they asked me to stay, and the storyline was that they would bring in a new love interest, and I would get married, etcetera. They wanted a state of conflict — which means that it had to be somebody opposite to myself, and that's when they brought in a white person, the Matthew character. I don't think they ever intended it to be like *Mixed Blessings* though. There were constant arguments about colour, because my family was against the relationship — my parents were not keen, and my brother, Darren, wasn't keen.

So we had two things happening in relation to the development of my character — first a mixed marriage, and then a potential wife-battering situation which developed later on. From my point of view as an actress, it was brilliant. I got to play a part that I had not played before. The conflict was a white man beating a black woman. I know it's easy for me to defend it, because you tend to get defensive about parts you play. But what many viewers saw, and what I was told, was that it was like slavery days. I was the domicile woman in the house, and there was the big master beating me. It was very strange hearing this because, if I had looked at it like that, I would never have done it. But I never saw it in that context. I saw a marriage breaking down, and I saw a classic wife-beating situation developing.

What would have been interesting is if it had been a black man and a black woman — what would have been the reaction then? Personally, I don't think I would have been happy if it was a black man beating a black woman. But then people were not happy with a white man beating a black woman. Therefore, does that mean we can never portray a wife-battering situation involving a black woman? It's questions like that to which I don't know the answers. They remain questions.

I think *EastEnders* has probably put itself out to be tested, because it has included black people in the storylines, unlike a lot of other soap operas. But you cannot just have black actors and hope that there will not be problems, or that all problems will be rectified, because you cannot fight a situation on your own. I can say, as an actor, that if I personally do not think something is right, and if there is enough time, the director will address it. But usually there is a short timetable and we have to move quickly. This is why we need more black writers and black directors working in television. They would be able to address problems before they get to

Judith Jacob and Stephen Hartley in *EastEnders* (BBC TV, 1988).

the floor, when everything starts to get confused. And I don't mean just one black director or one black writer. It's horrible to have just one black person always having to fight situations on his or her own. We need a couple of black writers, a couple of black directors.

In general, I think *EastEnders* is doing something positive and it's good. I understand that a couple of black writers have joined the team, though I don't know what's happening on the directing side. But there is still a long way to go right across the whole of television output, a very long way to go.

In the end, I stayed with *EastEnders* for three years. I had no intention of staying longer than that. I feel too young. I don't want to go through my life saying 'If only . . . if only . . . if only . . .'. But if they offer me a part when I'm forty-five or fifty, I'll take it and I'll stay!

The lack of continuity ● Personally, I feel that, for black people, television goes in circles. There is a period when we think that it's all happening, and then it goes quiet again. So it seems to come down to when you're in vogue. A typical example was when we were doing *No Problem!* and the BBC had nothing. Then they decided to do *The Frontline.* We then stopped doing *No Problem!* and they stopped doing *The Frontline.* Suddenly there was no more black television, no more black programming. I would love to think that there's some sort of continuity happening because – I have to be positive – I'm in this business. But when I talk to people who have been in the business a lot longer than me, and I see the circles that they've been through, I do begin to wonder whether things will ever change.

There aren't any British black actors that you could say are named black stars, like a Denzil Washington for instance. We could say that Norman Beaton, Carmen Munroe, and Rudolph Walker are those people; but they are not stars in the same way because there is no continuity in this business. And I think that black women probably suffer more than black men, because men get more parts than women and, therefore, they get more opportunities. I hope it will get better, because it has to. But I think it comes back to the writers, directors, and producers. That's where the power is, that's where we need more black people employed.

Whenever I watch a television trailer for a new series – or when they advertise a whole new season of stuff – I watch to see how many black faces there are. And then I say 'Interesting, a whole new series is starting and not a black face to be seen'. This is especially true when television goes into the classics. Britain is currently going through a recession and has become very patriotic, so the emphasis is on showing British culture again, which means in effect omitting anything that is not white. By the look of what's currently happening on British television we seem to be going through one of those phases.

Paul J. Medford was born in London and trained at the Barbara Speake Stage School. He made his film debut at the age of eight opposite Norman Beaton in the film *Black Joy* (1977) and later worked as a session singer with Kid Creole and the Coconuts.

Paul was in the original cast of the BBC soap opera *EastEnders* which was launched on 19 February 1985. He played Kelvin Carpenter for over two years before leaving the cast on 3 September 1987.

In 1990 Paul appeared on stage at the Theatre Royal, Stratford, in the hit musical *Five Guys Named Moe*, which transferred to London's West End Lyric Theatre on 14 December 1990. Paul's performance as Little Moe earned him critical praise and a nomination for a Laurence Olivier award for Outstanding Actor in a Musical.

My background in acting is, I guess, quite unconventional in the normal sense, but pretty conventional in a theatrical sense. My parents sent me to the Barbara Speake Stage School when I was about four. It was the sort of school where you did maths in the morning and tap or drama in the afternoon, and, in between that, you were sent out for a commercial audition or a television audition. I think between the ages of about five and thirteen, I played lots of African princes in various episodes of *The Professionals*, *Minder*, and so on. That's how it began, really.

Black Joy (1977) ● I can remember *Black Joy* distinctly, because it went to the Cannes Film Festival and it was my first major film. In fact, it was my first role where I had to speak and actually know what on earth I was doing. It was shot on location in Brixton and it had a pretty strong cast which included Norman Beaton and Floella Benjamin. It was shot over about six months on a really tight budget. But, of course, I was completely unaware of all this at the time. I was just going out every day and having fun, with a tutor every now and again giving me some lessons.

I didn't realise how important the film was, or how much effect it had, until I began to notice the publicity on the buses. There were lots of pictures everywhere and the whole black population around where I lived, realising that I was in the film, went to see it and really enjoyed it. And when it went to Cannes, I mean, that was just a wonderful experience. I can actually remember going to the festival and enjoying all that went with it, and seeing another film which I think was up against us, called *Car Wash*. It was a wonderful experience. That's when I decided that I was actually going to be in this business for the rest of my life.

EastEnders (1985-7) ● *EastEnders* was something else again. I had just won a scholarship to the Duke Ellington School of Art in Washington, DC and I was waiting for my visa to come through. I had just left school in London and basically wanted to do some work before I went to the States. I had nothing to do and was session singing. But I was bored with doing that and thought I would do a quick acting job. I got my agent to send me up for a few things, including *EastEnders*. I was told that it was a BBC2 drama serial, because, it was all very hush-hush at the time and nobody was supposed to know what was really happening. And I thought 'Oh, that'll be great. BBC2, no one will see it. I'll get some money and then that'll be that'. I went along to the audition, but there were no readings as such. The producer (Julia Smith) just took one look and said 'Yeah', and I got the job.

I then went to America and came back a few months later, in time to start on *EastEnders*. I arrived on the lot and there was a barrage of press and actors, and I thought 'Hang on, what's going on here? I thought this was a BBC2 drama serial about this one character'. I had no idea that it was a soap opera with dozens of other people in it. And then there were press reports in the papers that afternoon and the following day, and I finally began to realise that it was actually going to be a bi-weekly soap opera, and that I had to live with it, certainly until the end of my contract. Once I realised that, I had a great time. It was a lot of hard work, but it was fun.

Refusing to do stereotypical things ● I refused to do a lot of things that are usually expected from black kids, but this wasn't actually written into my contract. I refused to breakdance, for example, though we kind of wound it down to a bit of roller skating every now and again. And I refused to walk around with a ghetto blaster on my shoulder. I just thought 'Why not let one of the other characters do it?' I mean, I wasn't really radical at that point, but I was kind of concerned about how my character was going to be viewed, especially as he was going to be on twice a week with a repeat on Sundays. I wanted to get it right, because it was my first television acting role and I didn't want to do things that were naff in my eyes, let alone in anyone else's.

EastEnders' ultra-good black family ● The Carpenter family in *EastEnders* were basically good people. The fact that there was no opposition to that image, that there wasn't a bad black character in the storylines at the time, made it appear that the Carpenters were too good to be true. I tried, as an actor, to play it as best I could – I mean, I was cheeky to the actor who played my father (Oscar James), and there were some moments of confrontation. But there were no drugs, no pimps, and no prostitutes – so from that point of view I think we appeared to be whiter than white. That's as much as I can say about the representation of that family in *EastEnders*. But I think at the time it was needed. We were a good family, people enjoyed watching us, and I got a good reaction from people of West Indian origin in the streets. So as far as I was concerned, I was doing a pretty good job.

Black co-stars of *EastEnders* were quoted in the national press accusing the BBC of racism • Well, I have never been quoted in the national press saying anything, because I think it's beneath me to do all that business with the tabloid press people. I don't understand their mentality. In any case, I wouldn't say the BBC are racist. I would say they are apathetic, perhaps. They tend to ignore situations and believe that they are not happening. They don't give black artistes enough breaks, and they certainly don't give them any career structure. They don't take an actor, see him or her in a little thing, and think 'God, s/he did really well in that, s/he ought to have his/her own series'. They don't do that. But then I don't know how many white actors they do that for either. They have a certain middle- to upper-class bracket of actors who they do it for, and that's it. That is the BBC, from what I can see.

I left *EastEnders* in 1987 basically because I was bored. I had two-and-a-half years there. I'd played my character as much as I could play him, and, unless they were going to turn him into a devil, I couldn't see any way I was going to have fun with him. I also wanted to do other things, and doing a soap opera doesn't leave you much time to go off and do a film or some theatre. I thought 'Well, if I'm going to stay with this show, I'm going to have to stay with it for the rest of my life, otherwise I should leave now and cut my losses'. And that's what I decided to do.

Developing stagecraft and joining *Five Guys Named Moe* • After leaving *EastEnders*, I went to the National Theatre to learn my craft. You have to remember that I went into *EastEnders* when I was seventeen, and, despite having gone to a stage school, I hadn't been to drama school, not that I regretted that in any way whatsoever. But I thought I actually needed some time to think about the direction of my career. I knew all about cameras and lighting and all that, but I actually needed to go up on a stage and deal with the art of acting. So I went to the National for eighteen months, and carried on with music, and writing, and doing the things that I enjoy most and get a tremendous fulfilment out of.

Luckily people became aware of my musical abilities. Clarke Peters called and invited me to join a stage musical he wrote called *Five Guys Named Moe*, which was playing at the Theatre Royal, Stratford. It then moved to the Lyric Theatre in London's West End. I was then nominated for a Laurence Olivier Award, which I was thrilled about because I don't think it had ever happened to a black actor in a musical in England. I didn't win, but then I didn't expect to. The people I was up against were pretty mature and established, and knew what they were doing. But it was nice to be nominated.

Black actors in quality television drama ● I think the position of black actors in television drama is getting better, but it's still nowhere near where it should be. One of my main concerns is highlighted by the fact that whenever I go abroad, I never get called an English person. People always assume I'm American or South American or African, or even Algerian, and French sometimes. This is simply because the dramas that are made in England don't reflect society here at all. They're mostly period dramas and they refuse to cast any black people in those. These are the programmes that are sold abroad. So people who come to England do not expect to see any black people at all, and they are sometimes pleasantly surprised – sometimes not – when they discover that there are black people here.

So that's my main concern, that they make these dramas, sell them throughout the world, and don't include black people in them. I know the agents and casting directors are pushing and working as hard as they possibly can. But I don't know if the directors and producers are trying very hard. I know television executives certainly don't work hard enough to schedule black drama or black sitcoms in a good position in the programme cycle, so that people can see and enjoy them. So it's not good. But to end on a positive note, I'll say that it's getting a lot better.

Treva Etienne is best known for his role as Fireman Tony Sanderson in the London Weekend Television series *London's Burning*. He has also appeared in a range of other programmes, including *Desmond's*, *The Lenny Henry Show*, *The Paradise Club*, and *Casualty*. His theatre credits include *Black Poppies*, and the lead in *Macbeth* at the National Theatre Studio. He also played the lead in *Some Kind of Hero* at the Young Vic.

Treva is a Director of the Afrosax Drama and Music Company, and he recently formed Crown Ten Productions, his own production company for developing scripts for British television.

The problem with integrated casting is that the people who are employing actors, the writers and the producers, aren't actually sure why they're doing it. They're either trying to fill a quota, or they're trying to look as if they're doing their bit. And once you're in that situation as an actor, the producers don't actually know how to deal with having a black actor in the scenario. So what happens is that we get a black actor walking around playing a part, but never really feeling involved or a part of the overall action. Frustration then builds up because the actor wants a fair crack of the whip.

And there's always this over-trying as well, to prove yourself, because when you do get something you want it to be good. You want to try and create something that people are going to remember. You want to leave a mark that's, hopefully, going to get you more work. But what happens is that producers look at it and think 'OK, we've done enough for now. Let's just have him around, and carry on with our motive of why we're doing the show'.

Black characters in scenarios like that get lost, because the writers don't know how to write for them; and even when they do, they think that they have to write 'a black situation' all the time. Unfortunately, so-called black situations on television always centre on things like drugs, riots, prostitution, all the negative aspects of how the establishment sees the black community. It never actually focuses on the positive things, such as the fact that we have lawyers and doctors, and that we have been very instrumental in supporting this country economically. There's a kind of contradiction in the sense that some writers want to incorporate black characters in their drama, but there's confusion because once the black character is in there, they don't actually know what to do with him or her. And it's very frustrating from an actor's point of view.

I remember doing a programme for the BBC in which they wanted me to play a drug dealer. I got the script and it was full of stereotypical things like the Rizlas, the hat with a feather sticking out of it, and so on. I thought 'No, I can't do this'. I remember very early on saying to the director 'Look, I see this character in this way, and I think he should wear a suit, and should be well-spoken, and so on'. Well, there was a struggle because they saw it another way. So I had to try and convince them that, culturally, I knew what I was talking about and that my way of doing it was the right way. After a lot of debate and discussion, I thought we had eventually got what I wanted.

Then, on the day that we were actually shooting it, the wardrobe person walked up to me and said 'You look great in your suit and everything, but the director would like you to wear this hat'. And, of course, the hat had a big feather sticking out of it! As I had tried to explain before, this prop actually changed the connotation of why this character is in the story — it made him out to be a pimp. But I could now feel my argument slipping away and I thought 'Oh, no, not again'. So I started having this discussion with the director all over again, with him saying how it works and me saying how it doesn't. Meanwhile we're losing the light and there were still a lot of shots to do, and I was getting really peeved because I knew this was not right. In the end, we came to a compromise: I had the hat on when they called 'Action!', but took it off during the scene, so most of the shot was played without the hat.

That's just one example of how you really have to fight for what you want. But there's always the fear that you shouldn't push it, because you don't want to get a bad reputation for being 'difficult', and you don't want to mar your chances of getting more work. Sometimes, however, I think you have to go for what you want and actually push for it. In that little experience I just mentioned, it was worth it because the end result was that the programme worked, the idea worked, the character fitted in the way that I wanted it to. It pleased them, it pleased me, and everybody was happy.

I think black actors have to start doing that sort of thing more often, and actresses as well, because I think black actresses get a particularly raw deal. Black actresses, black women generally, are still not seen in television terms as viable, commercial, saleable products. We men go through a hard time, as men, but women get an even rawer deal in this business. When black women do get good parts, they show that they can excel in those parts and do the job. It's just unfortunate that there aren't as many roles for black women as there are for black men in television — especially as there are some good actresses out there.

Taking more control ● I've never really seen myself solely as an actor. When I started acting, even in youth theatre, I was writing plays and getting them performed. And when I left the Anna Scher Theatre and was doing a lot of youth theatre, I teamed up with another actor, Larrington Walker, and for six years we ran workshops at a community centre called Dick Shepherd. A lot of the black actors and comedians you see now in mainstream television came out of that workshop. We always had a huge influx of talented people coming to the workshops – it was just incredible, a very vibrant atmosphere.

But then I started to get more television work and I found that I didn't have as much time to invest in the workshops. Also, through the frustration that I felt as an actor, especially working in television, and just looking at the theatre scene and the kinds of roles that were being offered to us, I decided that the only way things were going to change was for us to actually start producing stuff that we wanted to do ourselves.

So I set up a production company with the aim of trying to create more ideas in the area of comedy and drama, because that was the world I was working in as an actor, and to try and filter into the mainstream and serve an audience and a market which I think has not been tapped. The kind of things the company wants to do are totally mainstream.

I think the climate is changing in so far as British society is slowly beginning to accept that there are black British people here who want to get involved in the media, just as they've accepted that there are black British people who are involved in sport and music. But my experience when I've tried to sell an idea to a producer or broadcaster, is that they usually think that I'm trying to sell them what they would term a 'ghetto' idea. Basically, this means that if you're a black producer, then they see you as only producing programmes for black people, which, in their eyes, represents a minority audience, or what a lot of people term 'a ghetto audience'.

My response to them is 'Well, it's not a black idea, because I was born here and I see myself as British. So if I present an idea to you, I see it as a British idea – in the same way that if John Barnes scores a goal for England, it doesn't become a black goal, the nation rejoices and everybody is happy because Barnes has scored a goal for his country'.

When Linford Christie and John Regis win a race, they run around the track carrying the British flag, the Union Jack. That's a statement which people accept because these black athletes have done something that's allowing Britain to be great again. I think new ideas can have the same effect – new ideas can actually make us, as black people, feel that we are part of this society, because we still don't feel that. For my generation of black people were born here – we speak the tongue, we went to school here, we are British and, when we go abroad, we say that English is our first

Treva Etienne as Fire Officer Tony Sanderson in *London's Burning* (LWT, 1988-90).

language. But then we come home and there's still a reluctance, not so much from ordinary people but from the establishment, that says 'We're not sure if we're ready to accept you people within our society'.

But if you look at what the Asians are doing in terms of supporting the economy, and what we're doing as black people in terms of paying our taxes and our TV licence fees, I think it's only fair that we get some kind of return on that investment. It's time that British society actually started looking at us as a viable market that's turning over a profitable amount of money, and started to invest in us seriously. We should not be patronised and nobody should think that we've got to be treated with kid gloves. We can take the knocks. We can learn from our mistakes, like everybody else, and we can go on to actually achieve from our mistakes. I think that's what British society has to start doing.

Initiatives like *The Real McCoy*, *Desmond's* and *The Lenny Henry Show* are essential because they help to put black performers on the map, and they actually allow us to reach the mainstream audience, which we would never otherwise get. What needs to happen now is for black people to start creating ideas that we can sell ourselves. What needs to come in the frame now is for us to start pushing more black writers and black performers into an arena where we can enter the mainstream.

There is no such thing as 'a black idea', or a project specifically for black people. With Europe opening up, people are going to start looking for new ideas and fresh people with a new approach to representing Britain in a range of films and television programmes. Hopefully, what will happen is that we'll slowly start to build a vibrant market, like the Americans have done, and this will start to promote what black people here are doing in this multicultural British society.

A Utopian vision ● Unfortunately, the financial element is something that is always going to have to come to the table. Without the money we can't create a Utopia, and we can't create the films that we want to make. We are always trying to convince the person across the table – who is usually white and Anglo-Saxon, with a lot of money or with the power to obtain the money – that the idea we have can sell, that it is mainstream, that it will attract an audience, and that it is a viable idea. What we also have to do is to create more black producers who are out there trying to finance their own projects, distributing their own material, and then invite white producers from all over the world to look at the way the projects can work and offer them a slice for their investment. It's time that people started to look at us not as a risk, but as professional, talented, experienced people who can deliver the goods.

We, as black people, need to give ourselves permission to attempt to write the screenplay, to become executive producers and researchers, to try and raise the money to produce a film, to direct something for television, the theatre, or whatever. It's only by attempting these things that we will learn if we can do them and if we can offer our services to the mainstream industry. We really need to get involved in the whole mechanics of how to do it. And I don't think that we should expect, because we're a minority, or because of the equal opportunities thing, that we should be treated with kid gloves.

What's more, I don't think that we should limit ourselves to just one market, because there's a world market out there. We, as black British people, tend to think that if we don't make it in Britain, then that's it. But there are other markets – America, Australia, Europe, the Caribbean and Africa – where we can utilise our skills and develop them, and then sell what we're making back to Britain.

— LENNY HENRY —

Lenny Henry was born in Dudley in the West Midlands. He made his television debut at the age of sixteen as a comic and impressionist in the talent show *New Faces*. After doing a stint with *The Black and White Minstrel Show* for several seasons, to gain stage experience, he appeared in the black sitcom *The Fosters* (1976-7) with Norman Beaton. A change in direction came in the late 70s with his regular appearances in the popular Saturday morning children's show *Tiswas*. Later he co-starred with Tracey Ullman and David Copperfied for three years in the BBC comedy series *Three of a Kind*, and this was followed by his own show *The Lenny Henry Show*.

In 1988 Lenny was the subject of a *South Bank Special*. He was the first British comic to make a live stand-up comedy film in the tradition of American comedians like Richard Pryor, Eddie Murphy, Steve Martin, and Robin Williams. In 1989 Lenny's show was filmed in front of a live audience at the Hackney Empire in London, and the resulting film was *Lenny Live and Unleashed*.

Lenny's 'Step Forward' workshop for new writers in conjunction with the BBC led to a new comedy series for BBC2 in 1991 called *The Real McCoy*. This was designed to present a black perspective through humour, sketches and musical numbers. Also in 1991 Lenny starred in the American film comedy *True Identity*, and in the BBC television drama *Alive and Kicking*.

Lenny is involved with Crucial Films, a company which helps to set up and launch film and comedy projects.

In 1984 Lenny was nominated for a BAFTA (British Academy of Film and Television Arts) award for The Best Light Entertainment Performance for *The Lenny Henry Show*. He has also received Variety Club Awards — in 1983 for Joint BBC Television Personality with Tracey Ullman and David Copperfield for *Three of a Kind*, and in 1989 for Show Business Personality of the Year.

After winning the *New Faces* talent competition, I started off doing various programmes like *The Golden Shot*. But my manager didn't really know how to place me. He didn't know how to get me any experience on stage because, really, I was only sixteen years old and I had no act. I had something like three minutes of material and it was just impressions. There was no substance at all – it was just different voices. Then I was sent along to see a well known impresario who was putting on things like *Holiday on Ice* and *The Black and White Minstrel*

Show at Victoria Palace, and summer seasons all over the country. I was told that he was very good, very wise, and that I had to talk to him.

So this guy shows up and he's like an old military colonel. We met at the Portland Hotel in London. And he says 'Ah, what you need is some stage experience'. And I'm saying 'Like what kind?' Bear in mind that I was only sixteen at the time, and there I was eating this food at the Hotel (I think I managed to eat all the sweet trolley!) and being very impressed, while they're talking about what shows I could do.

For some reason there was a choice between going to Morecambe and doing *The New Faces All Stars* summer season, or doing a club tour with *The Black and White Minstrels*. It was the second club tour *The Minstrels* had done. I wasn't really aware of them at that time. They were something friends' parents might watch. I'm not from variety. I mean, when I was a kid I was into Elvis and whatever else was going on at the time, like Northern soul and Glitter rock. I didn't really watch *The Black and White Minstrels*.

So anyway, the guy says 'There's *The Minstrels*' club tour, you could do that. You'll get experience, and you'll be protected because the audience comes to see the songs and the costumes'. I wasn't really presented with what it actually meant, so I said 'OK, I'll do it'. I thought 'It's six weeks work in all these big clubs, which I would never have had the opportunity to do on my own. Six weeks work and I've only got to do ten minutes of material. If the show starts at eight o'clock, I'll be finished by eight forty-five. It's got to be a decent night'.

It wasn't until a press call, when the press showed up and the photographers started shouting 'Here Len! Here's a funny picture – why don't you wipe the make-up off him, and why don't we put some cream make-up on you, and it'll be like you're both taking your make-up off!' That was the joke, you see. So I kind of went along with it, because I was sixteen and very very stupid! And I'm thinking 'Oh well, this is obviously the kind of joke that's going to happen'.

So I went along and did *The Minstrels*' club tour, and that was all right. And when I saw what the show was, basically these guys blacking up and singing songs, I thought 'Well, it's quite innocent in a way. But deep down it comes out of a racist principle. Why don't you hire real black people, for instance?' Part of me was saying this is weird, but I didn't really know how to deal with it because I was very young. So I did several seasons with them, till I was about twenty-one. Then I finally said 'Look, I can't do this any more. I feel wrong about it, the whole thing about the Stephen Foster songs on the Mississippi, mispronouncing words, and these guys having to black up and everything'. Although they were very talented singers, I just felt that it was wrong.

So I left *The Minstrels* and went and did *Cannon and Ball*, and that was a

Lenny Henry in *New Faces* (ATV, 1976).

huge leap for me. First of all, it didn't have the stigma of all these people with weird make-up on, and secondly people were coming to see the comedy and not all the wacky costumes and the burnt cork. So, ironically, it was like being set free working with Cannon and Ball. It was a very weird time!

But I was very young and I needed the experience. Whatever was wrong with the work, I needed the stage time. I was doing places like the Blackpool Opera House and the Britannia Pier in Yarmouth, and these were three thousand seater halls. If I'd carried on doing what I was doing when I won *New Faces* I'd be playing to a hundred people, so this was definitely a valuable time. It's just a shame that it was surrounded by this stigma. But in the end, I was glad to be out of it, really.

The Fosters (1976-7) ● The late 70s to the late 80s was a great learning curve for me. The beginning, I guess, was *The Fosters* where I was suddenly involved in the first ever black situation comedy with people like Isabelle Lucas, Norman Beaton, and Carmen Munroe. And I was going to see plays at the Royal Court and at the National. It was a really good learning time for me. Norman was very strict, you know. He would suggest books for me to read and plays to go and see. I remember going to see him in various things, and really being impressed with how professional and how great he was. Learning how to act from people like Carmen, Norman and Isabelle, was such a great discipline because they would tell you off if you were standing in the wrong place or couldn't remember your lines. I mean, they would really go off at you.

Working with Norman was also very exhilarating, because he was just so alive. When he came on the set you had to really run to keep up. He had a fatherly influence on everybody in the cast, and just watching him gave me a really good sense of what acting was all about — that you've got to learn your lines, and invest them with energy and intelligence.

And it was the same with Carmen Munroe. She said to me 'Learn as much as you can because you're going to use it. Learn to dance, sing, study plays'. I didn't do any of those things, of course. I was like 'Yee-ha! I'm twenty-one and in London, forget that!' And I was off. But Carmen was very strict with me as far as learning how to do stuff. She kept reminding me that if you're going to be an actor, if you're going to be in showbusiness, then you've got to learn how to do it properly. So learning how to behave on a television set, that was basically my main experience in *The Fosters*.

Tiswas (1979-81) and *Three of a Kind* (1981-3) ● I went on to do one-off things like *Seaside Special*, and then I was on *Tiswas*. *Tiswas* was an anarchic children's television show in which I was the only black person, apart from the bands that used to come on, like 'The Specials' and 'Fun Boy Three'. I was doing characters like Algernon Razzmatazz, Nat West the preacher, and some others.

When we came up with Algernon, it was like 'Oh well, I want to do this happy-go-lucky Rastafarian who eats bread and condensed milk'. Now, the bread and condensed milk idea wasn't such a big stretch because nearly everybody in my family ate bread and condensed milk. It was something you ate when you were a kid, something your dad took to work, so it wasn't like a huge stereotypical thing. It was just something that came out of my family experience.

So I did *Tiswas* and that got very cultsy — fifty-four per cent of the audience were over eighteen. I remember going to do some live shows with Chris Tarrant, Bob Carol Gees, John Gorman and Sally James and it was like 'The Beatles'. I mean, there were queues round the block and people dying to be covered in water. It was the most bizarre experience of my life. And I enjoyed that and got quite a reputation for being a live performer and being able to adapt. I got a lot of that off Chris Tarrant, really, just being able to adapt to a live situation.

And because of that, I got involved with things like *Three of a Kind*. I think I was spotted to do the first programme which was originally called *Six of a Kind*. Again I was the only black person in the cast. We did several programmes but they didn't really work, because there were too many people in the cast and they didn't really know what to do with these six people. And so the BBC decided to cut it down to three and recast another woman. They got Tracey Ullman who was appearing in *Four in a Million* at the Royal Court at the time.

So, once again, it was a safe package in a way – we've got two white people and we'll have this black guy in the middle. We don't want to frighten anybody. It was almost like being spoon-fed to the British public. In some respects that was an advantage, in others a disadvantage, because if you're the only black guy on the block, you have to really prove yourself, push yourself, and show that you deserve to be there. So I was constantly pushing myself, and learning, and trying to figure out how to be better.

I've always learnt from working with good people like Tracey Ullman, David Copperfield, Chris Tarrant, Norman Beaton – all the people I've worked with. I always sat and watched what they did, and how they did it, how they rolled with the punches and stuff. Tracey was one of the first people who actually showed me how to get into a character in depth. She really would break down a character and say 'She's got Susan Penhaligon hair. Her mother talks like this . . . She probably went to this kind of school' . . . And I'd be going 'God, is that how you do it?' Because before that, all my characters were 'put on a hat and there he is'. I was like that! So it was great to work with somebody who showed you how to sketch it in a bit more.

New Comedy and *The Lenny Henry Show* ● We finished *Three of a Kind* and I now wanted to do my own show. At first I wanted to do six half-hour comedies where I played a different character each week. But it was decided, not by me, that that was too risky because people were used to seeing me in sketches. So I went into another sketch show called *The Lenny Henry Show* and that was a huge breakthrough for me, because it was my own series. Also, the alternative comedy thing had happened, so I changed my style as a comedian.

From *The Black and White Minstrels* to *OTT*, I guess the kind of material I was doing was very self-deprecating, very self-detrimental – some of it, not all of it. There were a lot of 'darkie jokes' – if I was perspiring a lot, I'd say I'm leaking chocolate. There were lots of jokes like that, which were very stupid and very immature. I remember doing a show in Hull and a guy shouting out 'Oi! You've got to do jokes like Charlie Williams. That's the kind of thing we expect from black comedians up here'. I wasn't doing that kind of stuff at the time, but then I realised that he was right. I would go and

Lenny Henry as Delbert Wilkins in *The Lenny Henry Show* (BBC TV, 1984-8).

see Charlie Williams pulling the house down doing stuff about 'darkies' and how 'you've been left in the oven too long', and things like that. I just thought 'Oh well, this is obviously what you've got to do if it's a predominantly white audience – you've got to put yourself and other people down'. This was all unconscious. I didn't sit down and go 'Hmm ....' It just happened.

By the time I'd got my own television series, I had seen alternative comedy. I was a huge fan of Richard Pryor, Bill Cosby and Steve Martin. So I took all these influences on board and was ready to try and do my own thing. And you could see me being very Alexei Sayle-like and very Richard Pryor-like and very Steve Martin-like in putting monologues in the show. But in the sketches, it kind of stretched out a little bit and I got to play a variety of characters. These stemmed from all sorts of influences – my family, from what I was seeing when I was out and about in the community, and from films and things like that. It all gelled much better in the second series, as you would expect it to do. I think a lot of very good work happened in that series and that's a tribute, really, to Geoff Posner and Kim Fuller who were director and script editor respectively at that time.

The Young Ones and The Comic Strip influence ● At the time you couldn't help but be influenced by *The Young Ones* and *The Comic Strip*. They were the most successful, not in television ratings terms, perhaps, but the most successful shows in public terms. People knew *The Young Ones*. They knew Rik Mayall and they knew *The Comic Strip*. They knew what was going on, that *The Comic Strip* were producing half-hour films, and that *The Young Ones* could have talking hamsters and you could hit somebody with a cricket bat. I mean, this was like a revelation.

The other thing about *The Comic Strip* was they were doing non-sexist and non-racist comedy. When I saw what people like Alexei Sayle, Dawn French and Jennifer Saunders were doing, I was like 'Oh, so you don't have to take the piss out of yourself. You can actually just do material that's funny about where you're from. You don't have to be racist and sexist, but you can be racy and sexy'. Once I understood that, which was the early 80s, and I started to hang out with Dawn and Alexei, and people like that, it was a direct influence. It was like getting all that *Black and White Minstrels* and early musical variety stuff out of my system. It was like getting rid of that and starting again with a real clean slate.

Promoting new talent ● In the last few years I have tried to encourage black writers and black performers, because it's just very sad that there aren't more black people in front of and behind the camera in our television institutions. And although there are, or have been, programmes like *Desmond's*, *The Frontline*, *Empire Road* and *Love Thy Neighbour*, they're very few and far between. They're always like this little novelty item. They'll run for two series and then that's it.

What would be great would be to have something that lasts like *Desmond's*, or *The Cosby Show*, where it would be no big deal to have an all-black or multiracial cast, and where you could show up on the first day of rehearsals and it would be no big deal to have a black camera person, or an Asian sound recordist, or a woman floor manager.

Having talked to Jonathan Powell (Controller of BBC1) about this, things are getting slowly more integrated at the BBC, but it's going take a very very long time. Once again, I'll say that things are not going to change, or the programmes that we see are not going to change until the people behind the camera reflect the ethnic variety in society. I mean, it's very difficult for white writers, directors and producers to understand the ethnic experience. I'm not saying that it's impossible, but I am saying that it would be much easier if there were black producers or directors to relate to. I've worked with white people for most of my career and I've enjoyed the experience. It has been great. But if I'd had a black director when I was doing *The Lenny Henry Show*, for instance, I'm pretty sure it would have been a lot different.

'Step Forward' comedy-writing workshops and *The Real McCoy* ●
About two years ago, I started my own production company. I had been to the Washington Film Festival in America, where I met an African film-maker who told me that it took him twelve years to make his film, and I thought it was a really good film. I said 'Do you think I could make a film?' And he said 'If people know you, if you've got your own television series, you can raise money to make films. But you should have your own production company'. He got very excited and I was thinking 'Yeah, maybe he's right'. So I came back to England, determined to have my own production company to make films. It started off as a development company and we've done a few things. We're going to do more stuff encouraged by the BBC and various other people.

At the same time, I was going through this thing about how all the sketches that were coming in were written by white people. I don't mind that, you know, it's great. But it's a tradition at the BBC that a lot of the writers come out of Oxbridge. So I thought 'Yeah, this is cool. But here I am, one of the only black performers on the BBC doing a sketch show, and there are no black writers except for me'. Then I thought 'Wouldn't it be great to have some kind of programme whereby you could get young black writers and young Asian writers to come in and figure out how to do sketch comedy – the whys-and-wherefores of the three-minute sketch, what the rules are, and so on'. That was always in my mind right from when I was doing *The Lenny Henry Show*.

So, last year, I went to Jonathan Powell and proposed running a workshop on comedy writing. I talked to various people like Charlie Hanson, Richard Curtis, John Lloyd and Trix Worrell – and they all said that they were interested and would come down, hang out and talk to these young writers. Jonathan put up the money for us to do it and it built up from there. We set up the workshop and called it 'Step Forward'. People were asked to send in five pages of sketch material, or a scene from a movie, or a play that they'd written, or a monologue, or whatever.

We received thousands of these sketches and read them all. We bussed all these readers in to help us read the material, and we managed to narrow it down to fifty. We had an 'AA' list and an 'AB' list, then we finally got it down to twenty-two people. We got them to come to this conference centre, and we just talked at them for three days. They all had to write something. Then, on the Sunday morning, we got Victor Romero Evans, Dona Croll, myself and various other people to perform the best of the sketches, and then we talked about the exercises. Jonathan Powell, Jim Moir, Robin Nash, Richard Curtis — all these great people also came down to talk to these young writers, and it was really good.

Around the same time, *Comic Asides*, which is the facility that BBC2 has to premier new shows, wanted to do a black show because there aren't any. Charlie Hanson was contracted to put that together. Charlie had done a lot of work with the Black Theatre Co-operative, and he worked on *Desmond's* and *No Problem!*, so he started putting this new idea together, while I was doing 'Step Forward'. I then mentioned to him that he should use some of the writers from 'Step Forward'. It all seemed to come together at the same time — we had these twenty-two writers, plus everybody on the 'AB' list who were really good but couldn't get in because there weren't enough places. Charlie decided to commission some of the really good ones, and, as a result of that, a lot of the material in *The Real McCoy* was provided by 'Step Forward'.

It's probably an obvious point to make, but there isn't that much quality black drama going around. You see the odd thing in the theatre that's impressive, but you don't get a sense that there's a constant bubbling of talent being nurtured by any of the big television or film companies. That's a major problem. It's certainly one of the reasons why I've predominantly worked with white producers and directors and have done scripts by white writers. There needs to be something instigated for black film-makers, writers, producers and directors to enable them to learn their craft. If it's a matter of learning how to do it, then it must be encouraged and pushed. If it's a matter of being given the opportunity, they must be given that opportunity.

True Identity ● It's strange that my first big Hollywood film involved me masquerading as a white person. But, on the other hand, having worn prostheses a lot — when I've done impersonations of the cast of *Cheers* or Michael Jackson with a long chin and high cheek bones, or Steve Martin and stuff like that, it didn't seem to be such a big jump for me. It was just a matter of wearing the make-up and being as convincing an Italian-American as possible. That was a big challenge for me. But it wasn't like 'Hey, I'm whiting up. Whoa, this brings back memories!' — because I never blacked up when I was in *The Minstrels*, I was just doing straight comedy. But it was weird because I felt that people were going to make some connection with *The Minstrels* here.

The reason I was contacted to do *True Identity* was that I had made a film called *Live and Unleashed*, which is a stand-up concert film co-written by myself, Kim Fuller, James Hendrie, Geoff Atkinson and various people like that. At the beginning of the movie I did impersonations of Richard Pryor, Steve Martin and Bill Cosby. Somebody from Disney Productions saw the film when we were exhibiting it at the Cannes Film Festival, thought it was great and liked the Steve Martin bit a lot. We met and talked about it.

A couple of months later he called my agent to say that his producer colleague in Hollywood had seen the movie and thought I was great. A few months went by and I was in New York – I've been going to New York on and off since 1983 to do stand-up and to try and write material – when my agent called me from Los Angeles and said 'You've got to get over here. They want to meet you at Disney. They've got this picture you might be interested in'.

So I went Los Angeles, and although they didn't know me, the people at Disney were very complimentary about my work. They had seen *The Lenny Henry Show* and *Work Experience*, which had just won an Oscar, and they wanted to do some stuff with me. They handed me the script for *True Identity* to read. It was written by a white writer, but they had a young black film director named Charles Lane in mind to do it, whom they wanted me to meet.

I was quite excited and read the script on my way back to New York. There were things wrong with it – the love interest, the girl I fall in love with in the movie was originally a maid, and Miles, the character I play, didn't have any black friends at all in the picture. So when I got back to New York, I went to see *Sidewalk Stories*, which Charles Lane made for $200,000. He shot it in twelve days, on a tight budget, and it was enchanting and lyrical, very funny, and very moving. It's about a homeless artist who finds a little girl wandering the streets, and he decides to look after her and help her track down her mum. I watched it and really liked it. I arranged to meet Charles and we talked about the *True Identity* idea – what we thought the picture was about and what we could do with it, and if there was any social commentary we could get in, however small, and if we could address the black/white issues properly.

The basic core of the movie is that my character can only evade the mob by masquerading as a white guy for a period of time. So the colour thing is a big deal. It's quite a big issue and we didn't want people saying 'Oh well, it's about a black guy who wants to be white'. We had to make sure that the character felt uncomfortable with it and questioned it throughout the movie. And basically that's what we did. We added that element to the movie and

Charles re-wrote it a bit. Various other people came in to re-write it as well. You know, the typical Hollywood thing where there are dozens of drafts of a script, each one in a different colour – the red draft, the blue draft. Some days there'd be the cement draft, the burnt amber draft, the plastic draft, and so on. Anyway, we agreed to make the film and entered this re-drafting cycle.

The American experience ● The thing I really notice about America is that when you're unknown over there, you have to keep proving yourself all the time. It's so difficult for people who've been on television in England and used to going out, getting laughs with everybody loving you and everything. Then suddenly you're in America on a movie set with all these people walking around with their long blond hair, eating sticky buns and talking about going to the beach and driving Porsches. It's very alien. You're not at home, you're not in lovely Shepherds Bush with everybody saying 'All right there? What's going on? You wanna bacon sarnie?' It's not that at all. Suddenly you've got to show what you can do. And I found myself having to prove myself a lot, because you get a lot of people questioning why you've been chosen to do this part. I think British artistes get that a lot when they go to America – 'Why did they choose this person? Why didn't they cast somebody else?' So I found it quite a stressful experience, but because my wife, Dawn, was there it was less stressful.

As a British black person, having to relate to American blackness is quite difficult, very tough. I mean, four hundred years of slavery doesn't make it any better over there. At least we, in Britain, were invited to come here by the Commonwealth, even though it was to do the jobs that nobody here wanted to do. We were invited, we worked and we kind of integrated. However difficult it has been, we've learnt how to deal with white society on the whole. But in America, things are much more polarised. People get very protective of their African-Americaness and their roots, and there's a lot of hatred. I met a very rich black American guy who owned an apartment building and he said to me 'I've got this apartment building because all my life white people have looked down on me, and now I can look down at them'.

I've never had a feeling like that in my life. I've never had feelings like that because of the way blacks arrived in Britain. It's a different experience. And when you watch films like *Boyz N the Hood* and *New Jack City*, you see that aggression percolating out onto the screen. You see the drug dealing, the heavy drug addiction, the relationship with the police, which is much more intense than it is in Britain. These new black American films are violent, aggressive and confrontational – and they are a direct parallel to what's happening in black communities all over America. It's like when

John Singleton says in *Boyz N the Hood*: 'There's a gun shop on every corner in the ghetto, but not in Beverly Hills'. And why is that? People are now starting to ask questions, and these movies are right in your face asking these questions – 'Why is it like this in my community, and not in the white community?'

When I'm in America I certainly feel much more 'the black guy' than I do in England. I just feel like Lenny in England – that's who I am. I look in the mirror and say 'Well, yeah, that's Lenny and my parents are from Jamaica' and so on. But when I'm in America, I feel like the black guy and that at any minute I might get stopped or slapped up against a wall or whatever, because that's the way it is in America. It's very deeply entrenched, and to get over it is a huge achievement. It's still tough in this country, but to a lesser extent.